MASTERING BUSINESS LAW

TERRY PRICE

MACMILLAN

First published by Pan Books Ltd in 1982 as *Practical Business Law* in the Breakthrough Series.

Fully revised and updated edition first published in 1989 by
THE MACMILLAN PRESS LTD
Houndmills, Basingstoke, Hampshire RG21 2XS
and London
Companies and representatives
throughout the world

ISBN 0–333–48799–0

A catalogue record for this book is available
from the British Library.

Printed in China

10 9 8 7 6 5
00 99 98 97 96 95 94 93

CONTENTS

CONTENTS

ACKNOWLEDGEMENTS

Acknowledgements are due to the following.

Keith Martin who made many constructive suggestions and kept me abreast of the changes in the law.

Susan Bennett, Pamela McMullen and Wendy Scott at Canterbury College of Technology library for their help in locating so much information.

David Hogg of Canterbury College of Technology's AVA section for his assistance.

Deborah Price, my daughter, a solicitor, who assisted me in the preparation of this book.

Rachel Price, my daughter, who helped in the preparation of the index.

Simon Beckwith, for some interesting comments on judicial precedent.

Finally, my wife Sheila whose encouragement and help made the preparation so much easier.

Any mistakes or omissions are of course my responsibility.

TERRY PRICE

The author and publishers wish to thank the following who have kindly given permission for the use of copyright material:

The Controller of Her Majesty's Stationery Office for extracts from the Sale of Goods Act 1979, Courts Act 1971 and Unfair Contract Terms Act 1977. Also SI 786, 917 and 1200.

Solicitors Law Stationery Society plc for Land Registry form 19J and other material.

Times Newspapers Ltd for 'Women's Entitlement to Equal Pay', a report on Industrial Tribunals, *The Times*, May 1988, © Times Newspapers Ltd 1988.

INTRODUCTION

Taking on a new employee, buying and selling goods or services, meeting health and safety regulations are three very important and vital activities in most businesses. All three of these activities have legal implications. Taking on an employee involves a business in a legally binding relationship, buying and selling goods or services will result in a business contract and failure to meet health and safety regulations may well mean criminal and/or civil court action. Law, in fact, underlies a great deal of what takes place in business. It is important therefore that those involved in business should have some understanding of those legal principles which might affect their work. It is because a study of law is considered so important to business that it is included in many business courses.

This book provides an introduction to a number of important business law topics. It is designed as a self-study guide and requires no previous legal knowledge. Each chapter and section of the book begins with a realistic example which helps to illustrate and explain the law. Throughout there is a series of self-check and review exercises. These exercises have been designed to assist readers with their learning. Readers who study each chapter carefully and work through the exercises should gain an understanding of some of the important legal principles underlying business activity. At the end of the book there is a review chapter which attempts to bring together the topics which have been covered. English law relies, as you will see, on decided cases. There are a number of references to cases throughout. When reading a section of the book try to remember the case and how it relates to that particular part of the law.

The book, which incorporates changes that have been made in the law up to January 1988, is intended for anyone who wishes to understand some of the legal aspects relating to business. It will prove useful to students studying on business courses which include business law, particularly those courses leading to BTEC qualifications. It should also be useful to those studying commercial law in Royal Society of Arts and the London Chamber of Commerce examinations. It will also be a useful introduction for a number of professional examinations requiring a knowledge of business law.

TABLE OF CASES

TABLE OF STATUTES (ACTS OF PARLIAMENT)

To Sheila

CHAPTER 1

LAW AND THE COURTS IN ENGLAND AND WALES

1.1 CRIMINAL AND CIVIL LAW DISTINGUISHED

Michael Jennings is a technical representative with Precision Engineering Co. Ltd. He is returning by car from a sales visit in the South of England and is travelling through a small town in the Midlands. Michael is thinking about the good order he has arranged during his visit and allows his concentration to lapse. John Evans steps on to a pedestrian crossing and Michael, failing to see the red light, is in collision with John. John sustains serious injuries and both an ambulance and the police are called. The police threaten prosecution and John also decides to sue Michael.

Michael is certainly in trouble with the law. On the one hand he is being threatened by the police with prosecution and on the other John has decided to sue. In this section we will be dealing with the meaning of the terms 'prosecute' and 'sue' and at the same time bringing out the important differences between the two major branches of our law, *criminal* and *civil*.

When the police say they will prosecute what they are really saying is that they believe that the person in question has committed a crime. In our situation the police could argue that Michael has committed the crime of driving a motor car on the highway 'without due care and attention'. The case would be heard in one of the Criminal Courts and in this situation it is most likely that it would be heard in a Magistrates' Court. If Michael is found guilty, he will be fined and have his licence endorsed. Michael then would have been punished for his wrong-doing. Criminal law is concerned with conduct of which the state so strongly disapproves that it will punish the wrong-doer.

Activity

Think for a moment about other crimes and about the punishments which the state imposes.

Many of you no doubt will have thought of theft as an example of a crime. Our society could not work if people were allowed to help themselves to the property of others and so the state imposes a punishment such as imprisonment. It is hoped that this threat will deter persons from committing the crime of theft.

The branch of law which deals with crimes is known as criminal law.

You will remember, however, that Michael is also threatened with being 'sued' by John Evans. When we talk of sueing we are concerned with that branch of law known as civil law. Civil law is concerned with settling disputes between persons, groups of persons or organisations such as companies or local authorities and providing a *remedy*, often compensation to the person wronged. Thus John Evans who is the person wronged would be anxious to receive compensation from Michael Jennings for the hurt and suffering as a result of the accident. The case that John is bringing against Michael would be likely to be heard in the County Court, which is one of the civil courts. The branch of law concerned with disputes between persons is known as civil law.

In the two cases brought against Michael the criminal case would be described as *R*. v. *Jennings*. *R*. stands for Regina which is a Latin term for Queen and signifies that the Crown prosecutes on behalf of the community. Jennings is the defendant. In some cases the prosecution is signified as the police and in this instance the case might be referred to as *Police* v. *Jennings*. On 1 October 1986 a Crown Prosecution service replaced the prosecution function of the Police. In the civil case the parties would be referred to as *Evans* v. *Jennings* signifying that this is a dispute between two individuals. John Evans would be the plaintiff and Michael Jennings again the defendant.

Exercise 1

1 Write down a short definition of criminal law.
2 Write down a short definition of civil law.
3 In each of the two cases that Michael Jennings is likely to face he would be the defendant; what would the other party be known as in (a) the criminal case, (b) the civil case?

The main differences between criminal and civil law might be summed up by means of the chart below.

Criminal law	Civil law
1 A set of rules dealing with conduct of which the state disapproves.	1 A set of rules dealing with disputes between individuals or businessmen.
2 A breach of the rules may lead to prosecution.	2 A breach of the rules may lead to the defendant being sued.
3 Cases heard in criminal courts, e.g. Magistrates' Court.	3 Cases heard in civil courts, e.g.County Court.
4 Parties involved: *R* (Regina) or *Police* v. *Defendant.*	4 Parties involved: *Plaintiff* v. *Defendant.*
5 Fines and/or imprisonment may result from prosecution.	5 Compensation/damages may have to be paid by the defendant to the plaintiff.

We have identified five differences between criminal and civil law. Try to remember the five by seeing if you can note them without reference to the book. If you cannot do this read the sections again and then try to remember the five differences.

Exercise 2

In each of the following say whether you think the situation would involve criminal or civil law.

1 Brenda Jardine is injured while shopping when some heavy packages fall against her.
2 David Neville owes a garage £95 for some motor car repairs they have done.
3 Deborah Prince has been stopped by the police for driving a car which does not display a tax disc.
4 Colin Richardson has been arrested and charged with having committed burglary.

1.2 CRIMINAL AND CIVIL COURTS IN ENGLAND AND WALES

We have already learned that criminal and civil cases are heard in different courts. In the situation relating to Michael Jennings the criminal case was heard in the Magistrates' Court while the civil case was heard in the County Court. In this section we will be dealing briefly with the system of courts in this country and at the same time learning about their various functions.

The present system of courts in England and Wales was set up in 1971 by the Courts Act as the extract below shows.

Courts Act 1971

ELIZABETH II

1971 CHAPTER 23

An Act to make further provision as respects the Supreme Court and county courts, judges and juries, to establish a Crown Court as part of the Supreme Court to try indictments and exercise certain other jurisdiction, to abolish courts of assize and certain other courts and to deal with their jurisdiction and other consequential matters, and to amend in other respects the law about courts and court proceedings. [12th May 1971]

BE IT ENACTED by the Queen's most Excellent Majesty, by and with the advice and consent of the Lords Spiritual and Temporal, and Commons, in this present Parliament assembled, and by the authority of the same, as follows:—

PART I

INTRODUCTORY

1.—(1) The Supreme Court shall consist of the Court of Appeal and the High Court, together with the Crown Court established by this Act. The Supreme Court.

(2) All courts of assize are hereby abolished, and Commissions, whether ordinary or special, to hold any court of assize shall not be issued.

Criminal Courts

Magistrates' Court. First of all let us look at the system of criminal courts in this country. All criminal cases are heard in the first instance in the Magistrates' Court. The magistrates only have the power, however, to try less serious cases and thus many driving offences are tried in the Magistrates' Court. The power of magistrates is governed by the rule that they can only impose fines up to a maximum of £2000 and imprisonment up to a maximum of six months. It is clear, therefore, that more serious cases must be heard elsewhere. However, even such serious cases as murder or rape will go in the first instance to a Magistrates' Court for what is called a preliminary hearing. The task of the magistrates in a preliminary hearing is to examine the evidence to decide whether or not a reasonable case can be made. If they decide that a reasonable case does exist they will send the accused to the Crown Court for trial or to use the legal term 'commit the accused to the Crown Court'.

Certain criminal offences can be tried by the magistrates or the Crown Court. They are known as hybrid offences and the defendant must be given the choice. He can elect to be tried summarily (i.e. by the magistrates) or stand trial at the Crown Court.

The famous case in 1981 involving the so-called Yorkshire Ripper began in the Magistrates' Court in Dewsbury, West Yorkshire. Following the preliminary hearing the magistrates committed the accused to Leeds Crown Court, although as you will no doubt remember, the case was actually heard at the Central Criminal Court, the Old Bailey in London. The Old Bailey is, in fact, a Crown Court which has become famous because many well-known cases have been heard there. Cases which have attracted a lot of publicity will often be heard in the Old Bailey rather than the nearest Crown Court. This case is referred to as *R* v. *Peter Sutcliffe* (1981).

Activity

In the next few days have a look at your newspaper to see if you can find reports of magnistrates holding preliminary hearings.

Crown Court. The Crown Court, which always has a judge presiding, will hear all those criminal cases which are too serious for the Magistrates' Court In some cases for the most serious crimes, such as murder, the judge will be a High Court judge, but less serious cases such as burglary will be tried at the Crown Court but may be presided over by a circuit judge or a recorder. Criminal offences are divided into four groups for the purposes of the trial. Class 1 offences are very serious and will always be heard before a High Court Judge. Whether before a High Court judge or circuit judge or recorder, when the accused pleads 'not guilty' the case will always be heard in the presence of a jury. It is the jury guided by the judge who gives the verdict of guilty or not guilty. If a verdict of guilty is given then the judge will pass sentence. If the defendant pleads guilty then the judge passes sentence and the jury is not required. There are Crown Courts in most of the larger towns in England and Wales which are usually open to the public and if it is possible to make a visit then this will help you to understand this branch of the law more easily.

Appeals Against Decisions of the Magistrates' Court

It is possible for a defendant to appeal against a decision of a Magistrates' Court. He may feel that he has been convicted wrongly. For example a person convicted of a speeding offence may feel that the evidence produced by the police was neither sufficient nor accurate. It may also be that a defendant could think that while he may have been fairly convicted the sentence he had been given was far too severe, i.e. too heavy a fine or too long a term of imprisonment. In each of these situations, i.e. an appeal against conviction or an appeal against sentence, the case would go before the Crown Court and be reheard before a circuit judge sitting with magistrates. There would be no jury. The Crown Court sitting as an appeal court in these situations could reverse the decision of the magnistrates in respect of the decision and also could reduce the fine or length of imprisonment. The Crown Court could equally uphold (keep the same) the decision of the Magistrates' Court.

There are, of course, occasions where the prosecution, often the police, feels that the defendant has been wrongly acquitted, which means he has been found not guilty by the magistrates. In some cases the police may feel that the sentence given has not been severe enough. The prosecution has no right of appeal in either of these situations. Thus the right to appeal to the Crown Court is available only to the defendant, not to the prosecution. There are, however, circumstances where both prosecution and defence can appeal against a decision of the Magistrates' Court where it is felt that in coming to the decision the magistrates made a mistake in their application of the law. The appeal is made to the High Court, to the Divisional Court of the Queen's Bench Division, and it is made on a point of law.

The Divisional Court consider the details of the case and if the judges feel that the magistrates have interpreted the law incorrectly, they will order the case to be reheard by the magistrates and at the rehearsing the magistrates must apply the Divisional Court ruling. The following example of the sort of appeal which might be made to the Divisional Court from the magnistrates may help you to understand this better.

R. v. *Marylebone Justices ex. p. Yasmin Farrag* (1980)
In a case before a Magistrates' Court at Marylebone, Yasmin Farrag had pleaded not guilty to an alleged offence of soliciting for the purposes of prostitution. The police acting for the prosecution gave evidence and were cross-examined by the barrister for the defendant. The defendant then gave evidence and the chairman of the magistrates indicated that the prosecuting police officer did not need to cross-examine and turning to the other magistrates said 'case proven' before the defence barrister had closed her case or addressed the magistrates. Yasmin was found guilty and sentenced.

The defendant's barrister decided to appeal as 'a case stated' because a defendant or the barrister acting for the defendant must be allowed an opportunity to address the magistrates. The Queen's Bench Divisional Court, after considering the situation, ordered a retrial because the magistrates clearly had wrongly applied the law.

When an appeal is made on a point of law as in the above example, it is known as an appeal by way of 'Case Stated' which means simply that the details of the case are laid before the divisional court.

A more recent case provides another good example of an appeal by way of 'Case Stated':

Erewash Borough Council v. *Ilkeston Consumer Co-operative Society Ltd* (1988)
The Queen's Bench Divisional Court in this case decided that the magistrates had wrongly convicted the society for trading on Sunday in contravention of the Shops Act 1950. It was held that the society was acting as a travel agency and that this was not a shop in the ordinary sense of the word, i.e. 'a place where anything is sold'. Unless this decision is challenged in a higher court, e.g., the House of Lords, then travel agents will be able to open on Sundays without risking prosecution.

Appeals Against Decisions of the Crown Court

In the case of more serious offences which, as we know, are heard in the Crown Court, the defendant may appeal against conviction or against sentence to the court of appeal (Criminal Division), as the following example illustrates.

Rachel Davis has been convicted in the Crown Court for the manslaughter of her husband and she has been sentenced to four years' imprisonment. Her lawyers feel that the sentence of four years is far to severe in view of the evidence of severe provocation by her husband. The lawyers seek leave to appeal; permission is granted and the case is reheard in the Court of Appeal (Criminal Division). Three judges review the case by looking at a record of the Crown Court proceedings from tapes or shorthand notes. They also examine carefully the Crown Court judge's notes. After careful consideration the three judges decide that the sentence imposed upon Rachel was far too severe and Rachel's sentence is reduced to one year. Since Rachel has already served six months of her sentence while awaiting the appeal we can see that she has only a short time further to serve.

From this example we can see the way in which the Court of Appeal (Criminal Division) operates. Just as with the magistrates, the prosecution has no right of appeal either against an acquittal or sentence. If a defendant such as Rachel in the case above appeals against sentence, it can only be reduced or stay the same; under no circumstances may it be increased.

In almost all cases the decision of the Court of Appeal (Criminal

Division) is final, though where it is thought that a point of law of considerable general public importance is involved then the prosecution or the defence may be given leave to appeal to the highest court in the English legal system, the House of Lords. When the House of Lords sits as a court, a minimum of three, but more usually five, judges, known as Lords of Appeal in Ordinary, sit to review the case in much the same way as described in relation to the Court of Appeal (Criminal Division). Very few criminal cases ever come to the Lords but since the House of Lords is the highest court its decisions are final.

Although criminal appeals to the House of Lords are rare, there was in 1981 an appeal in a case relating to 'causing death by reckless driving'. The case *R*. v. *Lawrence* concerned a motorcyclist who ran into and killed a pedestrian who was crossing the road. The prosecution alleged that Lawrence was driving at between 60 and 80 mph within an area restricted by a 30 mph limit. In coming to their decision in this important case the Law Lords stated what constituted 'driving recklessly' and indicated that two elements must be proved: (i) that the driving in question created what an ordinary and prudent driver would regard as 'an obvious and serious risk of causing physical injury to another or of doing substantial damage to propery'; (ii) that the driver was 'reckless' as to whether physical injury or substantial damage to property resulted from his driving. This means that the driver realised the risk but nevertheless took it or he failed to think about it.

In this case it was clearly felt that such was the general and public interest in what constituted 'reckless driving' that by making the appeal to the Lords it was hoped that the law could be clarified on this subject.

House of Lords' decisions are binding (must be followed) on all other courts but the House of Lords is not bound by its own decisions and it will sometimes overrule (change) its previous decision and therefore the law as the following case shows:

R. v. *Shivpuri* (1986)

In this case Shivpuri thought he was bringing in to the UK prohibited drugs. In fact the material was not a drug but quite harmless and certainly not illegal.

In a previous case, *Anderton* v. *Ryan* (1985), the Lords had applied the Criminal Attempts Act 1981 and concluded that if the act itself was innocent even though the defendant thought it to be illegal he/she could not be convicted.

In *R*. v. *Shivpuri* the Lords overruled their previous decision and found Shivpuri guilty of a criminal attempt.

It might help you to understand the organisation of the criminal courts by looking at the chart on p. 30. If you are not sure of any of the terms used in the chart read back over the text and when you are sure then answer the review questions which follow in Exercise 3.

Exercise 3

Read the following and say for each example which court is likely to hear the case.

1 Roy Goldstein has been convicted on a charge of drinking and driving. His lawyers decide to appeal because they think the magistrates have not applied the law correctly.
2 Michael Moore is charged by the police of having exceeded the speed limit of 70 mph on the motorway.
3 John Smith has been charged with the offence of 'causing death by reckless driving'.
4 Jennifer Jones having been convicted on a charge of manslaughter decides to appeal against the conviction.
5 James Johnson has been convicted for an offence contrary to the Official Secrets Act 1939. He has appealed unsuccessfully against his conviction but because of the great legal importance of the case a further appeal is allowed.
6 Syd Mason has been sentenced to four months' imprisonment by the magistrates for being drunk and disorderly in a public place. Syd decides to appeal against what he regards as too severe a sentence.

County Courts. We have now considered the main criminal courts in England and Wales but, as we have already learned, the other major branch of law is civil law and this branch also has a system of courts. Civil law is concerned, as you will remember, with settling disputes between individuals, businesses or companies and it is with such a dispute that the following example is concerned.

Peak Building Supplies Co. Ltd is a small company which supplies a range of building materials and equipment to builders. The company has supplied materials to the value of £1750 to a small building firm known as Woodruffe Renovations. Despite a number of reminders to the owner of the business Mr Woodruffe, the bill remains unpaid and Peak Building Supplies Co. Ltd decide to take legal action to recover their money. Peak Building Supplies Co. Ltd write to Mr Woodruffe explaining that they will start proceedings in the local County Court unless payments is made in full within seven days.

Here then, we have an example of a dispute between a company and a small one-man business. This is a clear example of a dispute which could be settled by reference to civil law. Civil law is concerned with such disputes and providing a remedy. The remedy which Peak Building Supplies Co. Ltd is seeking is the recovery of the £1750. If Mr Woodruffe decides to ignore the letter from Peak Building Supplies then the company could begin proceedings to sue Mr Woodruffe by sending to the local County

Court particulars of the claim. Because this is an action to recover money it is known as a 'default summons'. Other types of claims, e.g. for compensation for injury, would be by means of an ordinary summons.

This particular case, *Peak Building Supplies Co. Ltd* v. *Woodruffe*, would be heard in the County Court because the claim does not exceed £5000. There are in England and Wales about 400 County Courts and they have the power to deal with most types of civil action where the amount claimed is not more than £5000. In addition the County Court may deal with disputes relating to land and property, bankruptcies and also undefended divorce actions. The upper limits in these disputes are higher. Defamation cases, that is libel or slander, are never heard in the County Court but always in the High Court. No doubt this is to discourage frivolous cases.

County courts are governed by the County Courts Act of 1984. The 400 County Courts in England and Wales are grouped in circuits of about fifteen courts. A Circuit Judge will preside over the circuit. You will remember that Circuit Judges also sit in the Crown Court.

Activity

Find out where your nearest County Court is. County Courts will supply, on application, a booklet entitled *Small Claims in the County Court*. This book will explain in more detail County Court procedure.

Exercise 4

1 In the case concerning Woodruffe Renovations and Peak Building Supplies Co. Ltd, name the plaintiff and defendant.
2 What is the main difference between a default summons and an ordinary summons?
3 Give three examples of the types of cases which might be heard by the County Court.

High Court. Although most civil disputes are settled without court action, of those that are heard by a court by far the majority are settled in the County Court, but as we have seen the County Court's power is restricted by the £5000 rule and also by the fact that certain cases such as those involving defamation of character (slander or libel) must be tried in the higher courts. Those civil cases which the County Courts have no power to deal with must go to the High Court. The High Court sits in London but there are also twenty-four centres throughout England and Wales where

High Court actions may be heard. The High Court is divided into three main divisions:

1 The Queen's Bench Division (QBD) which deals with the majority of cases such as failure to perform a contract, e.g. where a pop group has failed to turn up for an engagement, causing losses of many thousands of pounds, or claims for damages in a serious road accident where injuries have resulted in permanent disability and the claim is more than £5000. The Queen's Bench Division also deals with libel and slander with which the County Court cannot deal.

2 The Chancery Division (Ch.D) which deals with financial matters such as disputes relating to mortgages, bankruptcies and company liquidation.

3 The Family Division which deals, as its name suggests, with family matters such as divorce, matrimonial property and settlements, custody of children and adoption.

Activity

Newspapers often carry reports on important civil cases and within the next few weeks you might find it helpful to look for those reports. *The Times* newspaper often has a special section for court business.

Exercise 5

Name the three divisions of the High Court and for each division name one sort of case which might come before it.

Appeals Against Decisions of the County Court and High Court

In a County Court case both plaintiff and defendant, if they feel that the decision reached was incorrect, may appeal to the Court of Appeal (Civil Division). This right of appeal to the Court of Appeal (Civil Division) is also available to plaintiff and defendant in a High Court case. A recent case which went to the Court of Appeal will help to explain how the appeal system works in civil cases.

Mr Eric Hyde, a man of forty-six, had been admitted to Ashton-under-Lyne Hospital suffering from acute pains in his neck and arm. Fearing that he might be suffering from cancer, Mr Hyde tried to commit suicide by jumping from a third floor hospital window. His suicide bid failed but he was left totally paralysed. Mr Hyde sued the hospital board, Tameside Area Health Authority, claiming the hospital had been negligent in allowing him to attempt suicide. At the Queen's Bench Division Court he was awarded £200 000 damages. The Area Health Authority, in this case the defendant, decided to appeal. The appeal was heard in the Court of Appeal (Civil Division) in 1981.

Three judges hear the appeals in the Court of Appeal (Civil Division), by looking through the judge's notes and the official short-hand writer's notes. In an appeal hearing the three judges never call witnesses, nor do they allow fresh evidence to be produced. The barristers representing both defendant and plaintiff may argue their cases. After considering the case the judges may reverse the decision of the court below, uphold it or change the amount of damages awarded. In some circumstances, though much less often, they may order a new trial to take place in the original court, i.e. County Court or High Court.

In this case, known as Tameside Area Health Authority v. Hyde, after carefully considering the evidence the judges reversed the decision of the Queen's Bench Division and stated that they did not feel the hospital had been negligent and no damages should be awarded to Mr Hyde.

This case illustrates the procedure which the Court of Appeal (Civil Division) uses in hearing appeals. It is interesting to note that in the description of the case above the defendant Tameside Area Health Authority is the first named party. Usually as we have learned the plaintiff's name is mentioned first. Where, however, an appeal is heard the name of the party appealing is the first mentioned name. Clearly it was the health authority which was appealing against the £200 000 damages payment.

As with the criminal branch of law the highest court is the House of Lords and where an important point of law is involved appeals may be allowed to the House of Lords from the Court of Appeal (Civil Division). The case is reheard usually before five Law Lords and majority decisions are given. Since 1969 it has been possible for cases to go directly to the House of Lords from the High Court by means of a device known as 'leapfrogging'. The device is so called because the Court of Appeal (Civil Division) is, as it were, 'leaped' over. There have however been few instances of 'leapfrogging' since 1969 when this process was allowed.

A good example of a case which went to the House of Lords is provided by *British Railways Board* v. *Herrington* (1972). This case involved a young boy of six who had got on to an electrified section of rail by entering through poorly maintained fences, and was injured. The boy's parents sued British Rail for negligence but British Rail claimed that since the boy was a trespasser they could not be held responsible. In coming to its decision the Lords stated that an owner of property could be responsible for injuries to trespassers especially children when insufficient attention had been paid to excluding or warning them. The British Railway Board's appeal failed and damages were paid to the boy. Two other recent cases provide good examples.

1. *Hill* v. *Chief Constable of West Yorkshire Police* (1988)
We have already mentioned the case of Peter Sutcliffe, known as the 'Yorkshire Ripper'. The mother of one of his victims sued the police claiming that they had been negligent in not apprehending Sutcliffe who subsequently murdered again. The House of Lords dismissed an appeal and in their judgement stated: 'as a matter of law and also of public policy an action could not be brought against the police in respect of their failure to identify and apprehend a criminal where that failure had resulted in him committing further offences'.

As we shall see (page 24) decisions of the House of Lords are binding on other courts and similar cases will result in a similar decision.

2. *Pearce* v. *Secretary of State for Defence* (1988)
The Court of Appeal sitting in 1987 had dismissed an appeal from Pearce who had suffered personal injuries when serving as a solider on Christmas Island where the UK Atomic Energy Authority were conducting nuclear tests. The Court of Appeal relied on the Crown Proceedings Act of 1947 in

The House of Lords overturned this decision and stated that the crown could not use this Act as a defence. Pearce's successful appeal may well open the door to further claims for damages from soldiers.

The following chart shows the organisation of Civil Courts in England and Wales. You will note the Magistrates Court, this court is mainly a criminal court but has some civil jurisdiction, for example in some matrimonial matters such as the enforcement of maintenance orders.

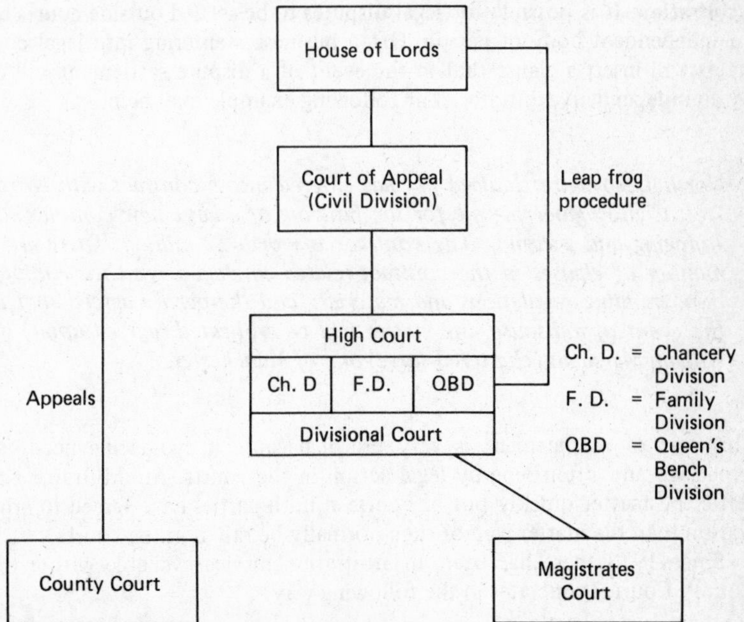

System of civil courts in England and Wales

Tribunals and Arbitration

Tribunals. From time to time new laws are passed by Parliament and it is decided that actions arising from the new laws would be better heard by tribunals - groups of people who are specialised in this area of law. Examples of this are industrial tribunals *or* actions heard by Income Tax Commissioners. The following example may help to illustrate how such tribunals operate.

Bob Dash has been working for Industrial Chemicals plc for 6 years. Following a slight disagreement with one of the supervisors Bob is called in to see the Plant Manager and is dismissed without notice.

In this situation, Bob would have recourse to an Industrial Tribunal which is usually comprised of a chairman who is a lawyer and two other people with specialised knowledge of the branch of the law. The tribunal can award compensation *or* order Bob to be reinstated.

In addition to unfair dismissal, Industrial Tribunals also deal with such matters as redundancy claims, discrimination on grounds of sex or race and other matters in respect of Employment protection.

The procedure for Industrial Tribunals is usually much simpler than the courts and for example Bob could take a trade union office to represent him rather than a solicitor.

The subject of unfair dismissal and other aspects of employment-legislation will be dealt with more fully in Chapter 4.

Arbitration. It is possible for legal disputes to be settled outside courts by an independent body or person. Often businesses entering into legal contracts will insert a clause that in the event of a dispute settlement will be by an independent arbitrator. The following example may help.

North Derbyshire Haulage plc has entered into a contract with North West Civil Engineering plc for the building of a large new complex for storaging and garaging. The contract is worth £2 million. There are a number of clauses in the contract related to stage payments, completion, building regulations and materials, and the parties agreed that in the event of a dispute, the matter will be arbitrated (agreed upon) by William Marshalls (chartered surveyors) of Manchester.

This sort of arrangement is very useful because it avoids the need for expensive and often lengthy legal action in the courts. An arbitrator can settle the matter quickly but of course if both parties have agreed to arbitration then the matter cannot then normally be raised in the courts.

Since 1973 there has been an arbitration service available within the County Court. It operates in the following way:

1 In claims of less than £500 the Registrar of the County Court, can refer the proceedings to arbitration. (A Registrar is a legally qualified person who administers the County Court and as we have seen acts as judge in arbitration proceedings but also can act as judge in the County Court in undefended cases and in cases where the amount claimed is less than £500.)
2 For claims of £500 or more if the parties concerned wish then the case can go to arbitration.

Arbitration is much more informal than court proceedings. The parties in a dispute sit around a table with the Registrar who then will give a decision. The procedure has been referred to as the 'small claims court' because it deals usually with cases where the sums of money contested are not large.

This system of arbitration has proved very popular and in 1986 1.5 million disputes were settled in this way. The civil justice review body has recommended to the government that the upper limit be raised to £1000 and that the small claims court become a local tier of justice.

A number of professional associations e.g. the Law Society, the British Medical Association have Disciplinary committees which have the power to expel a member, making it impossible for him/her to practice his/her profession. These are known as domestic tribunals.

Judith Black is a Solicitor in a small country town. Her clients include a large number of elderly ladies who are wishing to sell their large houses to move to smaller houses. Judith persuades them to sell to her. She then resells them at a profit and pays her clients the agreed price. She has made over £700 000 in this way.

This very unprofessional practice is discovered and she is asked to appear before the Disciplinary Committee of the Law Society. She is found guilty of unprofessional conduct and is struck off the Law Society register. This means she cannot practice as a Solicitor.

Activity

You may often read examples of solicitors or doctors being dealt with in this way. Try to find an example from your newspaper over the next few months or so.

Exercise 6

Read the following examples and for each say (a) whether you think it comes within civil or criminal law, (b) which court is likely to hear the case.

1 Peakdale Engineering Ltd has been taken to court by one of its employees, John Duffy, who was injured while using a faulty piece of machinery. John is claiming compensation of £4500 for the injuries suffered.

2 A famous pop group, the Rocker Billies, have been sued by Music Productions Ltd for failing to turn up for a concert in which they were top of the bill. Ticket money had to be refunded to the audience.

3 David Lomax has been found guilty of causing death by dangerous driving and decides to appeal against the verdict.

4 Four months' imprisonment for a minor shoplifting offence is felt by Martha Jackson to be too severe and she decides to appeal against the sentence.

5 Paula Johnson, financial director of Fortrax Ltd, has been accused of fraud and embezzlement to the tune of many thousands of pounds.

6 Because of the great public and legal importance of the case the Queen's Bench Division allow a libel case between *Conway (Publishers) Co. Ltd* and *Edward Tagg*, to go to the highest court in the land.

7 Jenny Wood has been refused promotion in her company on the grounds that the managing director prefers to see a man in a position of responsibility.

8 Hartley & Sons (Residential homes for the Elderly) has made a claim against the Phoenix Assurance Co. The insurance company decides to use the arbitration clause in the agreement to settle the dispute.

1.3 SOURCES OF THE LAW

1 Peter Howell and his wife Andrea have just returned from an afternoon's shopping and Andrea is anxious to try on a new pair of boots that she has purchased from a shoe shop, Town and Country Shoes Ltd. When she tries on the boots one of the heels comes apart from the boot. Andrea is very upset and Peter decides to go straight back to the shop with the boots to demand a refund of the £48.50 he had paid. The manager of the shop, though sympathetic, refuses to refund the money but says he will have the boots repaired. Peter decides to take the shoe shop to court.

2 Pauline Beckwith is shopping in a large department store and while stepping from an escalator she trips over a metal plate which has become loose and sustains a fractured arm and serious internal injuries. Pauline is advised to take the department store to court to gain compensation for her injuries.

Sale of Goods Act 1979

1979 CHAPTER 54

An Act to consolidate the law relating to the sale of goods. [6th December 1979]

BE IT ENACTED by the Queen's most Excellent Majesty, by and with the advice and consent of the Lords Spiritual and Temporal, and Commons, in this present Parliament assembled, and by the authority of the same, as follows:—

PART I

CONTRACTS TO WHICH ACT APPLIES

Contracts to which Act applies.

1.—(1) This Act applies to contracts of sale of goods made on or after (but not to those made before) 1 January 1894.

(2) In relation to contracts made on certain dates, this Act applies subject to the modification of certain of its sections as mentioned in Schedule 1 below.

(3) Any such modification is indicated in the section concerned by a reference to Schedule 1 below.

(4) Accordingly, where a section does not contain such a reference, this Act applies in relation to the contract concerned without such modification of the section.

PART II

FORMATION OF THE CONTRACT

Contract of sale

Contract of sale.

2.—(1) A contract of sale of goods is a contract by which the seller transfers or agrees to transfer the property in goods to the buyer for a money consideration, called the price.

In both of these civil actions it will be necessary for the County Court judge in situation (1) and the High Court judge in situation (2) to find out what the law actually is.

In the first case the judge would look at an Act of Parliament, the Sale of Goods Act 1979 (see pp. 17, 102).

This Act, which is the source of the law in this situation, will tell him that goods sold by shops must be of 'merchantable quality' and if they are not then shoppers are entitled to a full money refund. In the second case, the judge will have no Act of Parliament to guide him and he will look at previous similar cases and will reach his decision based upon decisions in these cases. It is previous cases which will be the source of law here. Pauline would be sueing the department store for negligence and there have been many similar cases.

In these two situations we have discovered the two main sources of law in the English legal system:

1 Acts of Parliament, or in other words *legislation*.
2 Decided cases, or in other words *precedent*.

We sometimes hear the expression 'he has set a precedent', which means that a person, by his actions, has provided an example for others to follow. This is exactly what judges do when they look at decisions in previous cases. They look for a precedent and since it is within legal cases that they look this source of law is often called 'case law'.

Legislation

The word legislation means a body of rules which have been formally made by Parliament and therefore have become an Act of Parliament and part of the law of the country.

Most legislation starts with the government. It usually has a majority in the House of Commons and can push through its legislation. Legislation starts as a Bill of Parliament which must be approved by both Houses, the House of Commons and the House of Lords. Both Houses receive plenty of opportunity to debate and discuss the Bill before voting upon it. Once it has passed both Houses it must receive the signature of the Queen, which is known as the Royal Assent. After receiving the Royal Assent the Bill becomes an Act and becomes law. An extract from the Sale of Goods Act 1979 is shown on page 17.

Delegated Legislation

Statutory Instruments and Orders in Council. There are circumstances where an Act of Parliament is passed which sets out in general what is required and then gives power to a minister to make detailed regulations. These regulations are known as Statutory Instruments. The term Statutory Instrument means really the instrument of a statute (in other words an Act of Parliament). These regulations have just the same force of law as legislation provided the minister acts within the power given to him by the Act of Parliament.

In a later chapter we will be considering the Health and Safety at Work Act 1974. This Act is an example of where Parliament set out the new law in general terms and then gave considerable power to the minister, in this case the Secretary of State for Employment, to make the detailed regulations. On page 21 you can see an example of a Statutory Instrument based upon the Health and Safety at Work Act. This particular example, which came into force 1 July 1982, deals with first-aid provision which must be made in places of employment. Failure to comply with this regulation may lead to criminal prosecution.

This Statutory Instrument is an example of delegated legislation. Delegated legislation is so called because Parliament has 'delegated' its power to make the law to a minister or Secretary of State. The delegated powers are contained in an Act of Parliament in this particular case, the Health and Safety at Work Act.

There are some instances where ministers will issue Orders rather than regulations. These have the same force of law and provide another example of delegated legislation. On page 22 there is an example of an Order issued by the Home Secretary, Douglas Hurd. This Order was issued on 12 July 1988 under powers given to the Home Secretary by the Police and Criminal Evidence Act 1984 and came into force on 29 July 1988. This Order, also known as a Statutory Instrument, was made in respect of tape-recording of interviews of persons suspected of having committed a criminal offence. As you can see, the Act gave the Minister the power to issue a code of practice to regulate the procedure. The Home Secretary now has the power under the 1984 Act to change the law in respect of these interviews.

There are some circumstances in which law is changed by what is called an Order in Council. This is yet another example of a Statutory Order but it is made by the Queen acting on the advice of her Privy Council, which effectively means acting on the advice of government ministers. The Order in Council on page 23 is one dealing with Antarctica and uses powers of the Antarctic Treaty Act 1967.

Bye-laws. Acts of Parliament will also delegate law-making power to local authorities. Local authorities use this power sometimes to make bye-laws. The Local Government Act 1972 gave this power to what are called district councils Each county has a number of district councils and they have limited law-making power.

An example of a bye-law is one made by Canterbury City council on 2 February 1979 and approved by the Secretary of State on 18 April 1979. This bye-law is concerned with the fouling of footpaths by dogs. A person in charge of a dog which fouls a pavement is liable on conviction to a fine not exceeding £50. Canterbury City council, by passing this bye-law, has created a new criminal offence in respect of that district. Similar bye-laws are in force in many districts in the country.

Regulations, rules and bye-laws of nationalised industries. There also are a number of examples where nationalised industries such as the British Railways Board and the various electricity boards have been given power by Acts of Parliament to make laws.

Activity

When next you travel by British Rail see if you can find examples of bye laws or regulations issued by this particular nationalised industry.

Delegated powers are only available through an Act of Parliament. Ministers local authorities, nationalised boards can only act within the powers attended them in the Act of Parliament. If they exceed these powers they are said to be acting *ultra vires* - 'beyond their powers' - and therefore illegally.

Statutory Interpretation

When Acts of Parliament are passed or changes made under delegated legislation, it is for the courts to interpret the law as laid down in the Act or Instrument. Parliament employs specialists known as draftsmen to ensure that the wording is clear and unambiguous, and usually courts must follow the literal meaning. Sometimes the literal rule leads to an absurd situation and in this case the judges apply the 'Golden Rule' which allows them to modify the language to avoid the inconvenience. Sometimes the judges will apply the mischief rule, that is they will attempt to find out what Parliament intended by passing the Act but this can only be used when the literal rule or the golden rule cannot. If Parliament is dissatisfied with the way its Acts are being interpreted, it can introduce new legislation to make its intentions clearer.

A good example of the application of the mischief rule is in *Gardiner* v. *Sevenoaks RDC* (1950). In this case the Local Authority sought to prevent Gardiner storing film without fulfilling certain conditions as laid down in the Act. The Act used the expression 'premises' and Gardiner claimed that since his film was stored in a cave, he was exempt since a cave was not premises. The court applying the mischief rule looked to see what was the intention of the Act and recognised that it sought to protect employees and others from fire risks. Sevenoaks RDC was successful.

STATUTORY INSTRUMENTS

1981 No. 917

HEALTH AND SAFETY

The Health and Safety (First-Aid) Regulations 1981

Made - - - -	*29th June* 1981
Laid before Parliament	*9th July* 1981
Coming into Operation	*1st July* 1982

ARRANGEMENT OF REGULATIONS

The Secretary of State, in exercise of the powers conferred on him by sections 15(1), (2), (3)(*a*), (4)(*a*), (5)(*b*) and (9) and 49(1) and (4) of, and paragraphs 10 and 14 of Schedule 3 to, the Health and Safety at Work etc. Act 1974 ("the 1974 Act") and of all other powers enabling him in that behalf and for the purpose of giving effect without modifications to proposals submitted to him by the Health and Safety Commission under section 11(2)(*d*) of the 1974 Act after the carrying out by the said Commission of consultations in accordance with section 50(3) of that Act, hereby makes the following Regulations:—

Citation and commencement

1. These Regulations may be cited as the Health and Safety (First-Aid) Regulations 1981 and shall come into operation on 1st July 1982.

Interpretation

2.—In these Regulations, unless the context otherwise requires—

"first-aid" means—

(*a*) in cases where a person will need help from a medical practitioner or nurse, treatment for the purpose of preserving life and minimising the consequences of injury and illness until such help is obtained, and

STATUTORY INSTRUMENTS

1988 No. 1200

POLICE

The Police and Criminal Evidence Act 1984 (Codes of Practice) Order 1988

Approved by both Houses of Parliament

Made - - - -	*12th July 1988*
Laid before Parliament	*13th July 1988*
Coming into force	*29th July 1988*

Whereas –

(1) in pursuance of section 60(1)(a) of the Police and Criminal Evidence Act 1984**(a)** (hereinafter referred to as "the Act") the Secretary of State is under a duty to issue a code of practice in connection with the tape-recording of interviews of persons suspected of the commission of criminal offences which are held by police officers at police stations:

(2) in pursuance of section 67(1) of the Act the Secretary of State has prepared and published a draft code of practice in connection with the said matter and has considered representations made to him thereon:

(3) in pursuance of section 67(3) of the Act the Secretary of State has laid a draft of the code of practice before both Houses of Parliament:

Now, therefore, the Secretary of State, in exercise of the powers conferred on him by section 67(4) of the Act, hereby orders as follows:

Citation and Commencement

1. This Order may be cited as the Police and Criminal Evidence Act 1984 (Codes of Practice) Order 1988 and shall come into force on the day after the day on which it is approved by resolution of each House of Parliament.

Tape-recording code of practice

2. The code of practice laid in draft before Parliament on 13th June 1988 in connection with the tape-recording of interviews of persons suspected of the commission of criminal offences which are held by police officers at police stations shall come into operation on the day after the day on which this Order is approved by resolution of each House of Parliament.

Douglas Hurd

Home Office
12th July 1988

One of Her Majesty's Principal Secretaries of State

(a) 1984 c.60.

STATUTORY INSTRUMENTS

1988 No. 786

ANTARCTICA

The Antarctic Treaty (Contracting Parties) Order 1988

Made - - - - *27th April 1988*

At the Court of Saint James, the 27th day of April 1988

Present,

The Counsellors of State in Council

Whereas Her Majesty, in pursuance of the Regency Acts 1937 to 1953, was pleased, by Letters Patent dated the 28th day of March 1988, to delegate to the six Counsellors of State therein named or any two or more of them full power and authority during the period of Her Majesty's absence from the United Kingdom to summon and hold on Her Majesty's behalf Her Privy Council and to signify thereat Her Majesty's approval for anything for which Her Majesty's approval in Council is required:

Now, therefore, Her Majesty Queen Elizabeth The Queen Mother and His Royal Highness The Prince Charles, Prince of Wales, being authorised thereto by the said Letters Patent, and in pursuance of the powers conferred by sections 7(1) and 10(7) of the Antarctic Treaty Act 1967(**a**) and all other powers enabling Her Majesty, and by and with the advice of Her Majesty's Privy Council, do on Her Majesty's behalf order, and it is hereby ordered, as follows:–

1. This Order may be cited as the Antarctic Treaty (Contracting Parties) Order 1988.

2. It is hereby certified that the Contracting Parties for the purposes of the Antarctic Treaty Act 1967 are as specified in the Schedule to this Order.

3. The Antarctic Treaty (Contracting Parties) Order 1986(**b**) is hereby revoked.

G.I. de Deney
Clerk of the Privy Council

(**a**) 1967 c.65.
(**b**) S.I. 1986/2221.

Precedent

This is a system where once a court has stated the legal position in a given situation then the decision reached by this court will be followed in all similar cases. We have already learned the system of courts in England and Wales and the rule is that decisions of the higher courts will be binding on the lower courts. This means that the lower courts must follow the decision of the higher courts, so for example the decisions of the House of Lords will be binding on all other courts.

Since the decision of one court may be binding on other courts, i.e. it will have to be followed, then it is important that judges make it quite clear why they have come to a particular decision. If we look back for a moment to the situation relating to Pauline Beckwith then the judge when giving his decision, assuming he agrees that Pauline has a good case, will say something like, 'I find for the plaintiff', but then he will go on to give his reasons for coming to the decision that the department store had been negligent. In his reason, known by the Latin phrase *ratio decidendi* (the reason for the decision), he will explain the legal principles he has applied in coming to his decision and he will no doubt refer to other similar previous cases.

It is, of course, possible that a situation arises where there have been no similar cases and there is no Act of Parliament to guide a judge. In this situation the judge must still come to a decision and give a reason. The decision must be followed by judges in similar cases in lower courts and may be followed by higher courts.

A good example of a case which has helped to make the law particularly as it applies to negligence (see Chapter 7) is the now famous *Donogue* v. *Stevenson* (1932) In this case the plaintiff suffered illness after drinking ginger beer containing the remnants of a decomposed snail. Lord Atkin, the judge in this case, established what has been called the neighbourhood principle when he stated 'who then in law is my neighbour. The answer seems to be persons who are so closely and directly affected by my act that I ought reasonably to have them in contemplation . . .'.

This *ratio decidendi* (reason for the decision) has been used in countless cases of negligence down to the present day and therefore used as a precedent. The court found for the plaintiff in this case – the manufacturer of the drink owed her a duty of care.

European Law

In addition to legislation, delegated legislation and precedent, there is one other source of law. Since the United Kingdom is a member of the European Economic Community (EEC) it is subject to certain rules and regulations made by the European Commission and the Council of Ministers. These regulations have the force of law and it is the only example of a source of English law being outside the country. One example of an EEC regulation which has become law in the UK is that relating to social security. The effect is if a person retires in the UK but has lived for periods in one of the EEC countries then they can enjoy the same pension benefits as if they had lived in the UK all their life and paid full contributions. In other words the national pension schemes of the member countries become harmonised in this respect when the European Act becomes law in 1992 it will have the effect of increasing the influence of European Community law on British law.

Activity

As explained earlier *The Times* newspaper often has a section on court cases. It will help you to understand this system of precedent if you look at this from time to time. An example of a case from *The Times* appears on pp. 249–50.

A very good example of the way in which a court outside the UK can influence the law in this country is provided by a recent case brought by the Commission of European Communities [EEC] against the UK and heard in the European Court of Justice.

Commission of European Communities v. *United Kingdom* (1988)
In this case the court in Luxembourg accepted the case brought by the EEC and said that zero rating for VAT purposes building construction and other goods and services such as fuel and power supplied to non-domestic users was illegal.

This ruling was the result, the court said, of an agreement signed by the UK government in 1977 and means for example that private schools and private hospitals will have to pay VAT on new buildings and other goods and services.

Activity

Over the next few months keep a look out for other examples of our law being influenced by this outside source. Remember however that the British Government by accepting membership of the EEC accepted this influence. It is likely that as we approach 1992 and after there will be quite a few examples of the situation we have described.

Exercise 7

1 Name the two main sources of English law.
2 What three stages must a Bill of Parliament pass before it becomes law?
3 Why is it important that a judge gives a reason for his decision in a court case?
4 Which court's decision is binding on all other courts?
5 Give three examples of persons/organisations that have been given delegated power to make law.
6 When the Queen, acting on the advice of the Privy Council, herself makes an order changing the law, what is this known as?
7 Give one example of laws which are made outside the UK but may have force within the UK.

Legal Personnel

In this section, we are more concerned with the work of solicitors and barristers, for it is with these two branches of the legal profession that businesses might often have to deal.

When, in Britain, we use the term Lawyer we could be talking of a Solicitor or Barrister. Their functions are different and the following example hopefully will help to explain the nature of the difference.

C. K. Patel Ltd is a private company which operates a number of retail newsagents shops in Surrey and Sussex. The company which comprises just three shareholders is managed and directed by the main shareholder C. K. Patel himself. The company now owns fifteen shops and salaried managers run them for the company. The company has two legal problems it seeks advice on.

1 C K. Patel wishes to purchase the freehold and business of a shop in Reigate which is being offered at £210 000.

2 In one of the shops in South London, one of the customers is claiming a large amount of compensation following an accident due to the collapse of some part of the building. The claim is in the region of £55 000.

In both instances, C. K Patel would consult a solicitor and he goes to Bennett, Brooke & Taylor, a solicitor near his main offices in Brighton. In the first case, the solicitor deals with the purchase of the property and draws up the necessary contracts and transfers. In the second case, the solicitor consults 'Counsel' as it is called and he goes to a barrister. Barristers are specialists in court work and advice will be given on the

£55 000 claim. If the barrister decides that C. K. Patel has a good case, they will receive instuctions from the solicitors.

Solicitors can be seen as the general practitioners of the legal profession. They deal with legal advice, the drawing up of legal documents, for example property agreements, wills, and they prepare cases for courts. Solicitors can appear in lower cours themselves i.e. Magistrates and County Courts, but only barristers are able to appear in High Courts.

C. K. Patel would not have been able to go to a barrister directly. A barrister must receive his instructions from a practising solicitor. Thus, in our example, Bennett, Brooke & Taylor will get advice (counsel) from a barrister on the £55 000 claim and then advise Mr Patel accordingly. If the case goes to court, then the solicitor will prepare a brief for the barrister.

In some cases leading barristers will be employed. These are recognised by the letters QC following their name which means Queen's Counsel.

Unlike most countries, the UK has two distinct branches in its legal profession and each receives quite different training.

1 Normally a solicitor qualifies by:
  (a) Obtaining a law degree
  (b) Passing Part II of the Law Society Examination
  (c) Serving 2 years as an articled clerk with a solicitor.

2 A barrister qualities by:
  (a) Passing examinations set by the counsel for legal education
  (b) Serving a period of pupillage (training) with a qualified barrister.

We will be examining the relationship betwen barristers and solicitors in more detail in the following section.

Court Procedure – A Civil Case

Many cases involving businesses are civil cases and in this section we will examine a situation where a case has gone to the High Court. The following example will help to explain the procedure.

Evans & Sons (Shopfitters) v. *Tudor Rose Ltd*

Margaret Owen runs a small chain of restaurants and tea shops known as Tudor Rose Ltd. She decides she wishes to refit one of her teashops to give it a sixteenth-century atmosphere. She employs a firm of shopfitters to do her work and a sum of £45 000 is agreed on completion. The work is completed on schedule and Evans & Sons submit their bill a week later. Margaret, however, is far from satisfied. Many of the fittings are not very realistic, several have already become loose and certain parts of the job are nothing like the original specification. The bill remains unpaid despite several reminders. Evans & Sons decide to take the matter to court and as we have already learned, because the claim is in excess of £5000, the case will go to the High Court.

Mr Alex Evans goes to see his solicitor to discuss with him whether it is worth pursuing and following counsel (advice) from Mr Walter Kitson a local barrister. Alex is advised to proceed but only after sending a formal letter to Tudor Rose Ltd asking for settlement and advising the debtor that legal action was likely. Tudor Rose Ltd reply and say that they have no intention of paying for what they regard as poor workmanship. (Individuals cannot approach barristers directly but must do so through a solicitor.)

The case is to be heard at the Queen's Bench Division and begins with a *writ* - a formal document setting out the nature of the claim. This is served on Tudor Rose Ltd, in this case by first class post - though it could be served by hand Tudor Rose Ltd by now have consulted their own solicitor and give notice that they have decided to defend.

Mr Kitson will now prepare a *statement* known as a Statement of Claim which sets out full details of what Evans & Sons are claiming and this is served upon Tudor Rose Ltd. Tudor Rose Ltd in turn prepare a defence which sets out in detail why they have not settled their bill. It really is an answer to the claim and must be made otherwise the defendant is admitting the claim. In the defence, Tudor Rose will no doubt comment on the bad workmanship, the poor fittings and the fact that the work does not seem to come up to specification. On receipt of this, Mr Kitson will then prepare a defence in respect of Tudor Rose's counterclaim. We thus have three documents:

1 A Statement of Claim (prepared by the Plaintiff or his lawyer)
2 A Defence (prepared by the Defendant or his lawyer)
3 A Defence to the Counterclaim (prepared by the Plaintiff or his lawyer).

These three documents are known as 'Pleadings'.

The next stage in the matter is known as the discovery process in which each party has to provide the other with any written evidence that either will produce in court. It so happens that Tudor Rose Ltd have a surveyor's report on the job done by Evans which supports some of Tudor Rose's complaints This document must be seen by Evans & Sons before the hearing. The discovery process has not posed any particular problems and the two parties make a brief appearance in the court when final arrangements are made for the trial. The trial is fixed for Friday 26 August 1988 at 10 30 a.m. This in fact is ten months following the serving of the original writ.

The case is heard before Mr Justice Tennant, a High Court Judge of the Queen's Bench Division. The judge finds for Evans & Sons and awards costs against Tudor Rose Ltd. However, he accepts Tudor Rose's counterclaim and finds for them.

The precise settlement is as follows:

To Evans & Sons		£32 500
	plus costs	£ 6 000
	Total	£38 500
To Tudor Rose Ltd		£15 000
	plus costs	£ 4 000
	Total	£19 000

Evans & Sons gain £13 500 after £6000 has to be paid to cover legal expenses. It might have been cheaper if Evans & Sons had dealt with Tudor Rose's complaints and not gone to the expense of legal action. As pointed out earlier, it is sometimes perhaps better if Arbitration is used – it would certainly have been quicker.

Exercise 8

1 Name the three documents which make up what are called Pleadings in High Court Actions.
2 The production of relevant documents by both sides is known as

3 High Court Actions always start with a
4 If Evans & Sons wished to appeal if this were allowed, which Court(s) would hear it?

Exercise 9

Try to answer all the following review questions without reference to the chapter. If, however, in checking your answer you find some areas you have not understood, then re-read the chapter or the particular section again

1 Give an example of a Civil case which has gone to the House of Lords.
2 By reference to Thameside Area Health Authority v. Hyde 1981, explain how the Court of Appeal (Civil Division) works.
3 Explain by reference to *Donogue* v. *Stevenson* (1931) the term *ratio decidendi*.
4 Explain the term 'Golden Rule' in respect of interpretation of Acts of Parliament.
5 What does *ultra vires* mean?
6 Explain the term 'prepare a brief' and 'take counsel' in respect of solicitors and lawyers.

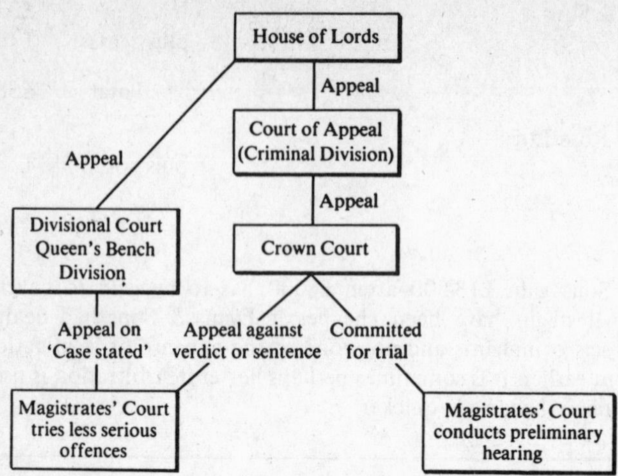

Criminal court structure in England and Wales

CHAPTER 2

BUSINESS AGREEMENTS

2.1 ESSENTIAL REQUIREMENTS IN A CONTRACT

Ian Wood has just been made redundant and he decides to use his redundancy money to purchase a business. The business which he purchases is a shop which sells do-it-yourself materials and items of hardware After just a few weeks in business Ian realises that he needs a van to make deliveries and to collect stock from suppliers. He notices in the local paper an E registered Bedford van advertised at £4960. The van is being sold privately by Alan Willis. Ian goes to see the van which is in very good condition and has done only 8500 miles. Ian makes Alan an offer of £4900 for the van and Alan accepts. Ian pays Alan by means of a cheque and Alan allows Ian to drive the van away.

This agreement reached between Alan and Ian is an example of a contract and in this chapter we will be looking at the main essential requirements which must exist in a legally binding contract. We will be concentrating particularly on business contracts but much of what is included here will be applicable to any legally binding contract. You will have noticed that the agreement between Ian and Alan was neither made in a solicitor's office nor in writing. In fact, although some contracts are in writing this is by no means a necessity and in practice only a very small percentage of contracts made are actually made in solicitors' offices. A contract is simply an agreement which the law will recognise.

Exercise 1

1 All contracts made must be made with the help of a solicitor. *true/false*?
2 All contracts must be in writing *true/false*?
3 Give a definition of a contract.

In order for an agreement to be a contract, that is something which the law will recognise, it must contain certain essential elements and it is with these essential elements that this chapter is concerned. A contract must begin with an offer. You will remember that Ian made an offer to Alan to purchase the Bedford van for £4900. An offer may be made to a specific person. In our example the offer was made to Alan. An offer however, may be made to a group of persons, for example when a company makes an offer to its employees. An offer may be made to the whole world as when an offer of a reward is made. It is important that the offer is communicated; thus in our example there is no doubt that Ian communicated his offer to Alan. When an offer is made the person making the offer is known as the offeror and the person to whom the offer is made is known as the offeree.

Exercise 2

In our example name the offeree and name the offeror.

It is very important to distinguish an offer from an invitation to treat. Goods in shop windows or on display and goods advertised are usually invitations to people to come in and make offers and are known as invitations to treat. Thus in our example the appearance of the van in the newspaper advertisement was an invitation to readers to come to Alan to make an offer. Only offers can be accepted; it is not possible to accept invitations to treat.

Exercise 3

If a shopkeeper displays in the shop window, by mistake, a radio for £5 instead of £55, what would be the legal position of the shopkeeper if he refused to sell the radio for £5 to a customer?

A well-known case illustrates the difference between an 'invitation to treat' and an offer.

Pharmaceutical Society of Great Britain v. *Boots Cash Chemist* (1953)
This was a criminal case which the Pharmaceutical Society brought against Boots Usually criminal cases are brought by the crown or the police acting on the crown's behalf, but individuals or organisations can bring a private prosecution. This prosecution was brought because the society argued that Boots had offered to sell drugs to the public without there being a qualified pharmacist present. This was contrary to Section 17 of the Pharmacy and Poisons Act. Boots, in their defence, argued that goods had been sold in a

self service store and that the goods on display on the shelves were merely 'invitations to treat', i.e. invitations to the customers to make offers which they made at the cash point. There was, Boots argued, a qualified pharmacist at the point of sale, i.e. at the cash desk, who could if he wished reject the offer. Boots were found not guilty and acquitted.

This case illustrates well that goods on display or goods advertised are not offers, indeed it is the customer who makes the offer and the shop proprietor or his assistant who accepts.

We have seen then from our example of the Bedford van that legally binding contracts must start with an offer and it was Ian who offered Alan £4900 for the van. The next stage in a contract is the acceptance which must match the offer completely. Thus, it is sufficient that Alan replies simply 'yes'. Alan's acceptance must be unconditional, i.e. there must be no 'ifs' or 'buts'. If Alan had said 'yes, but I want £4950' this would not be an unconditional acceptance and therefore not an acceptance at all. When the two parties, Ian and Alan, had offered and accepted respectively there was an agreement.

The next stage in our agreement was the two-way exchange; Ian gave Alan the money, in this case a chpque for £4900, and Alan gave Ian the van In this example the money (£4900) and the goods (the Bedford van) were the 'consideration' Consideration is the legal term for something of value which exchanges between the parties as a result of the agreement.

Consideration must be two-way and must be of value. In the example the consideration in both directions was of value.

Exercise 4

If Frank offered one of his employees a gift of £200 which the employee accepted, would this be a contract?

Exercise 5

In the following example identify the offeror, the offeree and the consideration.

Good Deal Motors Ltd have displayed in their showroom a 1987 Rover 2.6 car priced at £5450. John Hardiman who is very interested in this car tells the salesman that he is willing to pay £5250. The salesman agrees and John collects the car giving a cheque for £5250.

We have now identified three essential ingredients of a legally binding contract, i.e. (i) an offer, (ii) an acceptance which matches the offer completely, (iii) two-way consideration.

In addition to these three ingredients several other ingredients must be present in order for an agreement to be legally binding.

It is essential that the two parties entering into the agreement must have the capacity to do so. By saying a person has the capacity we mean that he is legally entitled to enter into a contractual agreement. In English law a person who has attained the age of eighteen has full legal capacity and therefore can enter into legally binding arrangements. A person below the age of eighteen has not got this full capacity and there are certain agreements entered into by young people who are under eighteen (to use the legal expression, who 'have not reached the age of majority') which are not legally binding because for these agreements the young person (the minor) has no contractual capacity. A good example of such an agreement is one where a young person enters into an agreeement to obtain credit. This agreement is not legally binding and therefore not a contract. This important fact serves as a warning to any business that it is dangerous to afford credit facilities to young persons. If the young person should default, i.e. not pay, then payment can never be enforced in the court. This is so because no contract exists; the creditor could not sue for breach of contract because there is no contract. The following case illustrates this well. In *Mercantile Union Guarantee Corporation Ltd* v. *Ball* (1937), an infant haulage contractor who took a lorry on hire-purchase was held not liable for arrears of instalments. Minor or infants as they are rather quaintly termed in law are now persons under the age of 18. Before the Family Law Reform Act the age was 21.

In our example we can safely assume that both Ian and Alan possessed full contractual capacity to enter into the agreement. If someone enters into a contract while drunk or temporarily insane then that person can 'avoid' the contract i.e. not be bound by it provided he/she can prove. (a) he/she was drunk or insane when he/she made the contract. (b) the other party knew that he/she was drunk or insane. The following example may help to explain this part of the law.

Gaynor Curzon has had six double whiskies and in her resultant state of drunkenness she agrees to sell her E registration Ford Fiesta car for £1200. Bill Usher is delighted with this deal but when he goes the next day to take delivery Gaynor refuses to hand the car over.

As we have seen Gaynor can 'avoid' the agreement provided she is able to prove: (a) that she was drunk when she made the agreement; (b) Bill knew she was drunk. It seems she is within her rights to refuse to hand it over.

English law will only recognise agreements which are legal, and therefore any agreement by one party, for example, to commit a crime in return for payment will not be recognised. Under no circumstances would a court allow a hired murderer to collect damages in the court if the person hiring him had refused to fulfil his side of the bargain, i.e. refused to pay for carrying out this illegal act. The hirer would not be in breach of contract because no legally binding contract exists.

There seems, however, nothing illegal in the arrangement to sell the E registered Bedford van mentioned earlier and therefore it would appear to have the ingredient of legality.

Exercise 6

We have now established the existence of five essential elements necessary to make a legally binding contract. Before we go on to consider the other essential elements try without reference to the book to list these five elements.

Although an agreement may contain each of these five elements the court may still not recognise it because, as it is sometimes put, there is between the two parties to the agreement 'no meeting of the minds'. This means that one or both parties had entered into the agreement either unwillingly or perhaps not knowing all the facts because they had been misled. For example in the Bedford van agreement, if the van was much older than suggested, i.e. it displayed false number plates because in fact it was a B registered vehicle and had done 27 500 miles not the 8500 indicated, then it is clear to see that Ian was entering into an agreement having been misled; indeed Alan had misrepresented the facts to Ian. There is little doubt that Ian would not have entered into the agreement had he the true facts before him. There would have been certainly no 'meeting of the minds' between Ian and Alan. The court would not uphold this agreement. In some cases of misrepresentation, courts will uphold the contract but award damages to the injured party.

Similarly, courts would not uphold agreements where one party had been forced against his will to enter into an agreement. Agreements will not be legally binding where there is clearly no 'meeting of the minds'. Often you will come across, in law books, a Latin phrase to describe this 'meeting of the minds': *consensus ad idem*.

As we have already seen, contracts need not be in writing; in fact in the majority of cases the court is not concerned with the form in which the contract is made. There are, however, several situations where the form of the contract is an essential element, and where if an agreement is not in a particular form it is not legally binding. The list below gives three examples of where the form of contract is an essential element.

1 A document to transfer ownership in land or property must be in a special form known as a deed otherwise it is not legally binding.
2 A hire purchase agreement must be in writing to be legally binding.
3 Some contracts are legally binding without being in writing but if not in written form will not be enforceable in the courts, e.g. an agreement to sell land or property. Note this agreement is to be distinguished from the actual transfer, see Chapter 11.

Agreements may contain all the seven elements as above, i.e. offer, acceptance, consideration, capacity, legality, *consensus ad idem* and be in the correct form, but nevertheless still not be legally binding. This is because there is one final element which must be present. Was there 'legal intent', i.e. did the parties to the agreement intend that their agreement should have legal consequences? There is no doubt that Ian and Alan intended this and in fact the rule in English law is that in business agreements which contain all the seven essential elements it is assumed that 'legal intent' is present unless it is specifically removed. In some agreements one party states that the agreement is 'binding in honour only' and in this case the legal intent has been specifically removed.

Exercise 7

A football pool coupon is an agreement lacking this essential element of legal intent. Obtain a coupon and try to find the clause which is contained on all football pools which removes the legal intent.

Although it is assumed that in most agreements 'legal intent' is present unless specifically removed, in domestic and social arrangements the assumption is the opposite, i.e. the court will assume the absence of legal intent unless it is specifically included. Thus if a father promises his son an extra £1 a week for digging the garden and then refuses to pay even though the son has fulfilled his side of the agreement, there will be no breach of contract because no contract exists because of the absence of legal intent. The following case sums this up well. *Appleson* v. *Littlewood Ltd* (1939), the plaintiff sued to recover money which he claimed to have won on a football pool. His action failed, because the printed entry form contained a statement that the transaction was 'binding in honour only'.

Exercise 8

Write down the eight elements essential in a legally binding contract. Check your answers. If you have missed any from your list then go over this section of work again.

It is important that you understand the elements necessary in a legally binding contract because a number of the chapters which follow are concerned with the law of contract. An understanding of contract forms a good basis for a number of topics included in later chapters. The following review exercise is an attempt to test your understanding of legally binding agreements and the essential elements within them.

Exercise 9

In each of the following examples there is one element missing; try to identify in each case why the agreement is not legally binding by stating the missing element.

1 Jim Frezier offers his wife £10 per week if she will clean his two cars regularly. Thelma, his wife, accepts the offer but Jim will not pay the £10 even though Thelma has performed her side of the bargain by regularly cleaning the cars.

2 Keith Martin buys a second-hand car from Good Deal Motors Ltd for £4200. The purchase is on a hire purchase agreement, £1400 down and 24 monthly instalments of £143.33 which includes 10% per annum interest. The manager explains the agreement to Keith saying that his firm does not believe in unnecessary paperwork. The agreement is a verbal one.

3 Woodruff Renovations Ltd offer to paint a customer's house free of charge. The customer accepts this offer but Woodruff Renovations refuse to do the job.

4 Michael finds a wallet belonging to Frank Dolman, a wealthy director. Frank's address is in the wallet and Michael takes it to Frank's house unaware that there is an offer of a £15 reward. Frank refuses to pay up despite getting his wallet back.

5 The Hotel Regal advertise two nights' bed and breakfast, double room with bathroom, for £25 each. John and his wife Barbara write asking for the first weekend in August. They do not hear from the Hotel Regal but assuming a booking has been made arrive at the hotel to find it fully booked.

6 Douglas Pochin is a technical representative for a machine tool company. He persuades Low Peak Co. Ltd to buy a lathe which he describes as a new German lathe of the most advanced design. In fact, it is an old lathe which has been reconditioned. Low Peak Ltd order the machine at a price of £8500.

7 Carol Latham (aged seventeen) has passed her driving test and buys a second-hand Mini for £2350 from Carsales Ltd. She signs an agreement to pay £350 deposit and the balance over two years at £100 per month which includes 10 per cent interest per annum.

8 Anxious to find more information about a rival firm's new revolutionary machine, Jack Lawrence, managing director of Engineering Developments Ltd, pays John Davey £2000 to break into the development office of the rival firm to obtain a photocopy of the plans for the new machine. John obtains this information but Jack refuses to pay the £2000.

If you have not correctly identified the element which was missing in any of these examples then read through this first section again so that you understand these eight essential elements.

2.2 THE MAIN CONTRACTUAL ELEMENTS

Offers

Commercial Vehicles Co. Ltd, which deals in the sale of both new and second-hand commercial vehicles, offers to sell Roger Kent, a market gardener who is visiting the showroom, a one-year-old lorry for £13 500. This is rather more than Roger wished to pay but he is impressed by the lorry's condition and asks the salesman if he can have a couple of days to think about the offer.

As we have already seen, all legally binding agreements must begin with an offer which must be communicated to the offeree. In this example Commercial Vehicles Co. Ltd have communicated an offer verbally to Roger Kent. An offer has then been made. Offers, however, cannot last indefinitely and we will be examining the ways in which an offer may come to an end by looking at our particular example:

1 If Roger decides to accept the offer of the lorry for £13 500 then the offer has ended by acceptance.
2 An offer can also come to an end if the offeror, in this example Commercial Vehicles Co. Ltd, decides to withdraw it. Sometimes the word 'revoke' is used instead of withdraw but it means exactly the same. The rule relating to revocation (withdrawal) is that the offeror may withdraw his offer at any time before it has been accepted. If this withdrawal is communicated directly or indirectly to the offeree, e.g. Roger, then the offer comes to an end. There must however be a definite communication of the revocation.

In our example you will remember that Commercial Vehicles Co. Ltd gave Roger a couple of days to think about the offer, yet despite this Commercial Vehicles Co. Ltd would be perfectly within their rights to withdraw the offer as soon as Roger left the showroom as long as the fact of the withdrawal has been brought to Roger's attention. The company may decide to sell the vehicle to another customer and they could do this because this would be the same as withdrawing the offer.

There is, however, one situation where the company would be prevented from withdrawing their offer before the allotted time of a couple of days had lapsed. This is if Roger had asked them to keep the offer open and he had paid Commercial Vehicles Co. Ltd let us say £300. In this case a contract has come into existence as shown below:

Commercial Vehicles Ltd | Roger Kent

Keep offer open for two days

Pays £300

As you can see, this contract is supported by two-way considerations. The company keeps the offer open and Roger pays £300. In business practice the £300 is used as a deposit and deducted from the purchase price. If Roger decides not to accept the offer then Commercial Vehicles Co. Ltd could keep the £300 since they kept their side of the bargain, i.e., keeping the offer open.

Exercise 10

1 Name two ways in which offers may be brought to an end.

2 Offers may be revoked at any time before . . .

3 How can an offeree ensure that an offer remains open for a specific period of time?

There are two additional ways in which offers may be brought to an end. If after thinking about the offer Roger decided that he could not really afford £13 500, or if he did not really think the vehicle was worth that, he could do one of two things. He could notify Commercial Vehicles that he did not wish to accept the offer - in other words he would be rejecting the offer. Or he could ask the company if they were willing to accept £13 000; here Roger would be making what is called a counter-offer and he would be rejecting the first offer. In fact, Roger would become the offeror because he is now making the offer and Commercial Vehicles would be the offeree. Offers may come to an end by rejection, by the offeree saying 'no' to the offer or making a counter-offer. This situation is summed up well by an old case *Hyde* v. *Wrench* (1840).

A farm was offered at £1000. The offeree thought this was too much and offered £950 but this was refused. The offeree, anxious to obtain the farm, then suggested £1000. The court decided that the offer of £950 was a counter offer and was the same as a rejection.

An offer may also come to an end by what is called lapse. If a specific time is put upon an offer, in our example two days, then when the two days have expired the offer comes to an end unless before that time it has been accepted, withdrawn or rejected. Where no time has been stated then the offer will come to an end after the expiry of a reasonable time. In a dispute it is for the courts to decide what is reasonable and clearly this will depend upon the subject of the offer. The offer to buy fresh fruit cannot remain open for too long for obvious reasons, whereas the offer to buy a motorcar may remain open for a longer period.

The Motor Agents' Association, to which many garages belong, has produced a standard form for motor car sales, which lays down certain time limits in respect of car sales.

The other way in which an offer can lapse is through death of the offeree before acceptance. Thus if Roger should die before accepting the offer of the vehicle then the offer would lapse and no other member of his family could accept. The offer will also come to an end if the offeror should die.

Exercise 11

1 Name the four ways by which an offer may come to an end.

2 If Roger offered to buy the lorry for £13 250 this would be a   and Roger would become the

3 Name two ways in which an offer might lapse.

Acceptance

All agreements must start with an offer but, equally important, offers must be accepted. In our example Commercial Vehicles Co. Ltd have made an offer of a lorry for £13 500. For Roger to accept it means that he must do so unconditionally, i.e. without conditions. As we have seen, it is not sufficient for him to say, 'I accept but I can only pay £13 000'. There must be no 'ifs' or 'buts'; Roger must say 'yes'. If he says 'no' or 'yes but' this is a rejection of the Commercial Vehicles Co. Ltd offer. The acceptance must match the offer completely. *Hyde* v. *Wrench* showed that a counter offer could not be an acceptance.

There are, however, special rules relating to postal acceptance, i.e. where the offeree decides to accept an offer by letter. The following example will help to illustrate this.

Arthur Williams is a technical representative working for Computer Power plc, a firm producing computers and word processors. On a visit on 1 June to a large firm of chartered accountants, Jordan & Sons, Arthur offers to sell the firm two word processors, each costing £7000, for £12 000. Arthur explains that the offer will remain open for one week; he leaves full details of the offer and suggests that Jordans write to his firm if they wish to accept the offer. On 2 June in the morning the partners of Jordans meet and decide to accept the offer and post a letter to this effect to Computer Power plc. The letter is posted at 11.30 a.m. In the afternoon of the same day Arthur is severely repri-

manded by his boss for making too 'good' an offer and is asked to ring Jordans to withdraw the offer. Arthur does this at 3.30 p.m. but Mr Philip Jordan who answers the phone replies 'too late'; we have already accepted'.

In this case Jordans have accepted the offer and a legally binding contract has come into effect between Jordans and Computer Power even though Computer Power has not yet received the letter of acceptance. The law, as it relates to postal acceptance, is quite clear; acceptance takes place at the time of posting, that is at 11.30 a.m. provided the letter has been correctly addressed and prepaid, i.e. has a correct stamp on it. Withdrawal takes effect when it is brought to the attention of the offeree, that is at 3.30 p.m., but this was clearly too late because as we have learned an offer cannot be withdrawn if it has been accepted.

The rules relating to postal acceptance are only applicable where either postal acceptance was suggested, as with Jordans and Computer Power plc, or where it is a normal means of acceptance. If the offeror specifies other means of acceptance, e.g. telephone, then the acceptance would be effective from the receipt of the telephone call and the letter would be irrelevant. It is for the offeror to specify if he wishes a particular form of acceptance. This is summed up well in the following case. In *Holwell Securities Ltd* v. *Hughes* (1974), an offer to sell required that acceptance be made 'by notice in writing to the intending vendor' within six months. Notice was posted but never arrived. It was held that there was no contract. The words of the offer showed that the offeror was not prepared to be bound until he *received* the written notice. The rules relating to postal acceptance were laid down in the judgement in *Byrne* v. *Van Tienhoven* (1880). In *Byrne* v. *Van Tienhoven* (1880), a firm in Cardiff offered by letter to sell tin plate to a firm in New York. Later, the firm sent another letter revoking this offer, but while this was in transit and before its delivery, the New York firm posted a letter of acceptance. It was held that the parties clearly intended the use of the post to communicate acceptance, and posting the letter of acceptance, therefore, brought the contract into existence, since this was done before the revocation arrived.

Exercise 12

1 An acceptance must match the offer completely. *true/false*?

2 Postal acceptance takes effect from the time the letter is received by the offeror. *true/false*?

3 The offeree can accept the offer by whatever means he wishes. *true/false*?

4 Withdrawal of an offer takes place when it is posted *true/false*?

Consideration

As we have already learned, all legally binding agreements must be supported by consideration in both directions.

> **Exercise 13**
>
> Identify the consideration in the following example:
>
> Commercial Supplies Ltd are selling a typewriter to Highgate Televisions Ltd for £450.

Normally, therefore, a promise of a gift can not be enforced because a gift is one-way consideration. It is possible, however, to make legally binding an agreement to give a gift by incorporating the promise of the gift into a deed which is simply a document which has been signed, sealed and delivered. For example, if David Beresford, a grocer, promises to give one of his employees, Philip Bagshaw, a gift of £200, the courts will not give any remedy to Philip if David breaks his promise. However, if David signs a document, such as the one below, the document becomes a deed and is enforceable against David in the courts. The seal is usually a red wafer fixed to the document shown in black in this example:

I, David Beresford, promise to pay Philip Bagshaw within 7 days of the date which appears on this agreement the sum of two hundred pounds(£200).

Signed, Sealed and Delivered

by the said DAVID BERESFORD ____ D. Beresford

in the presence of

Name JULIA EVANS **Signature** J. Evans

Address 56, WILLIAMS ST, CANTERBURY KENT. CT2 4DJ

Occupation SALES ADMINISTRATOR

Date 9th December. **1988.**

The rule therefore is legally binding agreements must be supported by consideration in both directions unless the agreement is made on a deed. This allows consideration to be only one-way.

Until recently, deeds of Covenant were often drawn up in favour of students by a parent in which the parent covenant to pay his/her daughter/son a sum of money. This allowed the money to be paid and the recipient in question to receive the tax which has already been paid back. (This tax concession was withdrawn by the 1988 Budget.)

There are, however, four more rules which must be understood relating to consideration and the four following examples will help to illustrate these rules.

1 Adam Bradd is a qualified accountant who has, on two occasions, helped a friend, Roy Spencer, who runs a small furniture and carpet business, with his tax returns. There has never been any mention of payment but Roy decides to make his friend a gift of a carpet and goes to Adam's house to measure up the lounge. However, Roy, before fitting the carpet falls out with Adam and the carpet is never delivered. Adam thinks of suing.

We have seen that consideration must be two-way and in this case Adam has done the tax returns and Roy is going to supply the carpet. However, the consideration supplied by Adam, i.e. the tax return, is in the past and the courts will not recognise past consideration. As far as the courts are concerned, the promise by Roy of the carpet is merely one-way and as suggested in the example merely a gift; Roy's promise is not legally binding.

Consideration can be present, i.e. if Adam had done the tax return and Roy had given him the carpet, or it can be future, i.e. Roy provides the carpet and Adam does the tax return in the future. It must, however, never be in the past. Promises for services rendered in the past are not legally binding.

If, therefore, you decide to assist a friend in some activity and you want payment for this it is always wise to discuss this at the outset. There are, however, many examples, of course, where work is done and payment made afterwards. If someone takes his car to the garage for repair the payment made after the repair will not be for past consideration for, in commercial dealings of this sort, there is an implied promise to pay for the repairs: the car repair is present consideration and the payment is future consideration because of the existence of the promise to pay.

2 Peter Hurwell is a hotel manager with a large hotel chain known as Leisure Hotels Ltd. He is, at present, manager of the Royal Hotel, a large hotel in the South West of England. There have been for some time certain problems at the Royal and the company feel that a lot is due to Peter's casual attitude to work. Peter is called to a meeting at

Leisure Hotels Ltd in which he promises to give up this casual attitude and to work to the best of his ability. In return the company agree to pay him a bonus of £2000 at the end of the year. When the company conducts its review at the end of the year there is no doubt that considerable improvements have taken place and Peter's new attitude has been the major contributory factor. Nevertheless, Leisure Hotels Ltd refuse to pay the promised bonus and Peter decides to sue his company.

It would seem that this agreement is based upon a two-way consideration, i.e. Peter's promise to work to the best of his ability and the company's promise of a £2000 bonus. If, however, we examine Peter's side of the bargain in more detail we will discover that in fact, Peter was only promising to do something which he ought to have done anyway. In other words, Peter was promising to fulfil an existing obligation and that in law is not consideration Therefore the agreement between Peter and Leisure Hotels Ltd is based only on one-way consideration; only the company is giving consideration and therefore the agreement is not legally binding and Peter could not sue.

The third rule, therefore, relating to consideration is that it must not be an existing obligation.

Exercise 14

Mary Goodwin has borrowed £400 at 20 per cent interest per annum for one year from East Credit Ltd. Her agreement is that she pays this sum off by means of 12 x £40 monthly payments = £480. By the end of the year Mary has paid just six instalments, making £240 in all. The credit company suggest she pays off £160 and they will let her off the interest. Mary pays this but East Credit Ltd decide to sue for the £80 interest.

What would your advice be to Mary remembering what we have learned about consideration not being an existing obligation?

3 Tony Hurnford and his wife Celia own a large detached house with a market value of about £120 000. Wishing for a quick sale because of financial problems they are in, Tony and Celia advertise the house at £90 000 and get a buyer immediately. Contracts are exchanged between the Hurnfords and the buyer, Timothy Lomas. The Hurnfords refuse to complete the sale because they argue the price was too low. Timothy decides to sue.

In fact, Timothy would be successful and it is likely that the court would order the Hurnfords to complete the sale. This is because while consideration must exist in both directions the court will never concern itself with the value of consideration. Timothy and the Hurnfords have entered into the agreement willingly and the court will not interfere with bargains unless there is any evidence that the agreement was obtained by Timothy unfairly, e.g. by threats. As we have seen, this was not the case and the agreement was willingly entered into. This then establishes our fourth rule that courts are not concerned with the adequacy of a consideration; they are only concerned with its existence. As long as consideration is two-way and is of some value the court will accept it.

Exercise 15

We have now learned four rules relating to considerations. State these four rules.

There remains just one more rule relating to consideration which can be explained by reference to this example:

4 XYZ Co. Ltd decide to give ten of their senior staff a special thank-you present for their efforts in a successful year. A weekend is booked for each of the ten staff and their wives or husbands. XYZ Co. book with the Regal Hotel on the south coast and pay in advance the bill which amounts to £2000. When the staff arrive at the hotel they find that the rooms are all fully booked. Keith Martin, one of the senior executives on the trip, threatens the Regal with legal action.

In fact, Keith could not sue the hotel since normally only the person supplying the consideration may sue on a contract. So XYZ Co. Ltd could sue because they supplied the consideration. Thus the final rule for us to learn is that only parties providing consideration can sue on the contract; in other words, only parties to a contract can sue on it. This rule is known as 'privity of contract', which means that an agreement is private to the parties who make the agreement. There is an important exception to this rule. This applies to motor insurance. A third party injured by a motorist can sue the motorist's insurance company even though the injured person was not a party to the insurance contract. Also the Road Traffic Act 1972 allows a person driving a car with the owner's consent to recover compensation from the insurance company with which the owner is insured. This is another example of an exception to the Privity of Contract rule.

Exercise 16

The following examples are provided to test your knowledge of the rules relating to offer, acceptance and consideration. Study each carefully and advise the party in italics of his legal position. Try to do this review exercise without reference to the text. Check your answers and if you have found difficulty with any of the exercises re-read the relevant section.

1 Marchant Machine Tools Ltd offer to sell a computerised milling machine to *Sterndale Engineering Ltd* for £15 500. Sterndale ask for a week to think the offer over and pay a deposit of £1500 and this is accepted. Subsequently, Marchant Machine Tools decide they cannot wait a week and sell the machine for £15 000 to another firm.

2 *The Palace Hotel* receive a letter from Deepdale Cash Registers Ltd wishing to book a suite of rooms for three days for a sales conference. The manager of the Palace writes a letter confirming the booking. Before receiving the letter Deepdale cancel the arrangements.

3 *Harpur Builders Ltd* decide to give each of their five employees a £100 Christmas gift. They send a written statement to the employees saying this gift will be in the next week's pay packet but in fact no gift is given.

4 *Paul Caffery* owns a cottage on the south coast and he decides to offer his solicitor a week's holiday in the cottage free of charge to thank him for legal work the solicitor has done in the past. The solicitor accepts the offer but when he presses Paul for a date Paul changes his mind.

5 Reg Pullin sells a two-month-old Rover 2.7 litre for £4000 to *Kearings Motor Supplies Ltd*. Reg then tries to recover the car saying £4000 is not nearly enough for a luxury car of this sort.

6 Julian Cartwright is injured while driving his friend's car. He tries to recover compensation from the Norwich Assurance but is refused because he has not made any contract with Norwich.

Capacity

We have already seen that one of the elements necessary in a legally binding agreement is capacity. In other words each party must be fully capable of entering into the agreement. The general rule is that everyone has full capacity but there are certain restrictions placed upon young people below the age of eighteen and upon drunks and insane persons.

Minors or infants. In a legal sense a person who has not reached the age of majority, i.e. eighteen years, is known as a minor or infant. Minors do not have full contractual capacity. The following examples will distinguish those agreements made with minors which are legally binding from those that are not.

Agreements which can be enforced against minors

Simon Beckwith (aged sixteen) orders a made-to-measure suit for his new job in a bank from Easifit (Tailors) Ltd. The tailors deliver the suit to Simon's house but Simon refuses to accept it saying he has changed his mind about the colour. Easifit decide to sue.

A legally binding agreement has come into operation and Easifit would be able to sue. Minors can make contracts for what the law calls 'necessaries', i.e. things which a minor needs. A suit for working in a bank is a 'necessary'. It is important to distinguish 'necessary' from 'necessity'. A 'necessity' is something which is essential, e.g. food and water. The courts will judge 'necessaries' against the criteria:

1 Is the article suitable to the minor's position in life?
2 How many items of this article does he have?

On these two grounds the suit would be regarded as a necessary.

This rule relating to necessaries is neatly summed up in a famous case *Nash* v. *Inman* (1908) where a minor (in those days under 21) was sued for £145 for the cost of eleven fancy waistcoats. The supplying firm could not recover this money because the court held that these were not necessaries. The boy's father had already supplied him with a full wardrobe of clothes.

Michael Pullen (aged sixteen) works for a large engineering company as an apprentice fitter. After a trial period of six months Michael is asked to sign an apprenticeship agreement which stipulates that he must remain with the company for four years, attending technical college one day per week, and for this he will receive a wage of £70 per week rising by £10 per week each year. Michael signs this agreement but after a year he decides to leave. The company sue Michael for damages for the money they have spent on his training.

This is an example of a legally binding agreement because although Michael is a minor the law lays down that agreements relating to employment, apprenticeship or education are for the minor's benefit. The company is likely to be successful in claiming damages although in practice the company would be unlikely to sue.

Exercise 17

Name two types of contract which a minor can make.

Contracts which are not enforceable against minors

Terence Clapham (aged seventeen) borrows £400 at 10 per cent interest for two years, from a credit company. After paying the initial payment of £20 Terence defaults and the credit company take him to court.

Unfortunately for the company no contract exists between Terence and the company because any agreement made by a minor relating to credit lacks capacity and therefore is void. It is easy to understand why shops will never enter into hire purchase or credit agreements with minors. As we have seen, another agreement with a minor which is void by virtue of lack of capacity is any agreement to supply goods which are not necessaries.

We have seen, therefore, that there are two types of agreement relating to minors; those which are valid and those which are void. There is, however, another type of agreement which if made by a minor is enforceable against him when he reaches the age of eighteen. We call this category of agreements 'voidable', which means they can be avoided by the young person before he reaches eighteen or a reasonable time thereafter. Three examples of such voidable contracts are:

1 Agreements to lease a flat or house.
2 Agreements to enter partnerships.
3 Agreements to buy shares in companies.

Example 18

Give one example in each case of an agreement made by a minor which is (1) valid; (2) void; (3) voidable.

Insane and Drunken Persons

We have already seen that this may affect a contract. The following example will underline the legal position.

Frank Browning owns a sports car worth about £6500. At a party at his office one of his employees seeing that he had had too much to drink persuades Frank to sell him the car for £650. Frank even signs a document to this effect. Frank, however, when he sobers up realises his mistake and refuses to release the car even though the buyer produces the £650.

In this situation, Frank could avoid the agreement because the court would say that at the time he made the agreement he lacked capacity. Frank must prove that (1) he was drunk; (2) the buyer knew he was drunk.

The same rule applies to someone who was temporarily insane, provided he can prove he was insane at the time he made the agreement and, secondly, that the other party realised this fact.

In certain cases persons suffering from mental illness cannot make any agreement because their property is subject to the control of the court. This device, introduced in 1960 by the Mental Health Act, is to protect the mentally sick from unscrupulous persons and removes completely their contractual capacity.

Legal Intent

Fortrex Office Supplies Co. Ltd draw up an agreement to supply a range of office machinery value £35 000 to Trenchard Manufacturing Co. Ltd.

Mrs Lynne Jones orders a bedroom suite at £785 from Fairfield Furnishings Ltd.

Both these agreements would, on the face of it, seem to contain the elements necessary to make them contracts and therefore legally binding. You will no doubt remember that one of the essential elements is the presence of legal intent, i.e. did both parties to the agreement intend that the agreement should have legal consequences? It would be fair to assume that each of the four parties concerned here – Fortrex, Trenchard, Mrs Jones and Fairfield Furnishing – had this intent. Indeed, the courts in this country will always assume that in commercial and business agreements the parties had legal intent. This assumption can only be removed if a clear statement accompanies the agreement such as: 'This agreement is binding in honour only and it is not intended that it should have any legal consequence.' An agreement containing such a clause could not become a contract for it would lack the essential element of legal intent.

Football pools coupons always contain a clause such as: 'This transaction is binding in honour only.' Therefore no contract exists between the punter and the pools company. If anyone feels he has won a large dividend he cannot sue the company for recovery should they refuse to pay because no contract exists for him to sue. Remember the case of *Appleson* v. *Littlewood* (1939).

There are some instances where an Act of Parliament has removed the legal intent, e.g.

1 The Post Office Act 1969 removes legal intent from agreements between Post Office and sender in respect of letters and packets. You might consider the implication of this if a valuable article is lost in the post.
2 The Law Reform Miscellaneous Provisions Act 1970 takes out the legal intent from promises to marry and therefore makes it impossible nowadays for a jilted fiancée to sue for 'breach of promise'.
3 Section 18 of the Trade Union and Labour Relations Act 1974 lays claim that an agreement between an employer and a trade union is

presumed not to have legal intent unless the agreement is in writing and contains a statement that the parties intend that the agreement will be a legally enforceable agreement.

Although apart from the exceptions mentioned the court will assume legal intent in commercial and business arrangements unless there is a statement to the contrary, in domestic arrangements, e.g. between husband and wife, the court will assume the absence of legal intent unless there is a statement to the opposite effect which is in writing.

Rachel Jackson has entered into an agreement with her husband John whereby she will decorate the lounge for half what it would cost if John employed a professional decorator. The sum agreed exclusive of materials was £120. Rachel completes the task to John's satisfaction but he refuses to pay the £120 and Rachel decides to sue him for breach of contract.

There is little doubt that Rachel would lose her case because the court would assume the absence of legal intent unless Rachel could produce strong evidence to the contrary. The courts may enforce agreements between husband and wife which are non-domestic – where for example a husband is in business, supplying his wife, also in business, with goods or services. This will be a normally legally binding agreement and intent will be assumed. This situation is neatly summed up in *Balfour* v. *Balfour* (1919), a husband promised his wife an allowance before he left to take up a post abroad. When he stopped the payments, an action by the wife failed on the ground that this was not a binding contract but merely a domestic agreement with no legal obligations attached to it.

Exercise 19

1 Buiness and commercial agreements are always legally enforceable because legal intent exists. *true/false*?
2 If a parcel posted at the post office is lost in transit the sender can claim the full value by sueing in the courts. *true/false*?
3 Domestic agreements between husband and wife are assumed to be 'binding in honour only'. Therefore they are not legally enforceable. *true/false*?

Legality

In the first section of this chapter we learned that an agreement could never be legally binding if it had within it any illegal element. Consider the following.

Francis Smythe is employed as an assistant director of finance by a well-known local authority. The post of director becomes vacant and Francis makes an application. He is desperate for this promotion and agrees to pay the chief executive of the local authority and the chairman of the county council £1000 each if he gets the post. Francis is appointed but refuses to pay the two £1000, as promised.

It is quite obvious that the court would never enforce this agreement because it was entered into for an illegal purpose and therefore lacks one of the essential elements, legality. Agreements tending to the corruption of public life are always illegal and the above agreement would fall into this category. Other types of agreement regarded as illegal are as follows:

1 Agreements to commit criminal acts.

2 Agreements involving sexual immorality; therefore, agreements between prostitutes and their customers are never enforceable. A decided case *Pearce* v. *Brooks* (1866) sums this up well.

3 Agreements to defraud the Inland Revenue, e.g. where a person contracts with a company not to disclose payments made to him to the tax authorities.

4 Agreements affecting public safety – therefore all contracts with persons living in enemy territory would be illegal.

Certain contracts are not illegal but may be declared void by the courts because they are said to be in restraint of trade. These sorts of contract fall into three categories as the examples below illustrate.

1 Deborah Price works as an articled clerk (trainee solicitor) with Dennett, Rooke-Naylor and Bright, a firm of solicitors in Dover (Kent). Deborah has signed an agreement that when she qualifies, she will not work within a 3-mile radius of this firm. On qualification, Deborah gets a job about 2½ miles from her former firm's office and Dennett, Rooke-Naylor and Bright sue her for breach of contract.

This is an example of a contract in restraint of trade and the court will only uphold it if it is reasonable. In other words, is it necessary to protect Dennett, Rooke-Naylor and Bright's business? Each case is treated on the basis of the circumstances. It is likely that this agreement would be enforced. However, if the restraint were too wide, i.e. the whole of Kent, then if Deborah worked next door to her former firm, then the court would not find for Dennett, Rooke-Naylor and Bright.

It is important in these situations for employers drawing up such agreements to ensure that they are reasonable and do not impose unnecessary obstacles to employees.

2 Gerald Nicholson has decided to purchase a newspaper and tobacconist shop near his home. He purchases the business rather than the shop itself which he will rent. The cost is £80 000 and he insists that the seller of the business signs an agreement that he will not start up in a similar business within a 2-mile radius. You will appreciate that it is important that this sort of arrangement is possible because if the seller started up a new business nearby, the £80 000 payment would be a waste. The court will apply the same ruling. Is it reasonable? This is another example of a contract in restraint of trade which will, in some instances, be enforced but if it is too wide, it will be held to be illegal.

The important aspect of transfer of business is dealt with again in Chapter 11.

3 Davis & Sons is a small paint shop in Kent. The owner, Bob Davis, signs an agreement with a leading paint manufacturer that in return for a grant for shop improvements, he will sell only this brand of paint for twenty-five years.

This is known as a 'solus agreement' and the courts will again, if it comes to a dispute, apply the rules of reasonableness.

Various Acts of Parliament have been passed, for example Fair Trading Act 1973 and the Restrictive Practices Act 1976 to assist in the regulation of arrangements and agreements to restrict competition.

Consensus ad idem

We have already met this small Latin phrase; try to remember what it meant in relationship to agreements. It is quite clear that agreements depend on both parties to the agreement entering into it willingly. We have already seen that where one party misleads the other and causes him to enter into the agreement then there would not really be a genuine 'meeting of the minds' and therefore no legally binding agreement.

There are three types of circumstances which prevent a genuine 'meeting of the minds'. The following three examples will help to explain them.

1 Gillian Smythe is anxious to purchase a genuine George III giltwood mirror and she is delighted when she finds one of these displayed at the showrooms of Peter Hanson (Antiques) Ltd. The owner of the business, although aware that this is a reproduction, assures Gillian that it is genuine and persuades her to buy it for £1500. Some weeks later Gillian discovers that the article she has bought is not genuine. She decides to sue the antique dealer.

This is a very good example of misrepresentation and the court will order Hansons to pay back the £1500 to Gillian. It is clear that there was no genuine meeting of the minds because Gillian was misled into thinking she was buying the genuine article.

2 Ernest Leigh is managing director of a printing firm which has recently advertised the post of foreman. One of his employees, David Mellor, a former boxer, has applied for the post and before the selection he threatens Ernest with a severe beating if he (David) is not successful. Despite some other very good applications Ernest, who fears for his safety, offers David the job and David accepts.

Again, there was no genuine meeting of the minds because Ernest did not really have a free mind when making his decision. The threat of force put him, as the law says, under duress and if necessary the court would uphold the situation if David was removed from the post.

We now have two examples of situations where *consensus ad idem* (meeting of the minds) is not present: (1) misrepresentation, (2) duress. In the second example we were concerned with force or the threat of force but there is a more subtle form of persuasion which might cause a person to enter into an agreement which was unfavourable to him, for example:

3 Mrs Beckford is an old lady of seventy-two who has extensive properties in the South of England. Her son wishes to borrow a large sum of money from her to set up a business and Mrs Beckford decides to sell some of her properties. She goes to see her solicitor of many years, Mr Graham Brooke, and asks him to dispose of several properties. Graham, anxious to make some money, decides to buy the properties himself and suggests to Mrs Beckford that she should accept his offer of £250 000 for the three properties. Mrs Beckford accepts this advice and the sale goes through. In fact, the properties were worth at least £450 000.

Although we have seen that the courts are not concerned about the value of consideration, in circumstances such as this where one party, i.e. Graham Brooke, has used his influence to get the agreement and where clearly Mrs Beckford trusted him, then the court will allow Mrs Beckford to get her properties back on the ground that 'undue influence' occurred. Undue influence may occur where one party has a dominant position over the other, e.g. doctor/patient, accountant/client, solicitor/client, father/son. Undue influence will only exist, however, where the dominant party uses his influence unfairly.

Exercise 20

1 Under what three circumstances might a court agree that there was no *consensus ad idem*?

2 List five types of agreement which might be void by reason of illegality.

3 What is a solus agreement? Is it illegal?

Form of the Contract

Generally, parties to an agreement can make this agreement in any form they wish and so, for example, they may make a verbal agreement or they may decide to set down the details of their agreement in writing. There are, of course, advantages in setting out an agreement in writing because if a dispute should arise it is easier for the party sueing in the court to prove that the agreement did exist if he has written evidence. However, there are certain agreements which must be made in a certain form.

1 Certain agreements must be made by a *deed*. We have already on p. 42 come across this term 'deed' and you will remember that it is a document which is signed, sealed and delivered. Examples of agreements which must be made by deed include:

(a) Agreements supported by only one-way consideration, e.g. a gift.

(b) Agreements to transfer or convey land or property. A transfer, an example of which is produced on pp. 55-6, transfers a property from Blackwell Estates plc to John & Jean Mitchell. Both sides of the document have been shown and the second page indicates how it has been signed, sealed & delivered.

We will be dealing with the subject of conveyance and property transfer in Chapter 11.

(c) Agreements relating to leases of three years or more. It is possible to rent a house or a piece of land. This procedure is often called a lease. Many home owners, in fact, have the land on which the house is situated on lease. These are usually for long periods, often 999 years.

2 Some agreements must be in writing because if they are not the con tract is void, i.e. empty, and therefore not legally binding. Three examples of agreements which must be in writing are:

(a) contracts to buy and sell shares in a company,

(b) contracts of marine insurance,

(c) contracts to buy certain consumer goods such as televisions by instalments, e.g. hire purchase agreements.

3 There are some agreements which need to be in writing to make them enforceable in the court. The absence of writing does not render the contract void but if one party does not fulfil his side of the bargain then the other party cannot sue. Probably the best known example of an agreement in this category is a contract to sell land. An agreement to buy or sell a house can only be enforced if it is in writing.

Exercise 21

Examine 'for sale' notices outside houses; some of them will have included the phrase 'sold subject to contract'. What do you think this phrase 'subject to contract' means?

An example of an agreement to buy property known as 14 Green Lane is shown on page 58. As you can see the agreement contains the name of the parties, the vendors or sellers, and the purchasers. Two identical copies of the contract are prepared. The sellers and the purchasers sign their copies and exchange them. This process is known as an 'exchange of contracts'.

Form 19(JP)

HM Land Registry **Land Registration Acts, 1925 to 1971**

Stamp pursuant to section 28 of the Finance Act 1931 to be impressed here.	*When the transfer attracts Inland Revenue duty, the stamps should be impressed here before lodging the transfer for registration.*

(1) *For a transfer to a sole proprietor use printed form 19.*

(1) TRANSFER OF WHOLE TO JOINT PROPRIETORS

(Freehold or Leasehold)

(Rules 98 or 115, Land Registration Rules 1925)

County and district (or London borough) } Canterbury, Kent

Title number(s) K 574506

Property 14 Green Lane, Canterbury

Date 28th August 1988 In consideration of One hundred and thirty two thousand

(2) *Strike out if not required.*

pounds (£ 132,000) (2)*the receipt whereof is hereby acknowledged*

(3) *In BLOCK LETTERS, enter full name(s), postal address(es) and occupation(s) of the proprietor(s) of the land.*

(3)I/We Blackwells Estates Plc.

(4) *If desired, or otherwise as the case may be (see rules 76 and 77).*

(5) *In BLOCK LETTERS, enter full name(s), postal address(es) including postcode and occupation(s) of the transferee(s) for entry on the register.*

(4)*as beneficial owner(s)* hereby transfer to:

(5) John Martin Mitchell of 56 High Grove Lane, Ashford, Kent college lecturer and Jean Vera Mitchell of 56 High Grove Lane Ashford, Kent, secretary.

(6) *Any special clause should be entered here.*

(7) *A transfer for charitable uses should follow form 36 (see rules 121 and 122).*

the land comprised in the title(s) above mentioned (6) (7)

(continued overleaf)

(8) *Delete the inappropriate alternative.*

The transferees declare that the survivor of them[8] can ~~cannot~~ give a valid receipt for capital money arising on a disposition of the land.

(9) *If a certificate of value for the purposes of the Stamp Act 1891 and amending Acts is not required, this paragraph should be deleted.*

~~[9]*It is hereby certified that the transaction hereby effected does not form part of a larger transaction or series of transactions in respect of which the amount or value or aggregate amount or value of the consideration exceeds* £~~ 132,000

(10) ***This transfer must be executed by the transferee(s) as well as the transferor(s).***

[10] Signed, sealed and delivered by the said Arthur John Tomlinson Managing Director, Blackwell Est Plc — A. J. Tomlinson

in the presence of

Name Martin Philip Owen Signature M. P. Owen

Address 34 Broad Street

Occupation Company Secretary.

[10] Signed, sealed and delivered by the said — Seal

in the presence of

Name Signature

Address

Occupation

[10] Signed, sealed and delivered by the said John Martin Mitchell — J. M. Mitchell

in the presence of

Name A K Brown Signature A.K. Brown.

Address 14 Grove Lane, Ashford, Kent

Occupation Technician

[10] Signed, sealed and delivered by the said JEAN VERA MITCHELL — J V Mitchell

in the presence of

Name A K Brown Signature A.K. Brown.

Address

Occupation

oyez The Solicitors' Law Stationery Society plc, Oyez House, 27 Crimscott Street, London SE1 5TS 12.85 F5167 5061122 * *

Exercise 22

1 What is a deed?
2 Give two examples of agreements which must be made by deed.
3 Give two examples of agreements which must be in writing.
4 Give one example of an agreement which will only be enforced if if it is in writing.

Exercise 23

We have now covered in some detail the main elements of contract and in the following exercise you will be tested on your understanding of this important part of law. If you have any difficulty with any of the following six review questions go back over the text.

1 Give four ways in which an offer can be brought to an end.
2 The Hotel Metropole receives a booking from an Alan Harrison and his family: one week, two double rooms, full board, cost £650. The hotel accepts Alan's offer by post which confirms the booking. Alan, before receiving the letter, decides to withdraw his offer but the Hotal Metropole say that the contract is binding on Alan. Advise Alan.
3 (a) Consideration may be past. *true/false*?
(b) Courts are always concerned with the value of consideration. **true/false**?
(c) Consideration must never be an existing obligation *true/false*?
4 Bob Walkden (aged seventeen) borrows £100 from his frend's father and says he will pay this back in a month's time. Bob, however, cannot pay this debt and the friend's father decides to sue. Advise Bob.
5 What three factors may cause the absence of a meeting of the minds (*consensus ad idem*).
6 (a) Agreements between husband and wife which are related to domestic arrangements are never legally binding. *true/false*?
(b) Give your reasons for your answer to (a).

CONTRACT OF SALE

The National Conditions of Sale, Twentieth Edition

Vendor

Blackwell Estates Plc

Purchaser

John Martin Mitchell and Jean Vera Mitchell
both of 56 Highgrove Lane, Ashford, Kent.

Registered Land		Purchase price	£ 132,000
District Land Registry:	Tunbridge Wells	Deposit	£ 13,200
Title Number:	K 574506	Balance payable	£ 118,800
Agreed rate of interest:		Price fixed for chattels or valuation money (if any)	£
		Total	£

Property and interest therein sold

All that freehold land and premises situated at and known as 14 Green Lane, Canterbury, in the County of Kent and registered with Title Absolute under Title number K 574506

Vendor sells as Beneficial owner

Completion date: 28th August 1988

AGREED that the Vendor sells and the Purchaser buys as above, subject to the Special Conditions endorsed hereon and to the National Conditions of Sale Twentieth Edition so far as the latter Conditions are not inconsistent with the Special Conditions.

*Signed J. V. Mitchell

Date 22nd July 19 88

J M Mitchell

***This is a form of legal document. Neither the form nor the National Conditions of Sale which the form embodies, were produced or drafted for use, without technical assistance, by persons unfamiliar with the law and practice of conveyancing.**

CHAPTER 3

THE TERMS OF THE BARGAIN

3.1 TERMS AND CONDITIONS

Excelsior Engineering Ltd is a small but very successful company producing a range of engineering products. The managing director Mr Kirkham is keen on buying a new up-to-date fully computerised lathe at a price of £18 500. He orders this from a firm of machine tool suppliers, Goodwin Machine Tools plc.

As we have already learned, an agreement such as this will be a legally binding contract provided all the essential elements are present. Goodwin Machine Tools plc decide to send to Excelsior Ltd a written agreement in which all the terms are included in connection with delivery dates, fitting and installation etc. The new machine is quite a complicated one and Mr Kirkham is happy to see that the supplier will be responsible for fitting and installation and also a training programme for his employees. A number of terms are written into the agreement including the following:

1 Goodwin Machine Tools plc undertake to deliver the machine to the premises of the purchaser by 31 August 1988.

2 Goodwin Machine Tools plc undertake to fit and install the machine and to provide at its expense a three-day training programme for up to three employees of the purchaser company. This undertaking to be effected within three weeks at least of the delivery.

The two terms which have been quoted here are examples of express terms. These are known as 'express' because they have been expressed, in this case in writing, though there would be nothing to prevent the terms being expressed verbally. Express terms are then those which have been mentioned and agreed by the parties at the time of reaching the agreement whether this be done in writing or by word of mouth.

Exercise 1

Express terms in a contract must always be in writing.
true/false?

Activity

You will find terms included in many contractual documents which you may have. For example look at an insurance policy, or a hire purchase/credit sale agreement and find the terms which are included.

The terms relating to a credit sale agreement with an electricity board are shown here and you will see that the board uses the expression 'terms and conditions'.

Terms and conditions of agreement

1 The Board shall sell and the Buyer shall purchase the goods at the credit sale price specified in the Schedule hereto.
2 The Buyer shall on the signing of this Agreement make the initial payment and thereafter shall make the subsequent payments specified in the Schedule hereto.
3 If the Buyer shall fail to pay any instalment within five days of its due date or in the event of any other breach by the Buyer of the terms and conditions hereof, the whole of the balance of the credit sale price then outstanding shall immediately become due and payable forthwith.
4 The property in the goods shall pass to the Buyer on delivery after which the Board shall not be responsible for any loss of or damage to the goods howsoever caused.
5 If the Buyer shall intend to vacate or shall vacate the said premises he shall forthwith inform the Board thereof and shall state his new address and shall during the period of this Agreement inform the Board immediately of any further change of address.
6 If the Buyer is the Tenant of premises in which the goods the subject of this Agreement are to be installed by the Board then the Buyer hereby indemnifies the Board against any claims for non-negligent damage to the said premises or Landlord's fixtures or fittings therein caused during the installation or removal of the said goods by the Board.
7 The Buyer hereby acknowledges that previous to the making of this

Agreement he was informed of and knew the cash price of the goods.

8 The Board hereby grants the Buyer the option to pay the cash price for the goods and installation stated on the face of this Agreement within three months of the date of signing this Agreement.

9 Any forbearance or indulgence shown by the Board to the Buyer shall in no way prejudice or affect the strict rights of the Board hereunder or otherwise.

10 Nothing herein contained shall affect diminish or extinguish any right or interest whether statutory or otherwise vested in the Board as an electricity undertaker.

11 This Agreement having first been signed by the Buyer shall become operative and binding upon the parties only upon being executed by or on behalf of the Board and shall be dated accordingly.

Although the document uses the words 'terms and conditions', in law 'condition' has a special meaning. Let us for a moment return to the two terms relating to the agreement between Goodwin Machine Tools and Excelsior. Both these terms are an important part of the agreement but there is a difference in the degree of importance as between (1) and (2). You will remember that in term (1) Goodwins agreed to deliver the machine on or before 31 August 1988. If delivery was delayed by one day and in fact took place on 1 September 1988 do you think that Mr Kirkham of Excelsior could treat the contract as breached? If the case went to court it is most certain that the court would judge that Goodwins had not really broken a term which lay 'at the heart of the contract' and the failure to deliver by 31 August was a breach of warranty for which Excelsior could sue if they could show that they had lost money as a result of late delivery.

If then a term is not considered important enough to effect the very basis of the contract it is regarded as a 'warranty'. However, some terms are so vital as to go to the heart of the contract itself. These will be considered to be 'conditions' and a breach of a condition will be treated in the same way as a breach of contract. Consider the following situation. You will remember in term (2) of the Excelsior/Goodwin agreement it was undertaken by Goodwins to fit, install and provide training in the use of the new lathe. If despite delivery on 1 September the machine had not been installed by December 1988, then Mr Kirkham would be correct to assume that this really was affecting the whole basis of the agreement. Indeed he would doubtless argue that he would have been unwilling to spend £18 500 of his firm's money had he known of such delays. If the case went to court the court would almost certainly treat this as a breach of condition and could order Goodwins to pay Excelsior back its £18 500.

Terms of an agreement may be conditions or warranties and this will be determined by their importance. It is important to realise that the mere using of the word 'condition' in an agreement does not in anyway guarantee that it is a condition. The test is, will 'non-observance' of the term affect the main purpose of the agreement? If the answer to this question is yes then it is a condition.

Two old cases in the same year sum the difference up very well. In *Bettini* v. *Gye* (1876), an opera singer agreed to attend for rehearsals six days before the first performance. He did not arrive until two days beforehand. This was held to be only breach of warranty, which entitled the management to recover damages but not to terminate the contract. Conversely, in *Poussard* v. *Spiers & Pond* (1876), Madame Poussard, a singer, failed to turn up for the first few performances. This was held to be breach of condition, which entitled the management to end her contract.

Exercise 2

1 Examine the terms and conditions of an electricity board credit agreement on page 59 and identify any which you would regard as a 'condition' in the legal sense in which we have used the word.
2 (a) Explain the meaning of the word 'warranty'.
(b) What will happen if a warranty is breached?

Exercise 3

Examine the four following examples and indicate whether you think the defendant is in breach of warranty or breach of condition.

1 John Martin a promising young cricketer has signed a contract to play for a well-known English county cricket club. One of the terms of the contract is that he must attend six practice sessions before the start of the playing season. John misses one practice session and the club threatens to sue him for breach of contract.
2 Michael Pullin signs a one-year contract to play for a First Division football club. One of the terms of the agreement is that he must play for any of the club's teams if selected. Michael decides to take his wife for a winter break and misses six key fixtures. The club decide to sue Michael for breach of contract.
3 Michael Mason has a small but busy insurance broker's office. Anxious to increase efficiency he orders a small computer. One of the terms of the agreement reached with the suppliers, Computer Supplies Ltd, is that a programme will be supplied with the machine which will allow a more efficient accounting system. Although the computer is delivered on time the programme is not supplied and Michael decides to sue.
4 H. & G. Heavy Haulage Ltd orders from a well-known truck manufacturers a tip-up lorry capable of dealing with lime supplies.

The agreement which is drawn up between the two firms expressly mentions the tip-up facility. When the lorry is delivered H. & G. Ltd find that the tip-up mechanism will not work. The firm decide to sue the manufacturers.

Implied Terms

We have been considering express terms, i.e. terms which are stated either in writing or verbally. There are, however, instances where even though the parties to an agreement have not made express provision on a point the courts nevertheless will imply a term. The following example will perhaps illustrate this point.

Keith Robinson owns a smallholding and he decides he needs the use of a tractor for a couple of weeks. He hires the tractor from Agricultural Hire Equipment Ltd at a cost of £267.50, payable in advance. When the tractor is delivered Keith finds that he is unable to use it due to a number of serious transmission faults and its unsafe condition. Keith decides to ask for the return of his £267.50. Agricultural Hire Equipment Ltd refuse saying that they had given no express undertaking that the vehicle was safe or suitable.

In fact in this instance if a case of this sort went to the courts the courts would say that this undertaking (term) existed by implication, or in other words there was in existence an implied term because clearly the agreement would make commercial nonsense without it. It is fair to assume that Keith would think that the goods would be fit for the purpose for which he was hiring them. This is summed up well by the following example. In *Liverpool City Council* v. *Irwin* (1977), the written tenancy agreements in a tower block of flats imposed no express duty on the landlord to keep the lifts and stairs in good repair! The court nevertheless implied such a term.

There are a number of examples where an Act of Parliament has stipulated that in certain agreements terms are implied. The best known example, which we will consider in detail in Chapter 5, is the Sale of Goods Act 1979 whereby it is implied that goods sold by a shop for example shall be of 'merchantable quality'; e.g. if you bought a new camera from a shop for £85 which you later discovered had such a serious fault that it would not take pictures, you could claim a full money refund because the shop had breached one of the essential implied terms that goods must be of merchantable quality.

Another example of terms implied by an Act of Parliament is where furnished houses which are let to tenants must be fit for human habitation. This is laid down by the Defective Premises Act 1972. We have therefore two types of implied terms: (1) terms implied by Statute (Acts of Parliament); (2) terms implied because it is necessary to give commercial sense to a business agreement.

Exercise 4

Advise the party in italics as to whether he/she would have a case in the following situations:

1 *Rachel Martin* buys a new motorcar which has two defective tyres, faulty brakes, broken headlights and badly chipped paintwork.
2 *Precision Engineering* hire a high quality lathe which has such a serious fault in it that a number of jobs are ruined with the consequent loss of materials.
3 *Mr and Mrs Goldstraw* rent a furnished flat which is rat-infested. The landlord, Real Estates Ltd, refuses to refund the advance monthly rent of £150.50.

3.2 EXCLUSION CLAUSES

Activity

During the course of the next few days look around to see if you can find examples of notices of the sort shown below:

> Vehicles and their contents are parked at the owner's risk and no liability is accepted for loss or damage to vehicles or persons howsoever caused.

The wording of notices you may see may be different but they all amount to the fact that one party to the agreement, the proprietor of the car park in this example, has excluded liability, i.e. taken out liability, by the introduction of what is called an exclusion clause.

The following example will help to explain the law relating to exclusion clauses.

Roger Lewis works as a representative for a pharmaceutical firm. As part of his work he has to spend three days at a seaside resort in the South West of England and he decides to book into a guest house which is owned by Mr Neil Nickson. When Roger arrives he is asked to sign a form which contains amongst other things a notice which reads:

> The proprietors of Maxstone Guest House cannot accept liability for personal injury to guests, loss or damage to guests' property howsoever caused which might arise during the guests' stay at this guest house.

This notice is also displayed very prominently at the reception desk in such a way that it would be difficult to miss. Roger has always been very careful and he reads the form carefully before signing. He feels that nothing is likely to happen to him in three days. However, this particular week must have been his unlucky one; on the first morning of his stay he leaves his wallet with £100, an expensive suit and some pharmaceutical samples in his room which he locks before going down to breakfast. When he does go back to his room he discovers the loss and reports the matter to Mr Nickson. Mr Nickson is sympathetic but draws Roger's attention to the notice he has signed. He does, however, agree to make an investigation.

The following evening Roger, having spent a day on business, has taken a shower prior to dinner. While walking from the bathroom to his room Roger trips on some loose carpet outside his room and falls awkwardly. He sustains a broken arm. Mr Nickson is informed and is most apologetic but again draws Roger's attention to the notice that he has signed.

What then is Roger's legal position? There is little doubt that at the time of making the contract to stay at the hotel Roger had agreed to the exclusion clause. Let us for a moment examine the first situation. If Roger took the guest house to court for recovery of his loss Mr Nickson would draw the attention of the court to the existence of the exclusion clause and the court would apply a number of rules to the situation to establish whether or not Mr Nickson could rely upon it:

1 Was it part of the agreement? The fact that it was incorporated in a form which Roger had every opportunity to read is a good indication that it was part of the contract. The general rule is that if a contract is drawn up in a written document which is signed by the party concerned then everything contained therein will be binding upon the signer whether he has read it or not.
2 If there is no signing involved then the court would need to be sure that everything reasonably had been done to bring to the attention of the other party the existence of the clause.
3 Was the clause introduced at the time the agreement was made? Under no circumstances will courts allow exclusion clauses to be relied upon if they have been introduced after the agreement has been made. In our situation Roger signed the form containing the exclusion clause at the time he booked in and therefore had an opportunity to say to Mr Nickson 'I do not agree to your terms'. If for example the notice had not been signed and was displayed in guests' rooms then this would be after the agreement was made and therefore could not be relied upon. For example, in a decided case *Olley* v. *Marlborough Court Hotel* (1949) the defendant tried to rely upon a notice in the guest room but the

hotel was of course unsuccessful. The exclusion clause in this case was introduced too late.

In fact in this situation the guest house had introduced the exclusion clause in the right manner. Roger had been required to sign a document but even if he had not then the guest house could still have relied upon it because the notice had been prominently displayed at the reception, i.e. it was introduced at the time the contract was made.

Unfortunately, Roger could not recover from the guest house the value of his lost property even though he might be able to prove that the guest house staff had been careless in leaving his room unattended and the door open while cleaning the rooms on his corridor. Mr Nickson had carefully indemnified himself against this claim. The exclusion clause is sometimes called an indemnity clause because it indemnifies the party introducing it. 'Indemnifies' means protects him against the possibility of any claim being made upon him. You may hear these clauses being referred to also as 'disclaimer' clauses because they disclaim liability.

Exercise 5

1 An exclusion clause in a contract is sometimes known as an clause or a clause.
2 An exclusion clause to be relied upon must always be part of a signed document. *true/false*?
3 Exclusion clauses may be introduced at any time during the operation of a contract. *true/false*?

It seems then that Roger would have little chance of success in an action to recover the value of his loss. However, you will remember that on the second day of his stay he fractured an arm tripping over some loose carpet. You will also remember that the exclusion clause which he signed sought to indemnify Mr Nickson against claims in respect of personal injury. If we applied the same rules to this second situation as to the first then it would appear that Roger would have no claim. This would have been the position prior to 1977. However, as a result of the Unfair Contract Terms Act 1977 Section 2(1) no one acting in the course of business can either by contractual terms or by notice given or displayed exclude his liability in contract or tort for death or personal injury arising from negligence.

In this second situation Mr Nickson has attempted to exclude liability for personal injury. He has done this by a notice and in the course of business. There is little doubt that Mr Nickson was negligent in leaving loose carpeting in the guests' rooms and Roger could successfully sue him for compensation for suffering resulting from his fractured arm and for any other loss incurred thereby.

The Unfair Contract Terms Act 1977, although it prevents a business from excluding liability for death or personal injury, still allows it to exclude liability for any other loss due to his negligence. Thus the notice given to Roger excluded Mr Nickson's liability for personal loss, i.e. in respect of the first situation, but not from liability for personal injury, i.e. in respect of the second. Therefore Roger would be most likely successful in an action based upon his personal injury - provided he could show that the guest house had been negligent. The law as it relates to negligence will be explained more fully in Chapter 7.

A section of the Unfair Contract Terms Act is shown below.

ELIZABETH II

Unfair Contract Terms Act 1977

1977 CHAPTER 50

An Act to impose further limits on the extent to which under the law of England and Wales and Northern Ireland civil liability for breach of contract, or for negligence or other breach of duty, can be avoided by means of contract terms and otherwise, and under the law of Scotland civil liability can be avoided by means of contract terms. [26th October 1977]

BE IT ENACTED by the Queen's most Excellent Majesty, by and with the advice and consent of the Lords Spiritual and Temporal, and Commons, in this present Parliament assembled, and by the authority of the same, as follows:—

PART I

AMENDMENT OF LAW FOR ENGLAND AND WALES AND NORTHERN IRELAND

Introductory

1.—(1) For the purposes of this Part of this Act, " negligence " means the breach— Scope of Part I.

(*a*) of any obligation, arising from the express or implied terms of a contract, to take reasonable care or exercise reasonable skill in the performance of the contract;

Activity

As we have learned, these exclusion clauses, sometimes known as indemnity clauses, may also be referred to as disclaimers - disclaiming liability. If you look around you will often find examples of these. Many still disclaim liability for personal accident but while it is not illegal to display such a notice it cannot be relied upon. Have a look for notices excluding liability and in the light of your reading of this section on exclusion clauses try to work out the protection afforded to the business seeking to rely upon the notice.

You may notice that in a number of cases notices have been changed to bring them in line with the 1977 legislation. An example of a notice displayed by Torbay Borough Council is shown below:

> The Corporation will accept no responsibility for any loss of or damage to any articles including articles of value brought into or left in this building whether such loss or damage is caused by the negligence of the Corporation, its officers or servants or otherwise.

You will note that in this example there is no attempt to exclude liability for personal injury. Even though it is possible to exclude liability for losses, in deciding whether an exclusion clause can be relied on, the court will attempt to see if it is reasonable. The cost of the service being provided will probably be taken into account as the following case shows. In *Photo Production Ltd* v. *Securicor Transport Ltd* (1980), Securicor contracted to guard the plaintiff's factory where paper was stored. The patrolman deliberately started a fire, and it destroyed the premises. It was held that an exemption clause in the contract protected Securicor. Both parties were established businesses that had negotiated the terms freely. The price of the patrol was modest. Both parties were insured, the plaintiff against loss of the building, Securicor against liability. The court was satisfied that both sides had intended Photo Production (or its insurers) to bear the risk.

Exercise 6

Examine the following examples and explain whether you think the person suffering the loss would successfully sue for compensation.

1 *Veronica Clapham* has to make a business trip to Austria and she books a flight with a British airline. Her luggage is put in the hold of the plane and during the early part of the flight from Manchester to Vienna she is handed a ticket which explains that the management cannot accept liability for any loss or damage of goods while in transit. Veronica's luggage is badly damaged due to the negligence of airline staff and she loses about £235 worth of property. She decides to sue the airline.

2 *Francis Harris* hires a touring caravan from Caravan Hire Ltd and at the time he makes the contract he signs a form indemnifying the company from claims in respect of personal injury resulting from the use of the caravan. Due to the negligence of one of Caravan Hire Ltd's staff Francis is badly injured and he sues the company who draw his attention to the form he signed.

3 *Electrical Components plc* has decided to move its head office from Derby to Ilkeston but for a short period they have to store office machinery in a furniture store known as County Store Ltd. The managing director of Electrical Components has to sign a document indemnifying County Store from claims should there be any loss or damage to the equipment while it is in the store. As a result of some very unusual storms some of the equipment is damaged. Electrical Components decide to sue County Store Ltd.

3.3 DISCHARGE OF CONTRACTS

Concorde Car (Sales) plc is a large car distributor with branches throughout the country. Anxious to boost sales it decides to hold a three-day sales conference for sixty of its senior sales personnel. The company decides to hold the conference at the Sceptre Hotel which has excellent conference facilities and is situated on the south-east coast. Terms are agreed whereby full board and conference rooms will be available at a total cost of £13 500. The dates agreed are 21 September to 24 September 1988.

As we can see a legally binding contract has come into existence between Concorde and the Sceptre Hotel. In this section we will be using this example to show how contracts may be discharged, i.e. brought to an end. There are basically four ways in which contracts may be ended (discharged).

1 If the conference goes ahead as planned and the bill of £13 500 is paid by Concorde then the contract will be discharged by performance. Each side has performed his side of the bargain, or to use the expression used in Chapter 2, each side has given consideration. Sceptre Hotel has provided accommodation, etc. plus full conference facilities for sixty persons and organisers and Concorde have paid the bill of £13 500. One way, then, in which a contract may be discharged is by performance – i.e. both parties fulfil their sides of the bargain.

2 It may be that at some time prior to 21 September Concorde decide that they do not wish to go ahead with the sales conference, perhaps because a number of their senior sales personnel cannot attend. If the hotel agrees to cancel the agreement then the contract is said to be dis-

charged by agreement. It is important to remember, however, that the agreement must be by both parties. If Concorde cancelled the conference but the hotel did not agree then the hotel could sue Concorde for the cancelled booking.

If the Sceptre Hotel had already spent some money on the arrangements then the hotel might still release Concorde but only if Concorde gave some consideration; e.g. the Hotel Sceptre might agree to the cancellation provided Concorde paid £400. Obviously, the nearer to 21 September it was the more likely it would be that the hotel would lose money by the cancellation, for it would give them less time to make alternative bookings.

It might be that the Sceptre, because of a number of problems, might wish to cancel the booking. If Concorde had time to make alternative arrangements it might agree to this. Thus a second way in which a contract might be discharged is by agreement, but the agreement must be two-way; it can never be one-sided, i.e. unilateral, for example where Concorde cancelled but the Sceptre did not accept.

3 There are circumstances where an event takes place, for which neither party to an agreement was responsible, which makes the agreement impossible or produces a radically different situation. In such circumstances it is possible that the court will regard the agreement as discharged by frustration:

(a) If prior to 21 September a fire occurs at the Sceptre Hotel which completely guts the building then the hotel would find it impossible to perform the contract and it would be discharged by frustration. However, as a result of the Law Reform (Frustrated Contracts) Act 1943, Concorde would recover money if they had incurred expense in arranging the conference prior to the discharge.

(b) Let us assume that Concorde are a major supplier for Japanese cars and prior to the conference as a result of government legislation there is a total ban on the import of Japanese cars, then it is easy to see the basis of the contract has been removed. There is little point in holding a sales conference to sell new cars when no more new cars will be forthcoming, and the courts might well allow the contract to be discharged by frustration. If the Sceptre Hotel had spent money on arrangements for the conference then this might be recovered.

A decided case will help to illustrate the law as it relates to frustration: *Krell* v. *Hentry* (1903). The contract was for the hire of a room in Pall Mall so that the coronation procession of Edward VII could be seen. The coronation was postponed due to Edward VII's illness. The landlord tried nevertheless to recover the rental. However, the court held that the contract was discharged by frustration since the basis of the contract had been removed.

The third way in which contracts may be discharged is by frustration. However, it must be remembered that courts will only allow a contract to be discharged by frustration exceptionally. It must be *impossible* to perform because some external event has so fundamentally changed the situation that the very basis of the contract has been removed. The courts will never allow frustration merely because it is difficult.

4 Finally one or other of the two parties may refuse to perform their side of the bargain. In our example if on 21 September Concorde's employees did not turn up and when the manager of the Sceptre rang the Concorde office he was told that Concorde had cancelled the conference, then if Concorde refused to pay their £13 500 the company would be in breach of contract, i.e. it had broken its side of the bargain. Similarly if the Sceptre Hotel refused to provide full facilities as agreed for the conference the hotel would be in breach of contract. Breach of contract can take place earlier than 21 September if one party unilaterally decided not to fulfil its side of the bargain before that date, if the Hotel Sceptre, for example, indicated before 21 September that it would not accept the conference.

The fourth way of discharging a contract is by breach. We will consider the remedies that a court may award for breach of contract in the next section.

Activity

During the next few days think of different contracts which you have made and then think of the way in which they have been discharged.

Exercise 7

1 List the four ways in which a contract may be discharged.
2 Name the Act which allows a party in frustrated contracts to recover some of the expenses incurred in respect of the contract.
3 Name a decided case which illustrates the law relating to frustration.

Exercise 8

Study the four examples below and explain in each how the contract has been discharged.

1 *Nigel Welch* has signed a contract with a well-known football club to play for three seasons. Before making an appearance he is injured

in a car accident and loses the use of his right leg which has to be amputated.
2 *Stanley Davey* is managing director of a large building firm; he orders timber from a timber merchant, Timber Supplies Ltd, at a cost of £9000. However, due to a downturn in trade Mr Davey asks Timber Supplies Ltd to be released from the contract and the timber merchant agrees.
3 *Precision Engineering Ltd* buys two large guillotines from Western Machines Ltd. The total cost is £12 500 inc. VAT. The machines are delivered on 1 August and Precision Engineering settles the account in full by cheque.
4 *Lawrie Taylor* is sales manager for a large firm producing leather, Leather Supplies Ltd. He signs a contract on behalf of his company to supply a consignment of leather to a company producing fashion shoes in the East Midlands. Delivery is agreed for 1 October 1988. Lawrie's firm cannot meet the delivery date and he rings the shoe manufacturer to say that delivery will not be until February 1989. As a result the shoe manufacturer loses important business.

3.4 REMEDIES FOR BREACH OF CONTRACT

Damages

Let us return for a moment to our example of the contract between Concord Car (Sales) plc and the Sceptre Hotel. We will assume for a moment that Concorde has made all its arrangements for the sales conference and has employed the services of a firm of marketing consultants to organise the conference on its behalf. On 20 September, that is one day before the conference, the manager of the Sceptre, Andrew Collier, rings Concorde to say that due to administrative errors over booking has taken place and that he has no alternative but to cancel the conference arrangements.

Clearly the Sceptre Hotel is in breach of contract and Concorde would sue for compensation for expenses incurred. It is obvious that Concorde has no chance of arranging alternative accommodation and the court will award damages, as they are called, to compensate Concorde for the loss incurred. If the cancellation had been made earlier and had provided Concorde with an opportunity to make alternative arrangements for their conference then the level of damages awarded would be reduced. It has always been the rule that the injured party (i.e. Concorde) should do what it can to minimise the loss.

Concorde's management would argue that because they have not been able to hold the planned conference sales of new cars will not increase as expected - as you will remember, this was the objective of the conference. However, courts will only award damages in respect of (1) losses that might be fairly and reasonably considered as arising naturally from the breach and (2) losses that might have been anticipated by both parties when the contract was made. It is unlikely that the courts would award damages in respect of possible loss of sales. This would be considered too remote. The following case illustrates the rules relating to remoteness of damage quite well.

Victoria Laundry (Windsor) Ltd v. *Newman Industrial Ltd* (1949)
The laundry firm ordered a new boiler which arrived late. The court awarded damages for loss of normal profits which should have been anticipated by Newman Industrial. The court would not award damages for loss by Victoria Laundry of a lucrative contract because the supplying firm would not possibly have known about this.

The three rules relating to the award of damages for breach of contract are as follows:

1 Damages are awarded so that the plaintiff will be compensated for the loss he/she has suffered.
2 Damages will be awarded only for loss that arises naturally from the breach and might have been anticipated by the two parties.
3 The injured party must do his/her best to minimise the loss resulting from the breach.

Specific Performance and Injunction

Courts may at their discretion give an alternative remedy for breach of contract. The following examples will help to illustrate this.

Alan Wilson is thirty-seven and he has already had a very successful spell with a leading American electronics company. A British electronics company, British Electrics plc, wishes to employ him and offers him a salary of £125 000 per annum plus a house of his choice in any part of England. Alan and his wife wish to live in Kent and they view four very expensive houses near Canterbury. They decide on one particular house which they like so much that Alan makes it as a condition of employment. The house costs £220 000 and the company immediately signs a contract to purchase it from the present owner, Mrs Angela Duffy. Angela, however, changes her mind and refuses to complete the sale. British Electrics plc do not want damages, they want the house.

Courts have the power in such circumstances to award a 'specific performance order', that is an order which compels Mrs Duffy to specifically perform her side of the bargain, in this case to sell the house.

Specific performance orders will only be granted where damages would not be an adequate remedy. In this case British Electrics plc did not want money they wanted the property. Specific performance orders will never be granted for any contract of a personal nature. Thus a person who contracts to work for a company and then refuses will never be made to do so. The company will only be able to claim damages.

Exercise 9

You might care to think for a moment why a specific performance order will never be awarded in employment contracts.

Entertainments Ltd have signed a contract with a well-known pop group, the Rocker Billies, whereby the group will give a live concert in a large Midlands town on 30 November 1988. The concert is a sell-out but one week before the event the Rocker Billies' agent John Beckwith rings Entertainments to say that the group will not be appearing because they have received a more valuable offer to appear in London.

Rocker Billies are clearly in breach of contract but as we have seen the court will never award a specific performance order for contracts of a personal nature. It is possible, however, for the court in this situation to award an injunction. An injunction is a court order directing a person not to do something. In this case an injunction would be awarded to prevent the Rocker Billies appearing elsewhere on 30 November. This order of course might persuade the group to appear for Entertainments Ltd but if they decide not to then Entertainments would still get damages for any losses incurred. The situation is neatly summed up in the following case. In *Warner Brothers Pictures Incorporated* v. *Nelson* (1937), an actress had contracted with the film company not to work as an actress for anyone else during her present contract. It was held that she could be restrained by injunction from breaking this undertaking.

When describing the two remedies, specific performance and injunctions, we used the phrase 'the discretion of the courts'. This means that in a breach of contract case, the court, if it finds for the plaintiff, must award damages, but it may award the other two remedies at its discretion. We call the order of specific performance and injunction, therefore, 'discretionary orders'.

Exercise 10

1 List the three remedies which might be available to a plaintiff in a breach of contract.
2 Specific orders may be awarded to enforce contracts of employment. *true/false*?
3 What is an injunction?
4 Explain the term 'discretionary' as it applies to specific performance and injunction orders.

Exercise 11

Examine the following examples and say what sort of remedy the court is likely to award for breach of contract.

1 Dovedale Motors Ltd agree to sell to John Bennett a new Astra 1300 hatchback for £500 below the list price which was at that time £6500. When the buyer John Bennett goes to collect the car he is told it has been sold to another buyer at the list price. John claims £6500 damages.
2 Chris Oliver has signed a lucrative contract to play for a well-known football club. However, prior to his first appearance he decides to sign for a club offering him better terms.
3 United Antique Dealers Ltd agree to sell a rare piece of furniture for £7500 to Tony Guest but when Tony arrives to pick up his furniture he is told that the company has decided to sell it for a higher price.
4 Associated Properties Ltd sign a contract to sell Mr and Mrs E. Disdale a three-bedroomed house for £82 500. The company refuses to complete the sale and Mr and Mrs Disdale seek a specific performance order. On the same estate there are about six similar houses for sale from another company for £85 800.

CHAPTER 4

CONTRACTS OF EMPLOYMENT

4.1 NATURE OF EMPLOYMENT CONTRACTS

Brian Webb is twenty-nine years old and has been employed as a workshop foreman for three years with Universal Machines Ltd. He is a very ambitious man and has been studying at the local technical college, where he has been successful in gaining good engineering qualifications. While reading through the local newspaper he notices the following advertisement:

High Peak Engineering PLC

A prosperous company producing machine tools in the North West of England require a man or woman as:

WORKSHOP ENGINEER

£11,500–£13,000 per annum to supervise the workshop. You should possess at least a Higher National Certificate or Diploma in Engineering and have had broad based experience in practical engineering and man management.

Applications in writing should be made within 14 days of the appearance of the advertisement to:

J. F. Honeywell
Personnel Manager
High Peak Engineering PLC
Castle Road
Dove Holes (Nr Buxton)
Derbyshire

You will note that the company has been careful to indicate that it requires a man or woman. It is important that every employer of labour is aware of the Sex Discrimination Act 1975 and the Race Relations Act 1976, which make it unlawful for a person in relation to employment in England, Wales or Scotland to discriminate against a man or woman on grounds of sex, marital status, colour, race, nationality or ethnic or national origins in:

1 the arrangements he makes for the purpose of deciding who should be offered the job; or
2 the terms on which the job is offered; or
3 by refusing or deliberately omitting to offer the job.

Not only in recruitment but also during the operation of a contract of employment an employer can face legal action if he practises discrimination on grounds of sex, marital status, colour or race. The following decided case illustrates this.

Nemes v. *Allen* (1977)
In a redundancy case the employer dismissed female workers when they married One such worker, Mrs Allen, was offered alternative employment which she refused and she was dismissed.

It was held that Mrs Allen had been unlawfully discriminated against, contrary to the Sex Discrimination Act 1975, because she was a woman and was married.

Discrimination is possible where it can be shown that it is a genuine qualification to be of one sex or of an ethnic origin. So, for example, it is regarded as lawful to reserve posts in Indian Restaurants for Indians. Some jobs require a man or woman, for example actors or actresses. Physical strength may not be regarded as a quality to justify discrimination. The following case sums this up well.

In *Shields* v. *Coomes Ltd* (1979), male counter-hands in a betting shop were paid more than women doing the same work, allegedly because it was the men who would have to deal with trouble or violence. This was held to be discrimination, because the men had no special training and, in any event, properly trained women could deal with violence equally well. The Court of Appeal upheld this finding.

Brian Webb decides to make an application for the post advertised in High Peak Engineering plc and writes a letter which gives details of his qualifications and experience. A few weeks later, Brian is invited for interview with the managing director, the chief engineer and the personnel manager. Following the interview, Brian is asked to wait in an adjoining office while the managing director and his colleagues discuss Brian's application. Deciding that Brian is the sort of man they are looking for, the managing director asks Brian to see him again and explains the terms and conditions relating to the job. The managing director then offers Brian the post and Brian accepts immediately agreeing to commence work in a month's time, on 15 August 1988.

A legally binding contract has come into existence between High Peak Engineering and Brian even though, as yet, there has been nothing in writing between the two parties to the agreement. Contracts of employment are simple contracts which need not be in writing, though it would be usual practice for High Peak Engineering to send a letter confirming the offer and asking Brian to reply confirming his acceptance.

For any agreement to be legally binding it must contain, as we have already learned, seven elements. It will be useful to examine this particular agreement to make sure that these elements are present. First, the managing director made an offer which Brian Webb accepted. The consideration, which is in the future, is Brian's services as workshop engineer and the wage of £14 500 paid to Brian by High Peak Engineering. As we have already discovered, in the absence of any statement to the contrary there is an assumption in situations of this sort that both parties intended their agreement to have legal consequences. There is nothing illegal about producing machine tools and we can assume that there is nothing illegal about this agreement. On the question of legal capacity, a man of twenty-nine has full legal capacity to enter into a contractual relationship of this sort, and we must assume that the managing director of High Peak Engineering had the right to act for his company in offering Brian the post. There is then just one final element which must be satisfied for this agreement to be legally binding and that is to ascertain whether the agreement between the two parties was real; was there *consensus ad idem*? Did Brian and High Peak Engineering enter into the agreement freely and in possession of the necessary information? We can assume that neither party felt threatened in any way and that both partners freely entered into the agreement but on the second point are we sure that there was no misrepresentation on either side which might have persuaded the other party to reach an agreement? You will remember that in the advertisement it mentioned the need for a Higher National Certificate or diploma in engineering and if Brian had stated he was in possession of this qualification when, in fact, he had not obtained it, then the company when they discovered this could dismiss Brian, or if they knew in time avoid the contract before Brian commenced work. It is important to remember that misrepresentation may cause an employee to lose his job. The following decided case illustrates this point very well.

Torr v. *British Railways Board* (1977)
In 1974 Torr stated on his application for a job as a guard that he had never been found guilty of a criminal offence. This was untrue since he had been imprisoned for three years in 1958. When his employers discovered this Torr was suspended and then discmissed. He was told that the dismissal was fair since this position is one of trust and responsibility.

As you will appreciate, it is often difficult for people who have been in prison to obtain work, and to assist them, the Rehabilitation of Offenders Act 1974 was passed. By this Act, it is possible for persons who have been convicted of offences for which sentence of up to 2½ years has been imposed (suspended or otherwise) to treat these as 'spent', i.e. they need not declare them even if asked. In the case just quoted, Mr Torr was outside the scope of this Act because his sentence was 3 years.

It is important to note that certain types of employment fall outside the scope of the Act, for example an application for the post of schoolteacher. However, in these cases, the fact of the exemption must be brought to the notice of the applicant.

We have now seen that a contract of employment, as any other simple contract, must contain the following seven elements:

1 offer;
2 acceptance;
3 two-way consideration;
4 legality;
5 each party must have capacity;
6 there must be legal intent;
7 there must be a real agreement, i.e. not based upon duress, undue influence or misrepresentation.

We have also learned that a contract of employment need not be in writing. Thus, if Brian decided, because for example his present firm were willing to make him a better offer, that he would not after all be joining High Peak Engineering, then he would be in breach of contract even though there had been nothing in writing. If High Peak Engineering decided to sue Brian for breach of contract, the company could be awarded damages. The court will never in these circumstances order Brian to work for High Peak Engineering because, as we have already seen, specific performance orders will never be awarded in respect of personal services.

There are just two exceptions to the rule that a contract of employment need not be in writing. Under the Employment Protection (Consolidation) Act 1978 young people entering an apprenticeship must be given a written contract; and under the Merchant Shipping Act 1970 a written agreement must be signed by both parties for the engagement of a seaman on a ship registered in the UK.

Although apart from these two exceptions contracts of employment need not be in writing, it has now become necessary as a result of the Employment Protection (Consolidation) Act 1978, which brought together legislation under the 1963 and 1972 Contracts of Employment Acts, for an employer to give each employee within thirteen weeks of his starting date a statement regarding his employment. This document is *not* a contract of employment. Thus it will be necessary for High Peak Engineering to give Brian Webb a written statement either when he begins his job or some time within the specified thirteen-week period. Certain particulars must be given and the following document gives an indication of the type of document which Brian might be given and it will also serve to show the requirements of this part of the Act.

EMPLOYMENT PROTECTION CONSOLIDATION ACT 1978

High Peak Engineering Co. Ltd

Name: Brian Frank Webb

Date of commencement of Employment: 15 August 1988
Date when particulars were given: 23 August 1988

1 You are employed in the service of this Company and your appointment is to the post of Workshop Engineer.

2 Your current salary is £14 500 per annum within the salary scale £14 500–17 000 rising by four annual increments of £625. Your salary will be paid at monthly intervals on the 25th of each calendar month and will be by direct transfer to your bank.

3 *Working week*. The normal working hours will be Monday–Friday 8.30 a.m.–5.00 p.m. with one hour lunch break to be taken between 12.30 and 2.30 p.m.

4 *Holiday entitlement*. This is calculated at the rate of two days' holiday for each month's completed service representing a total annual holiday entitlement of 24 days in addition to the normal statutory holidays. If an employee's contract is terminated the company will pay that employee a sum equal to the holiday entitlement due to date.

5 *Sickness allowance and procedures*. Entitlement to sick pay is based upon 30 days' full pay and 30 days' half pay except where sickness or injury is directly attributable to your employment with the company in which case a minimum of 6 months' full pay and 6 months' half pay is payable.

6 *Pension*. A pension scheme operates in the company which is contributory. Full details of this are set out in the company's Pension Scheme booklet, a copy of which is attached. A contracting out certificate is in force in respect of the company's pension scheme.

7 *Notice*. Except in cases of serious breaches of conditions the employment to which these particulars refer is terminable by one month on either side.

8 *Disciplinary arrangements*. Disciplinary arrangements applicable to this employment are to be found in the booklet 'Disciplinary Procedures in Relation to Salaried Staff High Peak Engineering 1984', which is available from the Personnel Office.

9 *Grievance procedure*. If you have any grievance relating to this employment, contact in the first instance Mr K. Martin, Works Manager.

10 *Changes*. Details of changes to these particulars will be notified to you or will appear in the Company's monthly staff bulletin.

Please note that this document is not a contract of employment. Your contract rests upon your letter of appointment and other implied terms and conditions relating to this post.

Signed:	B. Hamilton, Company Secretary
Date:	23.8.88

The above document which refers specifically to B. F. Webb and his employment with High Peak Engineering gives some idea of the sort of information which these particulars must provide. It has now become necessary for all employees to receive such a document with the following exceptions:

1 Part-time employees working less than sixteen hours a week.
2 Employees of the Crown, e.g. civil servants.
3 Where an employee works wholly or mainly outside the UK.
4 Where an employee is husband or wife of the employer.
5 Where written particulars have already been embodied in a written contract, e.g. as required in apprenticeship contracts.

It is very important to understand the significance of the written particulars which must now be provided in most cases to employees. As our example stated, the particulars are not a contract and a binding contract of employment is still in existence even though an employer fails to provide the particulars within the designated thirteen-week limit. If Brian Webb had not been supplied with this document he could make an application to an industrial tribunal and once the tribunal has ruled on the particulars to be supplied then they will become part of Brian's contract of employment. It is in the interest of both employer and employee that a written statement is provided because either party could find himself at a serious disadvantage in any legal proceedings which might arise out of the contract. In the particulars supplied to Brian Webb reference was made to the company's monthly bulletin in which details of changes might be given. Alternatively, it was suggested also under point 10 of the document that changes would be notified directly to Brian. However, it must be emphasised that even where the changes have not been notified they still may be operational and part of a legally binding contract. This important point is neatly summed up in the following case.

Parkes Classic Confectionery v. *Ashcroft* (1973)
Ashcroft's written particulars of her employment stated that she was required to work for twenty-two hours per week. When she was dismissed for redundancy her employers contended that the redundancy payment should be based upon the shortened number of hours she now worked, written particulars of which had not been given to the employee.

It was held that the employer's failure to give the appropriate notice of the changed conditions of employment as required by the Contracts of Employment Act 1972 (now replaced by the 1978 Act) did not make the change ineffective, thus her redundancy payment should be based upon the current number of working hours.

As well as emphasising the changes need not be notified to be part of a contract this case also illustrates well that the particulars are not part of the contract.

Exercise 1

Read the following examples and say whether or not a legally binding contract exists.

1 Matthew Brown is an accountant and he agrees to prepare the accounts of his father's small retail business. He does not intend to make a charge for his services saying it is a way of saying thank you for all the help his father has given him. A few weeks later, following a family dispute. Matthew refuses to fulfil his promise and his father decides to take legal action against him.

2 Vic Woodruffe sees an advertisement for a foreman bricklayer in his local paper and he writes to the firm of builders in question agreeing to work for them at a wage of £135.50 per week.

3 Keith Robinson is a works engineer at Harpur Engineering Ltd. Knowing that his firm is about to advertise for a workshop supervisor he decided to interview a friend and neighbour, Roy Spencer who is a qualified engineer. Keith offers his neighbour the post and Roy accepts.

4 Michelle Bennett, a graduate in Russian Studies and a fluent Russian speaker, accepts a post as translator with a consortium of government scientists who have made arrangements with the Soviet Union to send to the USSR regular information regarding British government defence research.

5 Tony Green applies for a job as a heavy goods lorry driver, a condition of which is that the person appointed shoudl have an HGV (Heavy Goods Vehicle) licence. Although Tony is a competent driver he does not have this licence but at his interview he claims that he does. Two months later his firm discovers that he does not, in fact, hold this licence and he is threatened with dismissal.

6 Pamela Webb has been offered and accepted a post as secretary to the personnel manager at Trenchard Industrial Holdings. Two days before she is due to start she phones the firm saying that she has changed her mind about the post and since she has received no confirmatory letter she is not bound by her agreement.

Exercise 2

In the following cases, advise the party in italics of his/her legal position.

1 *Stephen Wells* has been a computer operator with a firm of merchant bankers for two years but he has never received a statement of particulars relating to the post. He decides to leave the firm without giving notice and decides to sue the firm for breach of contract.

2 Because she has received no written particulars in relation to her post as accounts clerk with Boston Furnishings Ltd even though she has been with the firm for one year, *Audrey Worsley* decides to take the matter to the industrial tribunal, which endorses a statement containing details of a monthly wage of £110.50 based upon a 34-hour week. The firm accepts this but two months later seek to reduce her wage to £100.50 and increase her hours to 37 per week.

3 In his application for a post as foreman joiner with Boscombe Builders Ltd, *Vivian Phillips*, a West Indian by origin, is told that because of his background he needs higher qualifications than British-born applicants.

4 After accepting a post with a travel company *Anne Moore* is told that the 50 per cent holiday discount is only available to married male employees.

4.2 TERMS OF CONTRACTS OF EMPLOYMENT

Pat Browne is employed as a typist for Associated Food Supplies. Her wage is £125.76 for a 37-hour week. From time to time, as part of her duties, Pat has to operate a guillotine machine which does not have the required guard attached to it.

Pat has never really hit it off with the office manager, Mrs. E. Smythe and Pat shows her dislike on frequent occasions by outright disobedience in respect of Mrs Smythe's instructions and also by completing tasks given to her by Mrs Smythe both carelessly and incompetently. Mrs Smythe reports the problem to the firm's chief executive, who has overall responsibility for the work of the office. He sees Pat and warns her of the consequences of her disobedience, carelessness and incompetence. Pat replies by pointing out that the company is not fulfilling its duty to her by asking her to operate an unguarded guillotine. The chief executive concludes the interview with Pat by warning her that the company has been considering terminating her contract because of her continued membership of a trade union when she had had ample opportunity to join the company's own clerical staff association.

Terms and Conditions Relating to the Employee

All contracts of employment will have within them express conditions or terms. These terms form the basis of the contract and if not upheld may lead the other party to the contract to treat the agreement as breached. Express conditions, as the words suggest, are those conditions which are actually expressed or stated either verbally or in writing. Thus in the example we have just read an express condition would be the £125.76 for a 37-hour week. There are, however, existing in contracts of employment a number of implied conditions. We have already learned that some contracts contain implied conditions and what they are; these are conditions which are not stated but nevertheless they exist and failure to uphold them may lead to breach just as with express conditions. When a person takes up employment he is bound by the implied condition that he must obey reasonable and legal orders given by his employer or someone designated by the employer. It is quite obvious that Pat has a legal duty to obey orders and continued failure to do so could lead to her contract being terminated. This fact is well illustrated in the following case.

Pepper v. *Webb* (1969)
Pepper, a head gardener, refused to obey an order to plant flowers to prevent them deteriorating over the weekend while he was off duty. When questioned on weekend arrangements for the care of the greenhouse, Pepper replied, 'I couldn't care less about your bloody greenhouse or your sodding garden', and walked away. There had been complaints about inefficiency and insolence preceding this incident. Pepper was instantly dismissed without notice or payment in lieu of notice. He claimed damages for breach of contract of employment which specifically provided for three months' notice.

It was held that by wilfully disobeying a lawful order Pepper had shown his intention not to fulfil his contractual duties, which together with his previous conduct justified instant dismissal. It is important to remember that disobedience is permissible when the instruction from the employer is illegal or unreasonable. For example, in *Morrish* v. *Henlys (Folkestone) Ltd* (1973), a driver was sacked for refusing to obey his manager's order to make false claims for petrol expenses. Disobedience was held justified, and his dismissal was unfair.

A second important implied condition is the requirement that the employee works competently and carefully, and if Pat insists on producing incompetent, badly typed, careless work she is clearly in breach of this term and therefore, in breach of contract of employment. The standard of care and competency expected of an employee will vary in the light of what is expected of the particular occupation. Higher standards may be expected of professional persons such as doctors, solicitors or architects. This is summed up well in the following case. In *Harmer* v. *Cornelius* (1858), a man who accepted a job as a scene painter proved quite incapable of painting scenes, and was lawfully dismissed without notice.

It is a further implied condition that an employee accepts the rules of the organisation by which he or she is employed. An employee who breaks the rules can be said to be misconducting himself and may be at risk of being dismissed for breach of contract. Thus if Pat arrived for work each morning at 9.30 a.m. instead of 9.00 a.m. and insisted on taking two hours for lunch instead of the allocated one hour, then her employer would be quite justified in dismissing her without notice.

Finally all contracts of employment contain the important implied condition that an employee shows 'good faith' to his employer. 'Good faith covers a whole range of aspects but it will suffice to give just two examples. In an office a good deal of confidential information is available especially among those engaged as typists; and if Pat decided to pass on information about her employer's new plans to a rival, then this would clearly be regarded as a breach of faith. Secondly, if Pat was aware that one of her colleagues was involved in financial activities detrimental to the firm's interest, e.g. embezzling the firm's money, then she would have a duty to her employer to pass on this information. Failure to disclose this information could be regarded as a breach of faith and therefore breach of an implied condition. Two cases sum this up very well. In *Hivac Ltd* v. *Park Royal Scientific Instruments Ltd* (1946), the appellants manufactured midget valves for hearing aids. Certain of their highly skilled workers began to work on Sundays for the respondents, a competing business which had been set up nearby. It was held that the workers were in breach of good faith, and an injunction was granted restraining the respondents from employment them. In *Reading* v. *Attorney General* (1951), an Army sergeant serving in Egypt used to accompany lorries which were smuggling liquor. Because he was wearing uniform, the lorries were not searched. It was held that the 'profits' accruing to him from this enterprise (some £20 000) belonged to the Crown.

Thus, in addition to any express terms in a contract, an employee is bound by implied conditions. An employee who breaks his contract of employment conditions may be dismissed. As we shall see, though, any employee who feels he has been unfairly dismissed may appeal to an industrial tribunal.

Exercise 3

List the four implied conditions that are always implied in a contract of employment which apply to an employee.

Terms and Conditions Relating to the Employer

Not only is the employee subject to express and implied conditions but employers are also in a similar position. It is, of course, necessary for Associated Food Supplies to pay Pat a weekly wage of £125.76 because this is an express condition. The employer is also bound by certain implied conditions. First, the employer has to provide a safe system of work and the absence of the regulation guard protecting the guillotine would suggest that this condition is not being adequately fulfilled. The law states quite clearly that an employee must not be discriminated against or dismissed because he is a member of a trade union. The mention of trade union activity by Associated Food's chief executive would clearly be inconsistent with this condition. As pointed out earlier, employers must also not discriminate on grounds of sex, race, or national origin.

Where an employee incurs expense in carrying out business on behalf of his employer, then the employer has an implied duty to reimburse the employee. Thus if Pat is required to travel to a branch office in a nearby town for her employer, then her company must pay her reasonable travelling and out-of-pocket expenses. It is an obvious but nevertheless an implied duty that an employer must deduct PAYE tax and national insurance contributions. Employers must provide a reasonable system of management.

Thus in addition to any express condition which is stated an employer is bound by implied conditions.

Exercise 4

List the implied conditions to which an employer is bound.

It is interesting to note that an employer is not obliged to give any employee a reference for another post. If, however, the employer does give an employee a reference it is usually confidential between one employer and another and is not, therefore, normally seen by the employee. If the employee does learn of the contents of the reference the employer is protected from a defamation action as long as there was an attempt to state his honest opinion and there was no malice. From what we have read it is unlikely that Associated Food would give Pat Browne a glowing reference, but even if some of the statements they made about Pat were not completely true, if Pat discovered this she would not be successful in sueing the firm. The law as it relates to defamation will be dealt with in Chapter 7. An employer who wishes to get rid of an unsatisfactory employee might be tempted to give the employee in question a good reference if he applied for another post. However, in giving references, an employer owes the other, prospective employer a duty of care; if he makes a statement negligently or dishonestly, and on the basis of this statement the employee gets another job, then, if the employee is unsatisfactory and causes his new employer some loss, the first employer might be sued for negligence. An employer who gives a good reference to get rid of someone may run a risk within his own organisation, e.g. In *Haspell* v. *Rostron & Johnson Ltd* (1976), the employer who gave a favourable reference was estopped from relying on inconsistent allegations when he later tried to justify dismissing the employee. 'Estopped' is a legal term meaning prevented from.

Sex and Race Discrimination

The Sex Discrimination Act 1975 and the Race Relations Act 1976 make it unlawful to discriminate on grounds of sex (or against married persons) or race in the fields of employment, education, housing, grants, facilities, services and advertising.

These two Acts also cover discrimination by employers in recruitment and in relation to existing employees. There are some examples where employers can show that it is necessary for a job to be done by a person of one sex (e.g. a warden of a female hall of residence should be a woman) or of one particular racial group (the employment of Chinese in Chinese restaurants). In these instances discrimination in selection is permitted. Decency or privacy may require discrimination. The courts will look closely at any case of discrimination as the following shows. In *Wylie* v. *Dee & Co. (Menswear) Ltd* (1978), an employer refused to employ a woman as sales assistant in a menswear shop. This was held to be unlawful discrimination. It could not be justified on decency grounds, because customers could change in a private cubicle. Contact such as inside-leg measurement was rarely required, and could be carried out by one of the other seven assistants, all male, if need be.

The Equal Opportunities Commission and the Commission for Racial Equality can conduct formal investigations and both Commissions have issued Codes of Practice for employers and employees. You can obtain these Codes of Practice from:

Equal Opportunities Commission,
Overseas House,
Quay Street,
Manchester M3 3MN

Commission for Racial Equality,
Elliot House,
10/12 Allington Street,
London SW1

Equal Pay

Following the Equal Pay Act it is necessary for employers to treat men and women equally in terms of pay and conditions. A man or woman can appeal to the Industrial Tribunal under the Equal Pay Act.

The case on page 249, which is an extract from *The Times* newspaper, shows very well the working of this Act. It also is an example of a case from the House of Lords. As you will see the case was heard in the Industrial Tribunal where Miss Hayward was unsuccessful and on appeal it was heard at the Employment Appeal Tribunal and at the Court of Appeal. Both these Appeal courts dismissed Miss Hayward's appeal. In May 1988 she was finally successful in what has become a famous case.

Maternity Rights

In April 1987 a system of statutory maternity pay was introduced. To qualify a woman must:

1 have been in continuous employment with an employer for 26 weeks;
2 have been in employment up to the 15th week before the expected date of confinement (the birth). This 15th week is known as the qualifying week;
3 have been earning at least £41 per week;
4 must give at least 21 days notice to her employer of her intended absence.

Benefits available. A woman will be entitled to 18 weeks maternity pay. This is payable from the 11th week before the expected date of confinement. There are two rates:

1 The higher rate which is calculated at nine-tenths her weekly wage.
2 The lower rate payable for 12 weeks at £34.25 per week.

(Note the higher rate is only payable to women who have worked continuously for two years for 16 hours or more. Also to those who have worked for five years at eight hours or more.)

A woman has the right to return to work at any time up to 29 weeks following the birth. This may be extended for four weeks with a Doctor's certificate. The maximum allowed is 33 weeks.

Statutory Sick Pay

An employer must pay sick pay to an employee who is away sick. No payment is due for the first three days of sickness but thereafter sick pay is payable on a wage of £41 or more. A scale of sick pay is laid down, which at present is:

Average weekly wage	*Sick pay*
£41.00–£79.49	£34.25
£79.50 or more	£49.20

An employee will be entitled to a maximum of 28 weeks SSP (Statutory Sick Pay) in any one period. Remember that, as with other aspects of employment law these are minimum requirements and in many jobs full pay is available for quite long periods of sickness.

Employers can recover the amounts paid from government funds. Employers and employees contribute to the funds from National Insurance contributions.

Data Protection

The Data Protection Act 1984 was planned to regulate the use of personal data which can be processed by equipment operating automatically. A Data Protection Registrar is now in post and data users must register with him details of data held. From 1987 individuals have the right to be informed about personal data held on them. This right is available on request and must be provided within forty days. Individuals may claim compensation if they suffer distress from disclosure of information to others.

This Act offers quite considerable protection to employees. There are a number of exceptions, particularly those relating to pay, etc. Also an employee can give his employer the right to disclose information.

Exercise 5

In the following examples advise the party in italics whether there exists a breach of condition.

1 Burlow Road Buildings Supplies Ltd decide to reduce the salary of their *office manager* from £120 per week to £100.

2 *Michael Moore*, a development engineer with Amalgamated Metals, is asked by the chief engineer to assist in painting the managing director's office. Michael refuses.

3 *Margaret Frances* is a confidential secretary to a solicitor and she is in the habit of discussing clients' legal problems with her friends.

4 *John Martin* is employed by a firm of motor engineers. He regularly takes home engine parts suitable for his own private car.

5 *Philip Hadfield* is a quantity surveyor with a large building contractor, and on three occasions he has made mistakes in working out estimates in jobs which have involved his firm in heavy losses.

6 *Richard Haigh* is a commercial traveller for Midlands Dairy Food but in the course of his work for one week he spends £123 on petrol and two nights' accommodation at a modest hotel. His firm refuse to pay out this expense.

7 *Fashion Textiles Ltd* cannot afford to provide protective guards and require all their employees to work on machinery which is unfenced and threaten them with redundancy if they complain.
8 *Reginald Pullen* has been with a TV rental firm for six years as an accounts clerk and has an excellent work record. He wishes to leave and applies for a post in London. TV Rentals Ltd refuse to give him a reference for the post.
9 Calculate the maternity pay due to *Diane Hodges* who has been with her company for three years earning £100 per week.

4.3 UNFAIR DISMISSAL AND REDUNDANCY

Notice

We have already seen that contracts of employment are just like any other contract, needing to contain the same essential elements. In this section we will be considering how contracts of employment may be brought to an end, what rights employees may have if they consider they have been unfairly dismissed, and the law in respect of redundancies.

Alan Phillips, aged thirty-seven, a married man with two young children, has been employed by Associated Engineering Co. in Newcastle-upon-Tyne for seven years as a storeman at a weekly wage of £150. Like many engineering companies, Associated Engineering are going through a very difficult trading position and a decision is reached to trim the wages bill. In the stores where Alan works there are six employees and it is felt by the management that this section is overmanned. Alan, despite seven years' service, is the newest recruit and he is told that he will have to leave. Associated Engineering give Alan a week's notice and an ex gratia *payment of £100. Alan feels he is entitled to more but is not sure.*

Most contracts of employment end by means of one party or the other giving notice. How long this notice must be depends upon the particular contract between the employer and employee. Alan would check to see what it says in the particulars of employment which he should have been given (see page 81). These particulars should give details of the length of notice that needs to be given.

The Employment Protection (Consolidation) Act 1978 lays down minimum periods which must be given. An employer must give notice related to periods of continuous service on the following scale:

Length of service	*Period of notice*
4 weeks up to 2 years	1 week
2 years	2 weeks
3 years	3 weeks

and so on up to a maximum of 12 weeks for 12 years' service.

An employee needs to give one week after four weeks' service, and one week remains the legal minimum to be given by an employee.

It is important to remember that these are minimum periods and contracts of employment can stipulate any length of notice as long as they are at or above the minimum. In our example Alan would be entitled to at least seven weeks' notice or, if Associated Engineering wished, seven weeks' pay 'in lieu' (instead) of notice, i.e. 7 × £150 = £1050.

Activity

If you are in employment calculate the minimum period of notice your firm would have to give you as set out in the Employment Protection (Consolidation) Act 1978.

Exercise 6

Calculate the minimum amount of notice and the amount of money payable in lieu required by the Employment Protection (Consolidation) Act 1978 in the following examples.

1 Reg Pullin has been employed at Aston Containers Ltd for fourteen years at a weekly wage of £150.
2 Carol Latham has been employed as a shorthand-typist with the local authority for eighteen months at £80 per week.
3 Ken Gould has been a lathe operator with Trenchard Machinings Ltd for just three weeks at £138 per week.
4 Tracey Armstrong has been an office typist for 2½ years with Fisk, Mason and Wood, Solicitors, at a salary of £85 per week.

Redundancy

Let us return to our example in respect of Alan Phillips - you will remember that in addition to a week's notice he was given an *ex gratia* payment of £100. *Ex gratia* means that it is a way for the company Associated Engineering to say thankyou to Alan for his seven years' service. It is, however, likely that Alan is entitled to rather more than a £100 thankyou. He may well be entitled to redundancy pay.

The Employment Protection (Consolidation) Act 1978 which incorporates the terms of the Redundancy Payments Act 1965 states that redundancy may arise where an employee is dismissed under one or other of the following circumstances:

1 the employer has ceased or intends to cease to carry on the business for the purposes for which the employee was employed by him; or
2 the employer has ceased or intends to cease to carry on that business in the place where the employee was so employed; or
3 the work needed to be done by the employee has either diminished or ceased to be necessary to the business of the employer (either generally or at the place where the employee worked) or is expected to diminish or cease.

The law also stipulates certain conditions whereby short-time working or temporary lay-offs can lead to redundancy.

Alan's situation would be similar to the third item. Alan has been dismissed because his work in the stores has diminished. There is no longer the need for so many storemen due to the fact that Associated Engineering have had a reduction in their business.

The Act also lays down the categories of employees who are *not* eligible for redundancy:

1 employees over retirement age, normally 65 for men and 60 for women;
2 part-time employees. For the purposes of the Act this means employees who work less than sixteen hours per week or if they have been employed with the firm for five years or more and work less than eight hours;
3 a woman employed by her husband or vice versa;
4 certain categories of employees, e.g. registered dock workers, government employees;
5 employees on fixed term contracts of two years or more who in the agreement establishing the contract or some time before expiry have agreed in writing to be excluded from redundancy payment at the end of their contract;
6 employees who have not reached their eighteenth birthday;
7 employees who have worked for the employer for less than two years.

Alan is a full-time employee, he has been with Associated Engineering for more than two years, he is not on a fixed term contract and he is not yet over retirement age. It would seem, therefore, that Alan would qualify for redundancy pay. The Employment Protection (Consolidation) Act 1978 lays down the following formula for calculating the amount of money that a person might claim for redundancy:

1 for whole years' service between the ages of 18 and 22 birthday, ½ week's pay for each year.
2 for whole year's service from the 22nd birthday for the 41st birthday 1 week's pay for each year.

3 from the 41st birthday until retirement age 1½ weeks' pay for each whole year's completed service.

At present the maximum number of years' service that can be included is twenty years. The maximum salary is £164 and the total maximum redundancy pay payable is (20 × 1½ × £164) = £4920. This maximum amount, i.e. £164 and £4920, is the present situation. It is likely to be increased from time to time to reflect current wage levels. Where a person's salary exceeds £155 then the amount by which the wage exceeds £155 is disregarded.

The wage which is taken into account is usually the wage of the last week before dismissal. Alan's wage was £150 and all his seven years' service is within the 22–41 age-band; therefore he is entitled to one week for each year, i.e. 7 × 150 = £1050. In calculating redundancy pay the firm must work back from a person's present age so as to give him/her maximum advantage. If Janet Evans (age forty-nine) had been employed for twenty years with a company at a wage of £100 she would be entitled to:

8 years at 1½ weeks × 100	=	£1200
12 years at 1 week × 100		£1200
A total of		£2400

A company is legally bound to give redundant employees full details of the way in which redundancy pay has been calculated.

Activity

If you are in employment calculate the minimum amount of redundancy pay, if any, you would be entitled to under the law if you were made redundant.

Exercise 7

In the following cases for each say (a) whether the employee concerned would be entitled to redundancy, under the Employment Protection (Consolidation) Act. (b) where appropriate calculate the redundancy pay due.

1 Frederick Langton (58) has been a tax officer with the civil service for twenty years at a salary of £8500 per annum. He is made redundant.

2 Bob Williams (24) has been with Associated Plant for eight years. His current wage is £110 per week. He is made redundant because of a serious fall-off in trade.

3 United Chemicals Ltd move from London to Manchester and

Frank Brown (age 67), a cleaner, is made redundant. His wage is £75 and he has been with the firm for thirty years.

4 Rita Harrison (50) has been with United Foods Ltd as an accountant for thirty years at a wage of £150 per week. The company discontinue business and she claims redundancy.

5 Susan Mason (26) has done part-time work for Security Insurance Ltd for three years. She has worked twelve hours per week at a wage of £30 per week.

Before we leave the subject of redundancy two further points need to be made. Firstly, what we have been considering is the minimum redundancy payment which firms must give. However, if a firm wishes to pay more than the legal minimum then this is in order. In fact many highly paid employees particularly, receive quite lucrative 'golden handshakes' when they are made redundant; much more than the legal minimum. Secondly, when employees are made redundant they are sometimes offered alternative employment with the same firm and in some cases a refusal might jeopardise their entitlement to redundancy pay. To return to our original example:

Let us assume that Alan is offered the same job in Associated Engineering's London division. If, after considering this offer with his wife, Alan feels that a move from Newcastle-upon-Tyne, where he had lived all his life, was not really satisfactory and therefore turned down the offer, would he lose his redundancy entitlement of £1050?

Whether an alternative offer is suitable and therefore refusal is unreasonable will be judged on the facts of the particular case. Suitability is judged in terms of (a) status and (b) location. The following two cases will illustrate the position.

Taylor v. *Kent County Council* (1969)
A head teacher became redundant when his school was amalgamated with another. Kent County Council offered the head teacher alternative employment in a mobile pool of teachers to be used to cover staff shortages. His salary would be unaffected but he would have to move to another part of the county. It was held that the inconvenience and loss of status were held to justify refusal and he was entitled to redundancy payments.

O'Brien v. *Associated Fire Alarms* (1969)
An electrician had lived and worked in Liverpool for many years. He was offered alternative employment in Barrow-in-Furness which is 120 miles away when the Liverpool branch closed. It was held he was entitled to redundancy payment.

It would seem that in the light of these two decisions Alan could justifiably refuse to move to London. It is likely that a man with family commitments such as Alan could more justifiably refuse a move than a single man.

It is then part of the law relating to redundancy that alternative offers of employment may be refused yet still redundancy pay may be claimed.

Exercise 8

Consider the following and say whether the alternative offer of employment is suitable.

1 Dr George Morris is a research chemist with Regency Chemicals Ltd. Due to a down-turn in trade the company offer him the post of laboratory assistant at the same salary.
2 Deborah Harrison is an accountant with a firm in Wolverhampton. The firm closes its branch in Wolverhampton and she is offered the same post at Walsall, about ten miles away.
3 Fred Merrick is a head waiter at the Royal Oak Hotel, York. Fred, who is married with three children, is made redundant and is offered a post with the same firm in Torquay at the Regal Hotel. After a discussion with his wife he refuses this alternative offer.

Unfair Dismissal

We have already learned that employees may be made redundant. There are, however, other reasons for which an employee may be dismissed. Since 1971 employees who have been dismissed for reasons other than redundancy may appeal against what they consider to be unfair dismissal. In this section we will be considering the question of unfair dismissal and the remedies available to employees if they consider they have been unfairly dismissed.

Activity

In the second section of this chapter we considered express and implied conditions which related to employment contracts. Try to list the implied conditions which bind (1) an employee, (2) an employer. If you cannot remember these then refer back to page 84–6.

The following examples might help to explain the law as it presently stands in relation to unfair dismissal.

1 Mrs Dorothy Armstrong has been employed as a coach driver for 15 months by United Coaches Ltd. In the last 21 weeks however she has been involved in no less than seven accidents. United Coaches Ltd decide to terminate her employment by giving her one week's notice.

2 Michael Hunter is an electrician with Adams Electrical (Contractors) Ltd. He has been employed by this firm for six months. The managing director Paul Adams is very much against trade unions and when he discovers Michael is a member of a trade union he warns him that continued membership will jeopardise his job. Michael refuses to leave the union and is given one week's notice.

3 Dorothy Williams has been a cashier with a large food store for three years. Her employer discovers that over the past year Dorothy has taken over £1000 of the firm's money. She is called into the manager's office and is dismissed without notice.

4 Philip Clapham has been with Northern Press for twenty years as a printer. He has been a most successful employee but on one occasion, even though he knows the firm's strict rule about outside work, he prints some cards for his local church. He is called into the manager's office and sacked without notice.

5 Sarah Thomas gets a job as an accountant with a large firm by saying she is a qualified accountant, having the qualification ACCA. Her firm finds that she has never gained such a qualification and she is dismissed after having been with the firm for one year.

6 Frank Clements is a solicitor having been employed by a small firm for three years. Over the last few months his work has deteriorated and he has made several quite serious errors. He is called in to see the senior partner of the firm and explains that he has had some domestic problems which may be effecting his work. The senior partner decides to dismiss him.

The Employment Protection (Consolidation) Act 1978 which consolidates the law on unfair dismissal since 1971 lays down that an employee can appeal to an industrial tribunal if he has been employed for 52 weeks or more. Since the Employment Act 1980, for firms employing twenty employees or less the qualifying period is 104 weeks (two years). In the light of this let us examine the six cases outlined above.

1 Dorothy could appeal against unfair dismissal because she has been with United Coaches for 15 months. It is unlikely that her appeal would be upheld because she is in breach of an implied condition, i.e. the need to work competently and carefully, and seven accidents in 21 weeks does not seem consistent with this condition.

2 The law lays down clearly that dismissal for trade union membership is inadmissable and therefore 'unfair'. In fact the 52 weeks' qualifying period is not necessary for this situation and Michael could appeal despite having been with the firm for only six months.

3 Although normally notice is required by law, serious cases of misconduct which this certainly is will justify instant dismissal and there would seem little likelihood of Dorothy's appeal against unfair dismissal being successful.

4 This is another case of misconduct but less serious than in the previous situation The law requires that an employee normally be given a warning before dismissal for misconduct and Philip would claim that he had been unfairly dismissed. Firms are expected to comply with Codes of Practice issued under the Employment Protection Act 1975 which are designed to promote good industrial relations. The industrial tribunal would consider that the failure to give a warning as recommended by the Codes of Practice was sufficient to justify a case of unfair dismissal.

5 Sarah certainly in this situation has misrepresented the facts in applying for the post. There was between her and her employer no 'meeting of the minds'. There is little doubt that the industrial tribunal would not uphold any appeal against unfair dismissal.

6 Frank's work has deteriorated but as explained earlier it would be necessary for a warning to be given so that Frank could try to improve. If Frank appealed it is likely that the industrial tribunal would consider that the failure to give a warning constituted unfair dismissal.

If an employee who considers he has been unfairly dismissed wishes to complain of unfair dismissal he must do so by means of the procedure set out below.

1 A complaint of unfair dismissal must be presented to an industrial tribunal within three months of the termination of employment.
2 A copy of the complaint must be sent to the Advisory Conciliation and Arbitration Service (ACAS) who will designate a conciliation officer to try to get a settlement which may involve re-engagement/reinstatement of the employee or compensation.
3 If the officer fails to get a settlement then the case will go to the industrial tribunal. The tribunal has the power to make a reinstatement order (the employee must be given his old job back) or a re-engagement order (the employee is given a comparable job). There are circumstances under which it would be impractical for an employee to be reinstated or re-engaged. In some cases firms refuse to re-engage or reinstate.

In these circumstances the industrial tribunal may award compensation. There is in the law provision for a basic award which is calculated in a similar way to redundancy awards, for a compensatory award, for an additional award and a special award. The maximum rate of pay for the calculation of the basic award is £164 and the maximum basic award is £4920.

The present compensation award is set at a maximum of £8500 which takes into account loss of earnings, loss of pension rights and loss of benefits. This compensation is awarded if the employer fails to comply with a reinstatement or re-engagement order. The additional award is payable when the dismissal was an unlawful act of sex or racial discrimination. The present maximum is £8528, which is payable in addition to the compensation award. A special award may be payable when the employee is dismissed for trade union membership. This rate is calculated at the rate of 1 weeks' pay × 104 weeks or £11 950 whichever is greater. The maximum allowed is £23 850.

Exercise 9

1 What are the three possible stages in an appeal against unfair dismissal?
2 What four types of award may be given in compensation by an industrial tribunal in an unfair dismissal case?
3 What is the length of service to qualify an employee for an appeal to the industrial tribunal against unfair dismissal?
4 Examine the following three cases and say whether you think the employee concerned would be successful in an unfair dismissal appeal, giving reasons for your view.
(a) Adam Crawford has been with Reliant Heating Supplies for five years. It has been discovered that he has been using his firm's materials worth £2000 to do a number of private central heating jobs. He is dismissed without notice.
(b) Jane Mason joins a trade union and is immediately given notice of dismissal. She has only been with her firm for two weeks.
(c) Roy Bright has been employed as a salesman for two years. His sales record has been good but the last month has been a poor one for him. He is given two weeks' notice.
5 Roger Harrop earns £175 per week as an engineer on a cross channel ferry. He is sacked because he is in a trade union. Calculate his special award in these circumstances.

Exercise 10

1 All contracts of employment must be in writing. *true/false*?
2 Apprenticeship contracts must always be in writing. *true/false*?
3 Written particulars of employment must be provided within
(a) 1 year of the start of employment;
(b) 2 years of the start of employment;
(c) 13 weeks of the start of employment;
(d) 4 weeks of the start of employment.
4 An employer must provide an employee with a reference if he/she wishes to apply for another post. *true/false*?

5 How much minimum notice is an employee entitled to if he has worked for a firm for fifteen years?
6 Calculate the redundancy payment entitlement for an employee of 46 years old who has been with his firm for ten years. His salary is £100.
7 If an employee refuses an alternative offer of employment he may not claim redundancy. *true/false*?
8 How long must an employee have worked at a firm to be entitled to appeal against unfair dismissal?
9 Mary Jones is a teacher in a school in the Midlands. She tells the head teacher that she is expecting a child and will leave at the end of the term but would like to return. The head teacher refuses to re-employ her and Mary seeks advice.
10 Michael Bevan sees his employer and demands to see details of all personal data held on him in the firm's computer. The employer refuses.

The whole question of employment law and unfair dismissal is very complex, and we have only been able to deal with it very briefly in this chapter.

CHAPTER 5

CONSUMER LAW

5.1 SALE OF GOODS ACT 1979

Rachel and Deborah both wish to purchase motorcars. Rachel buys a E registered Mini from Associated Motor Sales Ltd for £4650. Deborah buys a similar model privately from a friend for £4350. Coincidentally within a month of their purchase both girls experience the same problems with their cars and are forced to have new gear boxes fitted at considerable cost.

In this case Rachel would be in a much better position because her contract to buy the car would be completely covered by the Sale of Goods Act 1979 because it would be considered to be a consumer sale. A consumer sale has been defined as such where the following criteria are satisfied.

1 The sale must be by a seller in the course of a business.
2 The goods must be of a type ordinarily supplied for private use or consumption.
3 The goods must be sold to a person who does not buy or does not hold himself out as buying them in the course of business.

If we apply these three criteria to the situation relating to Rachel then it is easy to see that this is a consumer sale. Associated Motor Sales Ltd are selling the car in the course of business; Rachel is buying it for her own private use and not in the course of business. Deborah's purchase, however, does not satisfy the first criteria. She buys the car from a friend, i.e. who is not selling in the course of business. This distinction is important because only consumer sales are completely protected by the Sale of Goods Act 1979 which we will be considering in this section.

Exercise 1

Applying the three criteria we have just considered which of the following would be regarded as a consumer sale?

1 Philip Latham buys a new music centre from Leisure Supplies Ltd for £450.
2 John Martindale a furniture retailer buys furniture from a furniture warehouse which he then resells in his shop.
3 United Food Ltd sell a consignment of biscuits to a grocery chain store, Supersave Ltd.
4 Malcolm Trent sells his motorcycle to a motorcycle dealer for £650.

If you decide to buy goods privately, that is not from a person or organisation in business, then you take a risk. The principle which covers private sales is *caveat emptor* which means 'let the buyer beware'. If the goods turn out to be faulty in some way and the seller has not misrepresented them in any way then there is nothing the buyer can do. In our situation Deborah would have no legal claim against the friend from whom she bought the Mini unless she could prove that he had in some way misrepresented the facts about the car's condition, for instance if he had said 'I have had trouble with the gear box but the one in now is a new one'. If this was not the case then he has misrepresented and as we have learned one of the essential elements would be absent, that is there would have been no *consensus ad idem*. If the friend knew about the gear box but said nothing or honestly did not know then Deborah would have to bear the full cost of a replacement gear box herself.

In the last chapter we learned that contracts may have within them implied (unexpressed) conditions. In any consumer sale the Sale of Goods 1979 implies certain conditions. If these conditions are breached then the buyer has the right to reject the goods and end the contract or sue for damages because of breach.

The following four examples will help to explain the implied conditions which exist in a consumer sale.

1 Barbara Dallow buys from London Road Motors Ltd a new Ford Escort GL. She trades in her present car which is a Ford Fiesta. London Road Motors sell the Ford Fiesta for £3200 to John Proctor. The Fiesta in fact had been stolen and belonged to David Beresford. The police trace the car and John is forced to hand it over to its rightful owner. John goes to see the manager of London Road Motors who explains that he had no idea the car was stolen and although sympathetic to John says he can do nothing.

There is little doubt that the contract between John and London Road Motors is a consumer sale and John is protected by an important implied condition of the Sale of Goods Act 1979, i.e. *that the seller has the right to sell the goods*. If the seller has no right to sell the goods then he is in breach of condition and must return the money. John therefore would be able to claim the return of his £3200 from London Road Motors Ltd.

Some of the cases which are quoted in this chapter are before 1979. The 1979 Act replaced a similar act of 1890 which was also known as the Sale of Goods Act. The following case shows that a buyer is able to reclaim a full money refund on goods that he has bought which are stolen.

In *Rowland* v. *Divall* (1923), the buyer of a car used it for about three months, but then found that it was stolen and had to return it to the true owner. He was held entitled to recover from the seller the full price which he had paid even though, when he had to part with it, the car was probably worth rather less. He had paid to become owner, he had not become owner, and he was, therefore, entitled to the return of his money.

2 Margaret Hamilton buys a pair of trousers from Fashion Wear, a small shop in town. The trousers cost £23.50. When Margaret tries the trousers on at home she notices a serious flaw in them and takes them back to the shop. The shopkeeper is sympathetic and says he will send them back to the manufacturers and asks her to call again in about two weeks' time. Margaret is not happy about this and asks for her money back. The shopkeeper refuses saying he will have to get in touch with the manufacturer before he refunds any money.

In this situation, which is similar to the one on page 17 in Chapter 1, Margaret could claim a full money refund. Fashion Wear is in breach of another implied condition of the Sale of Goods Act 1979 that *goods must be of merchantable quality*. Merchantable quality will vary with the price of the goods in question but for £23.50 for a pair of trousers you would not expect to find a serious fault in them. Incidentally, the manufacturer is of no consequence to Margaret; she made the contract with Fashion Wear and although shopkeepers often try to push the problem away from themselves and on to the manufacturers in fact legally they are the supplier to the customer and it is they who must comply with the implied conditions. This is an important point to bear in mind when you have to return faulty goods to a shop. Remember the quality to be expected depends on the price paid and in the case of second-hand goods, the age. In *Bartlett* v. *Sidney Marcus Ltd* (1965), a second-hand car was sold with a defective clutch. The seller had warned the buyer of the defect, and the price took account of this. The car was held to be of merchantable quality in the circumstances, even though repair cost more than the buyer expected.

Exercise 2

Look back at the situation in relation to Rachel and the Mini. Do you think Rachel might have a case under the Sale of Goods Act 1979?

3 Janet Beckford buys three pairs of cotton sheets in lilac from a large store in Oxford. The shop assistant gets the sheets from the shelf and they are already packed with a label indicating that they are 85 per cent cotton and are lilac. The full cost is £47.50. When Janet gets home she finds on unpacking them that the sheets are nylon and are yellow. She returns to the store with the sheets and demands a full money refund. The supervisor for the section is called and he apologises to Janet but says since she has opened the parcels she will not get a refund and suggests she should have checked before leaving the store.

In this case the supervisor is quite wrong because the store has breached an implied condition of the Sale of Goods Act 1979 which provides that where there is *a contract for sale of goods by description there is an implied condition that the goods shall correspond with the description.* The sheets in our example certainly did not and the shop would be wise to refund the money because the court would certainly find for Janet in this situation. The following case shows an example of the application of the rule 'goods bought by description must correspond with the description.' In *Beale* v. *Taylor* (1967), a car was advertised as a 'Herald Convertible, white, 1961'. The buyer saw the vehicle before buying it, but only discovered some time later that, while the rear part had been accurately described, the front half had been part of an earlier model. The seller was held to be in breach of section 13 of the Sale of Goods Act.

Sometimes persons will buy from a sample, for example a shopper may inspect goods on display ask to buy them but in fact may be given goods from the shelves or from the storeroom. In this situation the shopper will be protected by section 15 of the Sale of Goods Act which states that where goods are sold by sample they ought to correspond with the sample. The rule relating to description will also apply where a customer buys goods by description from a newspaper or catalogue.

4 James Frazier has just bought a large house with a large garden. He is a keen but rather inexperienced gardner and he decides to go along to the garden centre of a large department store. The store advertises regularly the fact that it has employed two staff in their garden centre who are expert gardeners and will give their advice to customers who ask for it. James is advised about a certain type of weedkiller to destroy weeds which are spoiling a very attractive rockery. James buys the weedkiller on the advice of the shop. Unfortunately he has been given the wrong advice and the weedkiller destroys all the plants on the rockery in addition to the weeds. James is upset and returns to the shop. The manager is sympathetic but reminds James that he did not need to accept the advice given him.

James is fortunate because he can rely upon an implied term incorporated in the Sale of Goods Act 1979 which states: *Where the seller sells goods in the course of a business and the buyer expressly or by implication makes known . . . to the seller . . . any particular purpose for which the goods are being bought there is an implied condition that the goods supplied are reasonably fit for that purpose.*

James would have to show that he relied upon the skill or judgement of the seller. It would seem that James could show that the seller had indicated that he could give advice and certainly James relied upon it, being inexperienced himself. James could claim breach of a condition and could claim damages. To use this condition a buyer would need to show that he relied upon the judgement and that it was reasonable for him to do so. A conversation with a shop assistant in a supermarket over a brand of washing powder would not come into this category.

We have now examined the five implied conditions which can protect a consumer in a contract of sale.

The Sale of Goods Act applies to goods but not to services. The Supply of Goods and Services Act 1982, the first part of which became law on 4 January, 1983, provides protection to purchasers of services. For example, motor car repairs and services must be of 'merchantable quality' and at 'reasonable rates'.

Weekend Breaks Ltd, a holiday firm, arranges weekend breaks in a number of tourist centres in the UK, namely London, Cambridge, Oxford, Bath, York, Edinburgh and Winchester. Each weekend has a fully inclusive price which includes first class rail fare and full board in one of the city's top hotels. It also includes three tours of the city. Hugh Lawler and his wife book a weekend in Canterbury which costs £250. When they arrive, they find that the hotel is fully booked up and are offered alternative accommodation at a small guest house. No tours have been arranged and Hugh and his wife return home thoroughly dissatisfied. Fortunately, under the Supply of Goods and Services Act 1982, Hugh can take Weekend Breaks Ltd to court for breach of an implied condition that the service must be of merchantable quality which clearly it was not.

Exercise 3

List the five implied conditions in the Sale of Goods Act 1979.

We have been concerned with consumer sales because a consumer is given complete protection under the Sale of Goods Act 1979 as far as the implied terms are concerned. As far as consumers are concerned sellers cannot exclude liability from the implied conditions by means of an exclusion clause. The following example will illustrate this point.

Sheila buys a new television from Video Supplies Ltd for £350. On taking delivery she is given a manufacturer's warranty which she signs. The warranty guarantees the set for six months but contains the clause 'This equipment is supplied subject to no implied condition nor to any statutory provision'. After seven months the set will not work and when Sheila returns it she is told the repair cost would be so great that she might as well buy a new one. Sheila, who knows something about the law, tries to use her rights under the Sale of Goods Act 1979, claiming the television set was not of merchantable quality. The manager of Video Supplies Ltd shows her the warranty she has signed which excluded her rights.

The Sale of Goods Act 1979 makes it impossible for suppliers to take away a consumer's statutory rights and Sheila could sue on the basis that after seven months the goods were not really of merchantable quality. Manufacturers' warranties or guarantees, as they are sometimes called, can only add to a consumer's rights under the Sale of Goods Act 1979. In fact often nowadays a warranty/guarantee will contain a clause such as: 'This statement does not restrict a customer's statutory rights under consumer legislation.' This really is a reminder to the buyer that the implied conditions of the Sale of Goods Act 1979 cannot be taken away.

Activity

Have a look at warranties/guarantees which you might have in connection with new goods you may have purchased recently. Try to find examples of clauses which remind you that your rights are not affected by the warranty/guarantee.

Exercise 4

Read the following examples and say whether you think the buyer in each example could sue for breach of contract under the Sale of Goods Act 1979.

1 David Harrison buys a tennis racquet from Sports Equipment Ltd for £63. After two games the racquet has to have new strings.
2 Brian Webb buys a new motorcar from Unicorn Motors Ltd for £7500. It has a twelve-month manufacturer's warranty. Fourteen

months following the purchase with only 8500 miles on the clock such serious faults develop that the car needs a new engine, gear box and clutch.

3 Muriel Wilshaw sees some delicious looking English apples displayed at a greengrocers. She buys 2lb but is given some prepacked apples. When she arrives home she discovers they are French Golden Delicious.

4 Caroline Fletcher sees a car advertised by Union Motors Ltd: Vauxhall Astra, hatchback, C registration, 1300cc, £3350. She purchases the car but finds that it is not a hatchback and is 1200cc.

5 Philip Bagshaw is a professional photographer. Relying on the advice of the manager of a photographic supplier he buys a new type of colour film for £4.50 which will give according to the advice excellent results. Philip uses the film for some wedding photographs and the results are so bad that the disappointed newlyweds will not accept them.

6 David Knowles, a Citizen Band radio fanatic buys some equipment from a local shop which he has to give to the police because it was in fact stolen property.

5.2 TRADE DESCRIPTIONS ACT 1968 AND 1972

Many buyers who may feel that they have been wronged in some way will often not do anything about it because they lack the knowledge of the Sale of Goods Act, or they lack the initiative or the energy. In some cases buyers are worried about the likely cost of proceedings. Consequently, many sellers of defective goods or services get away with it. Consumers are given, however, additional protection by the criminal law. Under the Trade Descriptions Act 1968 certain criminal offences were created in relation to false descriptions of goods or services. The Trade Descriptions Act, which only applies where the sale is in the course of business and therefore does not apply to private sales, attempts to protect the consumer from four main types of abuse. The following examples will help to illustrate how the Trade Descriptions Act tries to deal with these abuses.

1 Dream Kitchens Ltd advertise new kitchens in the following way: 'Free Formica worktops when you purchase an Eastham Kitchen from us. Offer applies August only.'

Mrs Sykes orders on 14 August a kitchen from Dream Kitchens but the firm does not supply the Formica worktops. When Mrs Sykes enquires into this she is told that supplies of the Formica have been used up and that Dream Kitchens Ltd can no longer afford to supply these.

Dream Kitchens have in fact committed a criminal offence because the Trade Descriptions Act lays down that it is an offence to apply a false description to goods. False descriptions may take many forms. This one falsely described what would be supplied with the kitchen, but such phrases as 'home-made', 'reconditioned', 'fitted with disc brakes', 'approved by AA', 'Staffordshire pottery', are all capable, if made falsely, of giving rise to the criminal offence of false description.

If trade description cases come to court the seller can try to show that they had genuinely made a mistake or had relied upon the information supplied by others. This defence is effective if disclaimer notices are used.

Activity

Look around a second-hand car salesroom. Many dealers protect themselves from criminal action by placing a disclaimer notice over the mileometer. See if you can find some examples of this look at the wording used.

2 Anxious to get rid of existing stock, Greenbanks (Men's Wear) Ltd offer a certain type of ready-made suit reduced from £100 to £50. A number of men including Kevin Quinlan take advantage of this apparently excellent offer. Kevin discusses his bargain with a friend who tells him that he bought the same suit from Greenbanks six months previously for £60. Kevin feels that Greenbanks have committed an offence but is not sure.

The Trade Descriptions Act 1968 makes it an offence to advertise price reductions of this sort unless the higher price had existed for a continuous period of twenty-eight days within the last six months.

The difficulty with this section of the Act is in proving that the higher price did not exist for the stipulated period. The prosecution has to prove this. It has been suggested that the law be changed so that the onus of proof lies on the seller, i.e. he/she has to prove that the higher price did prevail for twenty-eight days, but the suggestion has not been implemented. In fact to date there have been very few successful prosecutions for this offence which is called 'double pricing'.

3 Leisure and Pleasure Holidays Ltd is a firm specialising in holidays in historical towns in England and Wales. A holiday is advertised for sixteen days which includes four days in each of the following towns – Bath, Oxford, London and Canterbury – at a cost of £350 per head, which includes transport and free entry into places of historical interest. The hotels arranged are high class hotels each room with twin beds, private bath, w.c. and shower.

Mr and Mrs Edward Harris book this holiday but find that in two of the hotels there is no private bath, shower or w.c. Surcharges are made for the coach travel of £30 per head and in at least three of the visits entry fees have to be paid. Mr Harris decides to complain but is told by the management that there is nothing they could do.

In fact Leisure and Pleasure Holidays could face prosecution under the Trade Descriptions Act 1968, which makes it an offence for a person in the course of business to make a statement which is false relating to services, accommodation and facilities. This section, Section 14, states that the statement must be made 'knowingly or recklessly'. Therefore, Leisure and Pleasure could in their defence say that they honestly believed the facts in the advertisement to be true, and had received no information to the contrary. It would seem from recent decided cases that it is somewhat difficult to get a prosecution under this section.

4 Because of his opposition to the South African government's policy of apartheid Harold Gilman will never buy goods from this country. He buys some tins of fruit from a supermarket; the label on the tin states that the goods were from South Australia. Harold notices that on the tin itself it states Cape Town, S. Africa.

In this situation the supermarket could face prosecution because Sections 16 and 17 of the Trade Descriptions Act 1968 state that it is an offence to import goods bearing a false indication of origin, and these tins certainly contravene this section because although the fruit is from South Africa it is labelled as a product of Australia.

Exercise 5

1 Contravention of the Trade Descriptions Act 1968 could lead to a civil action. *true/false*?
2 Name the four main criminal offences created by the Trade Descriptions Act.

Enforcement of the Trade Descriptions Act 1968

Prosecutions under this Act are brought by local authorities usually by trading standards inspectors. Prosecution may lead to the normal penalties such as fines and sometimes imprisonment. Neither fines or imprisonment of the offender is much consolation to a person who has for example had a holiday ruined as a result of a false description. Magistrates' Courts, however, have the power to award compensation to a person who has suffered. This compensation is limited to £2000, but it does provide some assistance to a consumer who may be reluctant for all sorts of reasons to pursue a civil claim in the courts.

Exercise 6

In the following examples say whether you think the seller in question has contravened the Trade Descriptions Act 1968.

1 Alan Harrison runs a small craft shop and he advertises crafts from the Third World. Most of the crafts are made in fact by a company in Western Germany although all bear a stamp 'Produced in the Third World'.

2 Torbay Holiday Flats Ltd advertise self-catering flats each with a sea view and only five minutes' walk from the seafront. In fact most of the flats have no outlook over the sea and are situated at least forty minutes' walk from the coast.

3 Sports Supplies Ltd advertise tennis racquets at half price.

4 Country Kitchen Bakery advertise home-made bread and cakes. The bakery in fact get all their supplies from a large bakery twenty miles away.

5.3 CONSUMER CREDIT

There are often occasions when individuals want to buy goods or services but have not got at that moment the money available to do so. It is possible to obtain from banks or finance houses credit to enable one to buy goods or services. There are a number of different types of credit arrangements which individuals can obtain and in recent years a number of Acts of Parliament have been passed to protect individuals from abuses and unfair terms. In this section we will deal with the law as it applies to consumer credit so that you will understand the main operation of the law in this respect.

The following examples will help to explain some of the main types of credit arrangements.

1 David Pritchard wishes to borrow some money for a number of purposes, e.g. he wishes to take his family on holiday abroad and also to buy some furniture for his house. He decides that he wants £2000 spread over three years. David can go to his bank or he may go to one of the many finance houses willing to lend money such as Mercantile Credit, Lloyds Bowmaker, United Dominion Trust. David will have to complete a form and if satisfied the finance house will make him an offer, e.g. £2000 at 12.5 per cent per annum over 36 months will mean a repayment of £76.39 per month. If David accepts he will in due course receive a cheque for £2000 and he must pay the £76.39 in 36 monthly instalments.

The company supplying the loan is known as the creditor because they supply credit. The person obtaining the loan is known as the debtor.

2 Tony Slack is very keen on boats and he sees a new boat advertised for £2500. He decides he wishes to buy this but hasn't got the money. He decides to apply for credit from a finance house. He completes a form specifying exactly why he wants the £2500. After making its normal credit investigations the finance company offer Tony £2500 over 24 months at 12 per cent per annum making monthly instalments of £129.16. If Tony accepts this offer he will receive a cheque for £2500 which he will use to purchase the boat. This is known as a credit sale. As soon as Tony takes possession of the goods he becomes the owner and the finance company can only sue him for recovery of the money if he does not pay the instalments; under no circumstances can the company obtain the boat. In legal terms Tony's loan is really exactly the same as David's.

Both these loans are unsecured in the sense that the lender retains no interest in the borrower's property. Sometimes loans will be made by credit companies to houseowners and the house is mortgaged to the credit company so the company has certain rights in it, and if the instalments are not paid then there are rights of entry and of sale of the property. This type of loan is known as secured, i.e. the lender has security in the house.

Activity

Newspapers frequently carry advertisements for credit companies anxious to lend money to houseowners. See if you can find some example of these.

An example of the sort of wording used in such advertisements is as follows:

Make your home provide a loan.

If you are a homeowner, you are probably sitting on quite a substantial sum of money – the increased value of your home since you bought it. You can use this increased value by raising a loan from £2000 to £40 000. The plan works just like a building society mortgage and our rates of interest are very competitive.

Send for our free brochure today or phone us on Sternfield 666 666.

3 Nicola Mallet wishes to buy a new car for £7500. She takes her old car along to the dealer who offers her £4500 in part exchange, therefore leaving a balance of £3000. Nicola wants to pay this by instalments and the dealer arranges hire purchase. The finance company requires that for the purchase of a car the buyer must give a minimum deposit of one third, which Nicola has done by means of the £4500 trade-in and payments must be over a maximum period of 24 months. At 12 per cent per annum this would mean monthly instalments of £155.00.

The common practice these days is for a triangular arrangement:

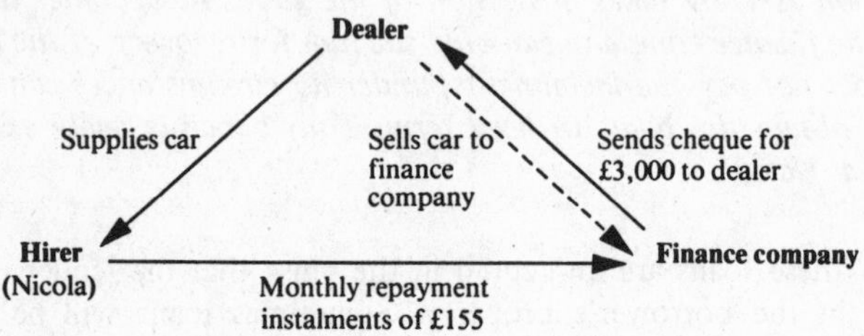

Nicola will complete the hire purchase forms at the garage and in effect the finance company buys the car from the dealer and then hires it to Nicola. When Nicola pays the final instalment ownership of the car passes to her. The finance company is the owner of the car and this means that unlike the credit sale arrangement if Nicola defaults in repayment then there are conditions under which the car may be returned to the finance house.

4 Philip Hargreaves decides to buy a suite of furniture for £550 using his Visa credit card. Philip is allowed a £1500 credit limit and since he only has £200 outstanding, then the £550 will present no problem. Philip buys his suite from Mammoth Furniture Stores plc. At the end of the month, he receives his statement from Visa which asks him for a minimum payment of £38.25. This is based upon £750 + 21 per cent interest (or 1.75 per cent per month) which will be £763.12. Credit card companies expect at least 5 per cent of the outstanding amount in repayment.

Exercise 7

1 Explain the difference between a secured and an unsecured loan.
2 In a credit sale agreement ownership of the goods remains with the company supplying the credit. *true/false*?

3 In a hire purchase agreement the person buying the goods becomes the owner immediately he/she pays the first instalment. *true/false*?

Consumer Credit Act 1974

An anonymous county court judge between the wars once commented that much of his time was taken up with 'people who are persuaded by persons they do not know to enter into contracts they do not understand to purchase goods that they do not want with money they have not got'. While this may well be an exaggeration, abuses certainly have existed and the company supplying the credit whether it be a credit sale or hire purchase agreement was in a position to use its stronger bargaining position to impose harsh terms on the debtor. It is because of this that various governments have passed legislation to protect debtors. The Consumer Credit Act 1974 attempted to bring together a good deal of the law as it applies to credit in various forms. All three of our examples would come within the operation of the Act which defined consumer credit agreements as agreements.

1 not exceeding £15 000 credit (i.e. £15 000 is the actual amount loaned);
2 that are personal, and the borrower is an individual or partnership not a company.

Agreements that come within the Act are known as regulated agreements. The borrowing of money to buy a house even though it is £5000 or less does not come within the Act and is known as an exempt agreement.

Exercise 8

Which of the following agreements would come within the Consumer Credit Act and are, therefore, regulated agreements?

1 Fortrax Haulage Ltd buys two lorries by means of a credit sale agreement.
2 Martin Thomas buys a £50 000 house with the aid of a £35 000 building society loan.
3 Julie Prince buys a music centre for £430 by means of a hire purchase agreement.
4 John Clements buys a new luxury car and borrows £18 000 to do so.

Protection under the Act. The Consumer Credit Act is administered by the Director General of Fair Trading whose duties under the Act include:

1 the administration and licensing under the Act;
2 to enforce the Act where necessary;
3 to supervise the workings of the Act;
4 to review the operation of the Act and to advise the Secretary of State from time to time.

Anyone wishing to engage in consumer credit business must first seek a licence from the Director General of Fair Trading. Licences will only be given when the Director is satisfied that the applicant is a fit person to engage in business of this sort. Engaging in consumer credit business without a licence is a criminal offence. Moreover, an unlicenced creditor will have great difficulty in enforcing a loan against the borrower should the borrower, for example, default.

Advertising of credit is subject to strict controls under the Act. False or misleading information is a criminal offence, as is canvassing by sending representatives to people's homes to persuade them to take credit.

The following example will help to explain the other protection which the Consumer Credit Act 1974 gives to the borrower.

Michael Field wishes to borrow £3000 over a period of three years and makes application to Ready Credit Co. Ltd, a licensed finance company.

Ready Credit Co. Ltd must firstly send to Michael details of the loan, e.g.

1 loan £3000 over 36 months
2 interest £1125
3 total payments £4125
4 36 monthly instalments of £114.58

If Michael is interested in the terms of this offer he will be sent an agreement form which must give particular details, e.g.

'I agree to borrow the sum of £3000 over a period of 36 months, repayable by 36 monthly instalments of £114.58. Signed . . .

'The loan of £3000 is made at an interest rate of 12½ per cent per annum (which represents an actual rate of 24.6 per cent). The total credit charge is £1124.58, making a total repayable sum of £4124.88.

'You may at any time pay off the balance outstanding and you will be entitled to a rebate of interest at rates shown in the enclosed booklet.

'Ready Credit Co. Ltd, Commercial House, 119/122 High Street, Manchester MC1 3XX.'

This example contains all the requirements of the Act, that is total interest charge, rate of interest, rights to termination. Usually there will be a bank mandate form attached which Michael will sign giving Ready Credit

Co. Ltd the authority to debit his account by £114.58 each month for 36 months.

The Act lays down that Michael must receive a copy of the form he has signed either immediately or if it has to be processed in some way within seven days of the signing. If finance companies do not comply with these regulations a court may refuse to enforce the agreement where (1) it is not in writing; (2) a copy has not been given to the borrower.

Where the agreement is signed on the business premises of the creditor (the finance company) or on the business premises of the supplier of the goods, which is often the case, the agreement comes into effect immediately. Where, however, the agreement is signed elsewhere then the Consumer Credit Act gives the debtor a period during which he can cancel the agreement - known as a 'cooling off period'. The right to such a period must be notified to the debtor in the credit agreement. The effect of the 'cooling off' period is that the debtor can up to the end of the fifth day after receiving his copy of the agreement terminate it. If he/she terminates the agreement within this period it is treated as though it never existed. If an agreement is ended in this way and it was for a money loan the debtor must return the money, but if goods are involved the creditor must collect the goods; the debtor must take reasonable care of them for a 21-day period. An agreement which can be cancelled in this way is known as a cancellable agreement.

Finally the Consumer Credit Act 1974 lays down that a court may interfere (the legal expression used is to 'reopen the agreement') and alter an agreement if it feels that interest rates are 'extortionate'. What constitutes extortionate will depend upon a number of circumstances including the prevailing interest rates. Courts will use the ordinary principles of fair dealing when deciding whether interest rates are extortionate.

The following case shows how courts can deal with high rates of interest. In *Barcabe Ltd* v. *Edwards* (1983), a low-paid man with four children had answered an advertisement, and been persuaded to borrow £400 at interest totalling 100 per cent per year. There was no evidence that he had defaulted on earlier debts, or otherwise was a bad security risk. The court reduced the interest to 40 per cent.

Exercise 9

Examine the following and explain the legal position of the person in italics in each exercise.

1 Jane Huxford borrows £1000 over 12 months from *Secure Finance Ltd* which is unlicensed. Jane makes only one payment of £96 89.

2 *John Hardy* borrows £1000 over 24 months from a licensed company but the agreement is made orally. John refuses to repay the loan.

3 *Ian Wood* signs a hire purchase agreement at his home for a television set with West Derbyshire Financing Ltd. Three days later he changes his mind but the company refuse to release him saying it is too late; he has already signed.

4 *John Lambert* borrows £500 for one year at a rate of interest of 50 per cent. He defaults on payment and asks the court to reopen the agreement.

Hire purchase agreements. In addition to the rights outlined above the debtor (hirer) in a hire purchase agreement has additional rights as the following example will show.

Richard Haigh decides to purchase a caravan for £5500. He pays a deposit of £2000 but obtains the additional £3500 by means of a hire purchase agreement which he signs at the office of Luxury Caravans Ltd The creditor however, is United Finance Ltd. His repayments are over two years at 12 per cent which amounts to £180.83 per month.

This agreement is based then on the usual triangular system:

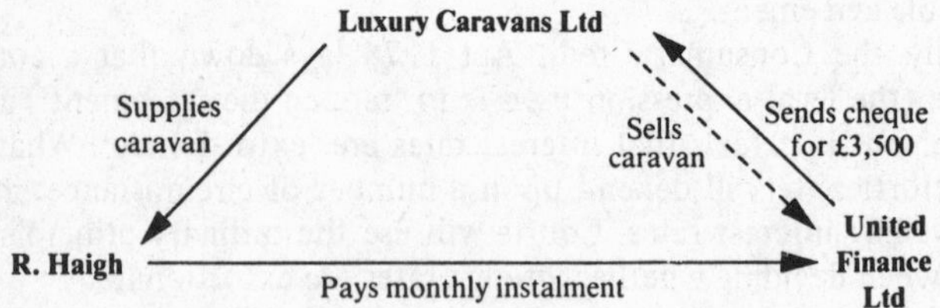

The agreement which Richard has signed is likely to have included the following notice duly completed with details relating to Richard's agreement:

THE STATUTORY NOTICE BELOW IS APPLICABLE AND MUST BE COMPLETED ONLY WHEN THE HIRE PURCHASE PRICE DOES NOT EXCEED £5000

STATUTORY NOTICE

As Required by The Hire Purchase Acts 1938, 1954 and 1964/65

Right of Hirer to Terminate Agreement

1 The Hirer may put an end to this Agreement by giving notice of termination in writing to any person who is entitled to collect or receive the Hire-rent.

2 He must then pay any instalments which are in arrear at the time when he gives notice. If, when he has paid those instalments the total amount which he has paid under the Agreement is less than £2170 he must also pay enough to make up that sum.

3 If the Goods have been damaged owing to the Hirer having failed to take reasonable care of them the Owner may sue him for the amount of damage unless that amount can be agreed between the Hirer and the Owner.

4 The Hirer should see whether this Agreement contains provisions allowing him to put an end to the Agreement on terms more favourable to him than those just mentioned. If it does he may put an end to the Agreement on those terms.

Restriction of Owners' Right to Recover Goods

1 After £1446.66p has been paid, then, unless the Hirer has himself put an end to the Agreement, the Owners of the Goods cannot take them back from the Hirer without the Hirer's consent unless the Owners obtain an Order of the Court.

2 If the Owners apply to the Court for such an Order the Court may, if the Court thinks it just to do so, allow the Hirer to keep either

(a) The whole of the Goods, on condition that the Hirer pays the balance of the price in the manner ordered by the Court: or

(b) A fair proportion of the Goods having regard to what the Hirer has already paid.

You will note that the hirer has certain rights.

1 Richard can terminate (end) the agreement by giving United Finance Ltd notice in writing. However, Richard will have to pay any arrears to make up if he has not already done so up to one half of the total hire purchase price. In Richard's case this will be £4340 ÷ 2 = £2170. The Consumer Credit Act lays down that the limit on minimum payment clauses in this context is one half (50 per cent).

2 If after termination the hirer receives the caravan he may sue for damage if it has been damaged due to Richard not having taken reasonable care of it.

3 If Richard did not pay his instalments regularly then since the caravan belongs to the finance company it has certain rights of recovery. However, Richard must be given seven days' notice of default. If Richard has not yet

paid one third of the total hire purchase price, i.e. £1446.66, then the creditor can 'snatch back' the goods though the creditor is not entitled to enter the debtor s property to get goods back which are subject to a regulated agreement as this is, without a court order. If the caravan was parked elsewhere then clearly it could be 'snatched back'. When, however, Richard has paid the third or more the goods become 'protected' and under no circumstances can they be 'snatched' back. A court order is necessary, and if the finance company took the matter to court the court might well give the hirer additional time to pay. Protected goods may only be recovered without a court order if they are abandoned by the hirer or returned voluntarily by him. The following case is an example of the effects of Hire Purchase Companies 'snatching back' unlawfully. In *Capital Finance Ltd* v. *Bray* (1964), a finance company took back, without a court order, a car which Bray had on hire-purchase. The car was protected goods and, when the company realised its mistake, it returned the car immediately. Bray used it for several months, refusing all requests for payment. Eventually the company sued for possession, and this was granted. The company could not, however, recover payment for Bray's use of the car after its return to him. Moreover, Bray recovered everything which he had paid.

Finally a hirer has similar implied rights in respect of goods when he buys under a hire purchase agreement as given to a buyer under the Sale of Goods Act 1979 (and the Supply of Goods and Services Act 1982). These rights, relating to quality title, fitness description, will give the hirer a claim against the supplier or against the creditor. Thus if Richard's caravan was not of 'merchantable quality' he could sue United Finance Ltd.

Exercise 10

1 In a hire purchase agreement the hirer is also the debtor. *true/false*?

2 A debtor under a hire purchase agreement can terminate the agreement at any time provided he pays up to a maximum of:

$\frac{1}{4}$ of the hire purchase price;
$\frac{1}{3}$ of the hire purchase price;
$\frac{1}{2}$ of the hire purchase price;
$\frac{2}{3}$ of the hire purchase price.

3 David Harrison buys a car by means of a hire purchase agreement. Having paid two thirds of the hire purchase price he decides he can no longer afford any further payments. The finance company send him notice of default and send a representative around who drives the car away despite David's protests. Has the finance company the right to do this?

Exercise 11

Explain the legal position in each of the following examples. Check your answers against those at the end of the book and if you have not really understood any aspect of this chapter read it over again.

1 Bob White buys a one-year-old motorcycle from a friend for £850. A week after the purchase Bob finds serious mechanical flaws in the machine.
2 Deborah James buys five bottles of French sweet wine from Spring Gardens Wines Ltd. When she opens the first bottle she finds it is Yugoslav dry wine.
3 Wainwrights (Domestic) Ltd offer fridges at 20 per cent discount at £65. The old price had been £70 for the last two years.
4 Mr and Mrs Taylor go on holiday in Malta and despite the advertisement which says that all rooms have sea views and that the hotel is close by the seafront, in fact, the hotel is nine miles from the sea and the sea views are only possible with the aid of powerful binoculars. They feel they have wasted the £450 which the holiday cost.
5 Marlene Ward borrows £1000 from a finance company but never receives a copy of the agreement. She refuses to pay the instalments and the company sues her.
6 Audrey Worsley buys a vacuum cleaner from a travelling salesman. She signs a hire purchase agreement. When her husband returns home from a business trip seven days later he is very angry so she decides to cancel the agreement.

CHAPTER 6

CONTRACTS OF INSURANCE

Keith Martin has, for the last ten years, managed a large shoe shop in the centre of a city. It has always been his ambition to run his own business but up until recently he has never had sufficient money to be able to purchase a shoe shop. Keith is, however, left quite a large sum of money and by chance a shoe shop near his home is put up for sale. Keith decides to realise his ambition and purchases the shop.

In taking on his own business Keith, like any other businessman, is taking certain risks. For example, the demand for shoes may decline and he may make no profit or his shop including stock may be completely destroyed by fire. Although no insurance company would insure against the first risk fortunately Keith could take out insurance against the risk of fire.

In this chapter we will be considering insurance contracts to see how they resemble any other business contract but also to examine some of their particular characteristics. In order to do this let us return to Keith's business and concentrate upon his need to insure it against the risk of fire.

Keith has heard that Safesure Insurance Co. has a very good reputation, so he decides to telephone the company to get a proposal form. A proposal form is really an application form on which Keith would need to give full details of the risk that he wishes the company to take on for him. It is on the basis of this information that the insurance company will calculate the premium, i.e. the amount of money which Keith needs to pay monthly, quarterly or annually to the insurance company. We will assume that Keith has calculated that if his business was completely destroyed by fire he would lose £400 000.

Safesure would assess the risk that they were taking on by pooling all similar risks together and estimating the amount of money they might have to pay out. These estimates will be based upon a number of criteria including past experience. The 'pooling of risk' concept which allows insurance companies to take on risks at a modest charge is illustrated by the diagram overleaf.

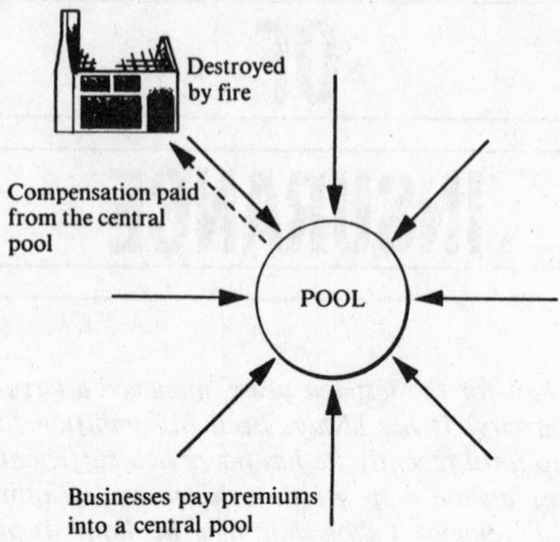

Assume that Safesure has 2000 similar risks on its books and that it estimates that £1 600 000 will be paid out in claims. The company has also estimated that each policy costs it about £80 per annum in administrative costs including profit. The premium that Safesure would quote to insure Keith's business would therefore be:

Total claims equal £1 600 000
Number of similar businesses insured is 2000
£1 600 000 divided by 2000 equals £800
Administrative cost per policy is £80
Total premium is £800 + £80 = **£880**

It is because the company can estimate with a reasonable degree of accuracy the likely number of claims that they can quote a premium. It would, however, be impossible for the company to calculate the number of claims for failure to make profit and therefore businesses cannot insure this risk because it is 'non-insurable'; whereas as we have seen fire is estimable and therefore insurable. Some risks are also non-insurable because it is illegal to cover them, e.g. it is unlawful for an insurance company to insure a person against imprisonment in the event of him committing an unlawful act.

Exercise 1

1 The form which is filled in by a person wishing to take out insurance is known as

2 Why is failure to make profits a non-insurable risk?

3 Insurance companies can keep their premiums low by putting all similar risks together. This is known as

Keith sends in his proposal form and Safesure Insurance will consider it in detail. Safesure Insurance will then make Keith an offer. Assuming that the detail he has put on the form does not suggest that his business is any different from the 2000 other similar businesses they are insuring then the offer will be that the company will take on the risk of fire at a cost to Keith of £880 per annum (the premium). If Keith accepts this offer – and remember that he must accept the offer unconditionally – then a contract is made, i.e. the company makes an offer, Keith accepts the offer, consideration is supplied by Keith in the form of a premium of £880 per annum and is supplied by the company in that the company promises to compensate Keith in the event of loss resulting from fire. A legally binding contract has come into existence and Keith will receive in due course a policy. The policy is in fact the contractual document and will contain the terms of the insurance.

We can safely assume that the other four elements essential for a legally binding contract also exist. There is nothing illegal about fire insurance; both parties, i.e. Keith and the company have the legal capacity; both parties intend that the agreement should be legally binding; and there was probably *consensus ad idem* (a meeting of the minds) as far as the agreement was concerned.

In addition to the seven essential elements which must exist in a contract, insurance contracts have other important characteristics. All insurance agreements must be based upon the principle of utmost good faith, the principle of insurable interest and the principle of indemnity.

Utmost Good Faith

When Keith completed his proposal form he would have been asked a number of questions about the premises in which the shoe business was conducted. If Keith had answered these falsely then he would be misrepresenting the facts to the insurer, i.e. Safesure Incurance Co., and the agreement as we have seen because it would lack *consensus ad idem* would not be legally binding. In addition in an insurance agreement Keith is obliged to disclose information which might be relevant even though the proposal form did not ask for it, e.g. if Keith's son Andrew was studying chemistry at university and used one of the rooms attached to the shop for his chemical experiments then it would be necessary for Keith to disclose this; or if the shop was next to a premises where inflammable liquids were stored then this would have to be disclosed.

This is an important principle because if Keith did not disclose what, after all, is a fire risk, he has failed to disclose what is very relevant information. Then if fire did cause damage, the insurance company could treat the agreement as voidable and refuse to pay out.

If we think about the principle of utmost good faith, then it is quite obvious that insurance companies, in order to assess a risk, must have all the relevant information. Conducting chemical experiments on the premises certainly changes the nature of the risk and would cause the insurance company to think rather carefully about the premium that it would charge.

All insurance contracts must be based upon the principle of utmost good faith, sometimes known by the Latin expression *uberrimae fidei.*

Exercise 2

In the following examples say whether the insurance company in each case could refuse to pay out.

1 Roger Allen (44) takes out a £50 000 life insurance with Security Insurance Co. but omits to mentioned on the proposal form that he spends a lot of time on his hobby of hang-gliding. He dies as a result of an accident in this activity and Security refuse to pay his widow.

2 Brian Webster keeps a small shop which sells sweets, tobacco and newspapers. It is a lock-up shop but Brian leaves a side window at the back open to let his cat get in. He has been burgled in fact five times in two years. Brian decides to take out insurance but forgets to mention either of these two facts. When he tries to claim for yet another burglary the insurance company refuses to pay out.

Insurable Interest

The following two examples will help to illustrate the meaning of this principle.

John Smith decides to insure his next-door neighbour Philip Green's life for £40 000. Most insurance companies refuse to accept such insurance but one company, Fidelity Co. Ltd, decides that for a monthly premium of £60 John can arrange this. Philip dies a year later and John seeks to collect £40 000. Fidelity refuses to pay.

In fact, Fidelity need not pay because this contract is void by illegality. The Life Assurance Act 1774 lays down that:

No Insurance shall be made by any person or persons . . . Wherein the person or persons for whose use, benefit or on whose account such policy or policies shall be made shall have no interest.

It then is illegal for such insurance to be taken out and clearly if such practices were allowed then there could be considerable encouragement to crime, e.g. life insurance could be taken out on a person and that person could be disposed of and the insurance collected. Generally, speaking you can only insure your own life or another person's in whom you have a financial interest. It is, of course, possible for a wife to insure her husband's life and vice versa. It is also possible for one partner in a business to insure another partner. In both these cases the death of husband/wife or partner would represent a loss to the person taking out the insurance.

Carol and Florence both own teashops in a small town. They are firm friends and decide in addition to insurance on their own shops they decide to insure each other's shop. Following a fire which completely destroys Carol's shop the insurance company pay her £80 000, the sum insured, but refuse to pay Florence.

Although what Florence has done is not illegal, i.e. she can insure someone else's business, in practice it would be a waste of money because insurance principles lay down that you can only collect insurance if you have suffered a loss. Florence certainly has suffered no financial loss as a result of Carol's situation and therefore could not collect. Insurance companies will not normally make agreements with persons who have no insurable interest in the risk they wish to insure.

The object of a contract of insurance is to protect the interest of the insured, therefore the insured must have an interest in the subject matter of the policy.

Exercise 3

In the following cases say whether you think the person taking out the insurance has an interest in the subject matter of the policy.

1 Michael borrows his friend's boat occasionally and therefore decides to insure it for £1000.
2 Mrs Yeomans insures her husband's life for £35 000.
3 Victor Wood insures his car by taking out a comprehensive insurance policy.
4 Sheila Pullin insures her best friend's life for £20 000.

Indemnity

Adam Cranston owns a house valued at £80 000. Being a cautious and careful man he decides to insure the house for £140 000. Shortly after taking out the insurance Adam's house is completely gutted by fire and he can either have the house rebuilt for £60 000 or buy a comparable property. Adam decides to buy another, superior property and claims the full £140 000 from the insurance company.

The insurance company pays out £80 000, which it claims is the value of Adam's loss. Adam feels cheated and decides to sue the company.

In this situation Adam would not be successful because one important principle of insurance is that of 'indemnity', which means the insurance company have a duty to compensate the insured for his loss but no more. It is an important fact of insurance that it is not intended that an insured person gains from insurance. The intention is that the insured person be put back in as near the same position as possible as that which existed before the accident. The £140 000 represents the maximum sum payable under the insurance, not what the company will actually pay. Since the value of Adam's property was only £80 000 the additional £60 000 cover represented for Adam a waste of money.

This, however, does not work in reverse; if Adam had only insured his property for £60 000 then in the event of a fire he could only get £60 000. The principle of indemnity states that an insured be compensated for his loss. The insured can only obtain, however, the maximum sum payable under the policy, i.e. £60 000.

This example perhaps illustrates the folly of being under-insured and the waste in being over-insured.

For obvious reasons the principle of indemnity can never be applied to life policies because the loss resulting from the death of a husband, for example, is not really assessable.

Exercise 4

1 What do you understand by the term indemnity in respect of insurance?
2 Why can indemnity never apply to a life policy?
3 Explain the terms 'over-insurance' and 'under insurance' in relation to property.

Linked to the principle of indemnity are two other principles of insurance contracts, 'contribution' and 'subrogation'. The following examples will help to explain them.

Contribution

Thelma Sheldon owns and runs a business offering secretarial services to local firms. She estimates that the total value of her equipment in the business is £65 000. Being a careful woman Thelma insures her business with two separate insurance firms, Security Co. Ltd and Northern Union Insurance. Unfortunately her business is completely lost by fire but Thelma is not really worried because she claims two lots of £65 000, i.e. £130 000.

If we think about this example we can see it goes against the principle of indemnity because Thelma has gained from the fire. In this situation the principle of contribution is applied. Each company would pay 50 per cent contribution to Thelma's loss. This example illustrates that double insurance is really a waste of money. Again, however, the principle of contribution does not apply to life insurance and in this respect a person may have as many life policies as he wishes and can afford.

Subrogation

David Ekin has insured his toy shop against fire with the Sapphire Insurance Co. for £80 000. As a result of fire and following an inspection of the premises David gets the full £80 000. However, David decides that he can advertise some of the toys as fire-damaged and he holds a sale which realises £5500.

It is easy to see that David has gained an extra £5500 and of course this is against the principle of indemnity. The principle of subrogation states that the £5500 belongs to Sapphire and if the company discovers that David has made an additional £5500 it can sue him for recovery.

Exercise 5

1 If Carole Newsome insures her house with two companies and it is damaged why can she not get double compensation?
2 After an insurance company has paid out for a loss in full any additional money obtained by the insured belongs to the company. The fact is based upon the principle of: (a) utmost good faith, (b) subrogation, (c) contribution or (d) insurable interest.

Exercise 6

In the following examples explain the legal position involved. Check your answers with those which follow and if you have not understood any of the points, read over this chapter again.

1 John Phillips forgets to disclose in an application for motor insurance that he suffers from epilepsy.
2 In a proposal for fire insurance for his business, Bob Brown forgets to mention his wife has had several convictions for arson all in relation to his business property.
3 Cyril Ruback's carpet warehouse is completely gutted. His insurance compensates him in full but Cyril sells off a large number of fire- and water-damaged carpets.
4 Pat Browett insures her cottage for £100 000; its value however is only £65 000.
5 Ann Bishop insures her neighbour's life for £45 000.
6 Bob Dash insures his new car with two companies. Following an accident his car is a write-off and he uses the money from both companies to buy a car for both himself and his wife.

CHAPTER 7

BUSINESS TORTS

7.1 THE TORT OF NEGLIGENCE

Mrs Fiona Sykes owns a grocery shop which is situated in the suburbs of a large town. During the last two years she has run her shop as a self-service store. Customers select the goods they wish to purchase, placing them in wire baskets, and then pay at the cash desk. On one occasion a customer, Sheila Hayward, is reaching to get some tins, when the shelf on which the tins are placed comes away from the wall and Sheila sustains quite a serious arm injury as a result of the shelf and its contents falling on her. Sheila's injuries cause her considerable discomfort and necessitate hospital treatment. She is also forced, because of her incapacity, to give up some typing she was doing at home for a local firm. Sheila decides to take the matter to court.

Incidents like this happen frequently, and lawyers and courts spend a lot of time dealing with claims for compensation such as Sheila is attempting to make in this example. In fact, Sheila will be sueing for the tort of negligence. Negligence is just one of a number of torts which we will be examining in this chapter. The word 'tort' is from a French word which means 'wrong'. As well as negligence there are torts of nuisance, trespass and defamation of character. As with contract, which we have already met, it will be the civil courts which deal with torts. In this section we will look at the tort of negligence. Using the example of Fiona and Sheila will help you to understand the main aspects of negligence and help you see how this important branch of law can be applied to business situations.

You will no doubt remember from your previous reading that in civil cases there are two parties involved; in our example Sheila will be the plaintiff and Fiona will be the defendant. If she is going to be successful in getting compensation, Sheila, as the plaintiff, will need to prove negligence; to do this she will have to prove three things. It is important to note that in negligence it is for the plaintiff to prove and therefore we say that the 'burden of proof' in negligence is on the plaintiff.

Exercise 1

1 What does the word 'tort' mean?
2 In the situation relating to Fiona and Sheila, who must do the proving?
3 The tort of negligence is criminal. *true/false*?

What then are the three things which Sheila will need to prove to be successful in negligence and therefore in getting compensation?

Duty of Care

First, Sheila must prove that the defendant, Fiona, owed her a duty of care: English law imposes upon people a duty to be careful in their dealings with others. In an extremely important case, *Donogue* v. *Stevenson* (1932), the principle of the duty of care was established. Mrs Donogue attempted to sue the supplier of a ginger beer drink, which she had drunk and which contained the remnants of a decomposed snail. In *Home Office* v. *Dorset Yacht Co* (1970), the neighbourhood principle relating to duty of care was used in this decision when the Home Office was held to be liable for damage to yachts when boys from a Borstal escaped and damaged property.

The judge, Lord Atkin, in *Donogue* v. *Stevenson*, defined the duty of care as being that owed to one's neighbour and then went on to define a neighbour as anyone who you might reasonably foresee could be affected by your acts or omissions, in other words by something you did or failed to do. In our example it is quite clear that Fiona had not adequately checked the shelving or had overloaded it and that she (Fiona) might reasonably have foreseen that anyone coming into her shop might have been injured as a result of this omission (failure to check) or act (overloading).

There are many examples in a shop situation which could give rise to negligence actions, and shopkeepers have a duty towards any customer coming into the shop. Not only can people be liable for careless deeds or omissions but it is possible for persons to be liable for careless statements. Thus it might be said that a professional person, e.g. a bank manager, solicitor, accountant, owes a duty of care to his customers or clients and can be held liable for negligent (careless) statements. So, for example, where a credit company takes up a reference from a bank manager in respect of an applicant for a loan then the bank manager must be particularly careful in supplying information – the bank could be liable should the person receiving the loan default. A case, *Hedley Byrne* v. *Heller & Partners* (1963) illustrates the principle well that a bank for example may be held liable for a negligent mistatement. In *Hedley Byrne* v. *Heller and Partners* (1963), a firm of advertising agents gave credit to a client in reliance upon a banker's reference, and suffered loss when the client became insolvent. The reference had been given carelessly but, since the bank had expressly disclaimed liability when giving it, the action failed. Nevertheless, the House of Lords stated that, contrary to what had pre-previously been believed, liability for negligence may extend to careless words as well as to careless deeds and that damages may be awarded for financial loss as well as for physical injury to persons and property.

Activity

To help you understand the concept of duty of care, you might think for a moment about all those people to whom you have owed a duty of care today.

You may be surprised at the large number of people covered by the term 'neighbour'.

Certain people have been exempted by law from owing a duty of care. For example, a barrister will never be liable in negligence for his careless handling of a case because he does not owe a duty of care to his clients; but clearly barristers will not get many clients if they gain a reputation for careless dealings. The law also says that occupiers of premises do not owe a duty of care to certain people. An occupier of premises owes a duty of care to all lawful visitors but he does not owe a duty of care to trespassers. A trespasser must take the premises as he finds them. So if Sheila had broken into Fiona's shop and had injured herself on the shelving while helping herself to goods then Fiona would not be liable because she would not have owed Sheila a duty of care.

There are two circumstances where an occupier might owe a duty of care to trespassers.

1 The law requires that a duty of care is owed to children who trespass on to property. The case of *British Railways Board* v. *Herrington* (1972) illustrates this. A young boy aged six wandered on to railway property through a hold in the fence and was injured on an electrified section of rail. The Board was held to be liable in negligence even though the boy was a trespasser.
2 There are some circumstances where people become so used to walking across property where the occupier has done nothing to prevent them that they could be forgiven for not realising they are trespassers. If one of these people had an accident then the occupier would be held to be liable because the courts would assume the existence of a duty of care.

Breach of duty of care. Having established the existence of a duty of care, and we have seen that a duty of care does exist towards Sheila, it is necessary to show that the duty of care has been broken, or to use the legal term, breached. In our example Sheila would need to show that the standard of care exercised by Fiona was not that of a reasonable person. In other words, Sheila would need to show that regular checks should have been made on the shelving and care should have been taken that the shelves were not overloaded. If Fiona could show that she had maintained regular checks or that she had recently employed the services of a competent joiner to look at the shelving then she might be able to show that she had not broken her duty of care towards Sheila. We will assume that this was not the case and that the duty of care had been breached.

Exercise 2

Read the following example.

Richard Huyton is a company secretary for a large company and is in a hurry to attend a meeting. He is driving far too fast and skids on an icy stretch of road injuring a pedestrian, David Pritchard.

1 Name the defendant and plaintiff.
2 Does a duty of care exist from the defendant to the plaintiff?
3 Do you think the duty of care has been broken?

Whether a duty of care has been breached will depend upon the circumstances. The courts use the concept of a reasonable man – one definition describes it as 'doing what a reasonable man would not do or failing to do what a reasonable man would do'. You don't, in other words, have to be perfect, just reasonably careful.

In some circumstances an accident occurs where the only possible cause is negligence. In *Richley* v. *Faull* (1965), the defendant's car skidded violently, turned round, and collided with the plaintiff's car on the wrong side of the road. It was held that this, of itself, was sufficient evidence of negligent driving. Since the defendant was unable to give a satisfactory explanation of his skid, he was held liable. In this case it was up to the defendant to prove he was not negligent. The court has applied the rule 'the facts speak for themselves' or to use the latin phrase often used by lawyers '*Res ipsa loquitur*'.

Loss arising. We have seen, therefore, that to prove negligence it is necessary to show (1) the existence of a duty of care and that (2) this duty has been broken. We have seen that Sheila could easily prove the existence of these two elements. However, it is also necessary for the plaintiff to prove a third element and that is that he/she suffered some loss as a result of the defendant's breach of the duty of care. The loss can include damage to property, personal injury and in some cases financial loss. There is little doubt that Sheila had suffered personal injury as a result of Fiona's breach of duty. Her injury also made it impossible for Sheila to continue with her typing work and therefore she suffered financial loss.

It would seem, then, that Sheila can prove the existence of these three essential elements, i.e. a duty of care, a breach and loss. She would be successful in an action for negligence and the court would award her damages. The damages awarded would be calculated to try to compensate her for the pain she suffered and also to compensate her for the financial loss she suffered as a result of her inability to engage in typing.

The question of resulting damage is well summed up in the case *Barnett* v. *Chelsea and Kensington Hospital Management Committee* (1969). The details of the case are as follows. Mr Barnett went to the casualty department late at night complaining of vomiting having drunk tea. The duty doctor did not examine him but sent him home and advised him to call his own doctor. Three hours later Mr Barnett died of arsenic poisoning. The doctor, and therefore the hospital committee, owed Mr Barnett a duty of care and had breached it by not examining him. However, since there is no cure for poisoning of this sort, the damage did not result from the breach and Mr Barnett's widow was unsuccessful.

Exercise 3

1 What are the three elements which a plaintiff must prove to be successful in an action for negligence?
2 George Shaw breaks a leg while shopping. Negligence is proved; George claims £400 loss of earnings. How would the court assess the amount of compensation (damages) paid?

Exercise 4

Examine the following cases carefully and say whether you think the person or organisation in italics would be successful in sueing for negligence. In each case apply the three elements (a) duty of care, (b) breach and (c) loss. If you feel that there is no case give the reason for your view. Spend some time on these examples making sure you get them correct before you continue.

1 *Michael Street* has broken into the offices of Buxted Engineering Co. While switching on a light Michael is injured from an electric shock caused by a faulty electric fitting.
2 *Mary Goodwin* has been interviewed for a post as secretary with Low Peak District Council. Coming down the steps from the office,

Mary slips, and reaches for the stair rail, which gives way. Mary sustains a broken leg.

3 Alan Harrison is managing director of Sparkes & Co. Ltd (Electrical Suppliers). He has always been a most careful driver and is driving down the main street of a country town at about 14 mph. A child runs on to the road and Alan brakes but skids on some oil on the road. His car collides with a pedestrian ***Rachel Martin***, who is injured. Alan is able to explain why the skid occurred, when he gets out of the car and sees the patch of oil.

4 Margaret Brown is suffering from an incurable disease and is likely to die at any time. While walking in the hospital ward she slips on some loose floor covering. A day later she dies. ***John Brown*** sues the hospital board for negligence.

5 An explosion due to a faulty process occurs in the laboratory of Filton Chemical Co. ***Michael Pullin*** a laboratory technician although nearby, miraculously escapes injury.

6 Andrew Knowles aged five wanders on to a building site and ignores the sign 'trespassers will be prosecuted'. He falls down a hole and is badly injured. His father, ***David Knowles***, decides to sue the builders, Easibuild Co. Ltd.

When you are satisfied that you have understood these five examples, go on to the next part which deals with defences which might be used in a negligence action. If you have any doubt go back over the section on negligence and then try to answer the questions again.

Possible Defences Against a Negligence Action

We have seen that for a plaintiff to be successful in negligence he must prove (1) the existence of a duty of care, (2) the breach of that duty and (3) loss or damage arising from the breach. Clearly it is for the defendant if he wishes to try to show that in fact one or other of these elements did not exist. If he can do this then he can show that there was no negligence. The defendant may claim for example:

1 that he owed no duty of care to the plaintiff; or
2 that although he owed a duty of care he had acted reasonably and had not been in any way careless and therefore had not breached the duty of care which he owed; or
3 even though he owed a duty of care and he had been careless his negligence did not cause the plaintiff's loss.

In these instances the defendant is countering the plaintiff's claim that negligence existed by denying the existence of one or other of the elements.

There are, however, two situations where although negligence does exist, because the three elements exist, nevertheless a defendant can offer a defence. These two situations can best be illustrated by examples.

Consent

Dove Dale Engineering Ltd have built a sports and social club for their employees and families. At the entrance of the club there is a cloakroom where members and guests can leave their coats under the charge of a cloakroom attendant. Clearly displayed at the entrance to the cloakroom is a notice which reads:

> Dove Dale Engineering Ltd cannot be held liable for loss or damage to any property which is left in the cloakroom. Persons leaving their belongings in the cloakroom do so at their own risk.

Brian Hamilton and his wife Margaret have spent an evening at the club. When they return for their coats Margaret finds that hers is missing and Brian discovers the loss of a cigarette lighter, car keys, cheque book and various credit cards from the pockets of his coat. When Brian makes further inquiries he discovers that the cloakroom attendant had been in the bar for fiteen minutes and had left the coats unattended. Brian is very angry and decides to sue Dove Dale Engineering Ltd.

Although all the three elements necessary to prove negligence exist here, the defendant, Dove Dale Engineering Ltd, would use the defence of consent and would draw the court's attention to the notice which disclaimed liability which is displayed at the entrance of the cloakroom. If a person consents to suffer damage, or consents to run the risk of it, he cannot then claim compensation. This consent is sometimes expressed by the Latin phrase *volenti non fit injuria* – 'to one who is willing no harm is done'. It is important to remember that the notice which disclaims liability must be brought to the attention of the plaintiff before the event; thus in our example Mr and Mrs Hamilton saw the notice before they deposited their coats. You will remember that although it is possible for firms or individuals to disclaim liability for loss they can no longer use as a defence a notice which disclaims liability for personal injury or death (Unfair Contract Terms Act 1977, see Chapter 3).

Contributory negligence. It is also possible for a defendant to attempt to show that the plaintiff was partly responsible for loss or injuries sustained. The next example will help to explain this.

Mrs Fraser is a secretary with Westshire County Council. On one cold and icy morning Mrs Fraser is rushing to get to her office on time and slips on a frozen section of a pathway in the grounds of County Hall leading to her office building. Mrs Fraser is injured and damages her coat in the fall. Despite the cold conditions Mrs Fraser is wearing boots with extremely high heels. Mrs Fraser decides to sue Westshire County Council in negligence, claiming that no attempt had been made to clear the pathway even though it was the only way to the office.

If we apply the three elements to this case it can easily be seen that the county council was negligent. The county council may argue, however, that the fall was partly caused by the wearing of inappropriate footwear. If the court hearing the case accept this it might well reduce the level of damages that would have been awarded to Mrs Fraser. This is known as contributory negligence, i.e. the plaintiff has contributed to the loss or damage sustained. The principle of contributory negligence is well illustrated by the fact that courts are becoming increasingly reluctant to award car drivers claiming negligence full compensation, arguing that they have contributed to their injuries by not using their seat belts.

A well-known case also illustrates the principle of contributory negligence: *Sayers* v. *Harlow UDC* (1958). Mrs Sayers found that she was locked in a public lavatory. Unable to get help she decided to climb over the door. To aid her climb she used the toilet-roll holder as a foot rest. The toilet roll rotated from her weight and she fell, injuring herself. The court held that Harlow UDC had been negligent in allowing a faulty lock to be on the door but that 25 per cent of the blame was Mrs Sayers' for attempting this climb. The damages awarded were thus 75 per cent of the total.

In recent cases drivers or passengers injured in accidents but not wearing seat belts have had damages reduced.

Exercise 5

1 List the five defences which a defendant may use in an action for negligence.

2 Disclaiming liability for death or personal injury is possible provided it is brought to the attention of the plaintiff. *true/false*?

Activity

Within the next few days look for disclaimer notices. See if you can recognise those which could be used as a defence in a negligence action and those that could not.

Exercise 6

Read the following and say whether you think that Alan would have a good case in negligence.

Alan Pilkington is staying at the Hotel Regal on the south coast. He books in at the reception desk and a porter is called to assist him with his luggage. When the porter and Alan arrive at Alan's room, the porter draws Alan's attention to a notice which reads:

> The Management cannot accept any liability for the loss of any guest's property while the guest is staying at the Hotel Regal; guests are advised to deposit valuable property in the safe at reception.

Alan is in a rush to get a meal and leaves some valuable property, worth £1000, in the room. While he is in the restaurant a member of staff with a known police record uses his pass key to get in the room and steals the £1000 worth of equipment, which is never recovered.

Occupiers' Liability

We have already seen that generally one is not liable for negligent acts towards trespassers. Occupiers' Liability Act of 1957 lays down that a duty of care is owed by an occupier to all lawful visitors and goes on to establish three categories of lawful visitors.

1 Persons with an express permission to be on the occupier's premises (e.g. friends invited for a meal, a person invoted for an interview for a job).
2 Persons with implied permission (e.g. customers in a shop, a door-to-door salesman).
3 Persons with a statutory right to enter (police to enforce the law with a search warrant, officials reading gas or electricity meters).

Activity

In this section we have examined in some detail the law relating to negligence. You may care to think of your own experiences and think whether you have been negligent recently or have suffered from the negligence of others. Relating this section to your own experiences will help you understand better the important tort of negligence.

9.2 THE TORTS OF TRESPASS, NUISANCE AND DEFAMATION

In addition to the tort of negligence there are a number of other torts such as trespass, nuisance and defamation. We will now look at these torts, especially as they may affect business.

Trespass – Trespass to Land

The following example will help to explain the law relating to trespass to land.

Associated Timber Supplies Ltd own a large store which is situated near a housing estate. The timber yard which forms part of the store provides a very good short cut to local shops. Despite the presence of a large sign 'trespassers will be prosecuted', two women, Mrs Rachel Wite and Mrs Doreen Saunders, persist in climbing over the wall so that they can get to the shops more quickly. The person in charge of the store, Syd Lambert, is concerned about the two women's presence on company property and on one occasion asks them politely to leave the company's premises and not to use the yard as a short cut. The women refuse to leave and are abusive to Syd, who attempts to use force to eject them. He reports the matter to the company secretary, who decides to start legal proceedings against the two women. The ladies when they hear this decide to sue Syd for assault and battery.

There is no doubt that Rachel and Doreen have committed the tort of trespass to land which is defined as 'direct interference with the land of another' Rachel and Doreen are unlawful visitors since they have never received any invitation to be on the property of Associated Timber Supplies Ltd. Thus because this is a tort the women in question can be sued in the civil courts. Despite the notice 'trespassers will be prosecuted' which one often sees, trespass is a civil offence and prosecution relates to criminal offences. Only occasionally is trespass a crime and this is, for example, when trespass takes place on military or railway property.

Recently, more and more trespass to land situations have been brought under criminal law. Trespass to local authority property has been brought under criminal law by an Act of Parliament. This was particularly to deal with the problems caused by trespass on school property.

It is likely that Rachel and Doreen would first receive a letter from the company's solicitors explaining that they are trespassing and warning them of legal action. If the women still persist in trespassing then court action would be taken and the company might get damages, but more likely an injunction would be awarded against the two women.

Exercise 7

With reference to Rachel and Doreen, explain what you understand by the term injunction.

When talking about Rachel and Doreen we used the term 'unlawful visitors'. It is important that you understand exactly what this means. There is little doubt that Rachel and Doreen are unlawful visitors but the definition is not so straightforward. In some instances someone may enter premises quite lawfully but then by his behaviour he becomes an unlawful visitor. For example:

Michael Moore is in the habit of going to the public house during the lunch hour and then returning to his factory where he is a toolsetter. On one particular occasion he returns to work and begins to act quite aggressively towards the supervisor and he is clearly the worse for drink. The works manager is called and Michael is asked to leave the factory. Michael refuses and becomes by his refusal an unlawful visitor and therefore a trespasser.

It is also important to understand the distinction between unwelcome visitors and unlawful visitors. The police have certain powers of arrest and powers to search property. They may not be welcome in a suspected criminal's house but they would not be unlawful visitors. Health and Safety Inspectors, as we shall learn in the next chapter, can enter a factory to inspect it without the permission of the owners.

In addition to the legal remedies against trespassers in the courts, i.e. injunction and damages, the owner of premises has the right to eject a trespasser using minimum force provided he has asked the trespasser to leave. It is thus likely that Rachel and Doreen would not be successful if they sued Associated Timber Ltd because as you will remember the supervisor asked them to leave and then tried to force them to leave. Provided the use of force was reasonable then this would be a defence.

Exercise 8

Examine the following examples and advise the parties concerned of the legal position.

1 Burlow Motors Ltd threaten to prosecute two youths who persist in wandering through their showrooms.
2 Marc Holburn, security guard at Weaving Brake Linings Ltd, asks a man who is acting suspiciously to leave the factory premises. He refuses and Marc forces him to leave. The man in question threatens

Weavings with legal action.
3 Complaints have been made about health standards at a food factory. Health Inspectors go to the factor to investigate and they are sued for trespass.
4 Bill Usher goes to his firm's dance. He has rather too much to drink and is asked to leave. He leaves under protest saying he will sue the firm because he has paid for his ticket.

Trespass – Trespass to Person

Frank Brown is manager of a supermarket near the centre of town. He is a man with a fairly short temper. In recent weeks he has been concerned about youths who are unemployed hanging around outside the store and generally being a nuisance. There has also been a spate of shoplifting in the store. One morning Frank is called outside to deal with two seventeen-year olds, Bob and John. Frank is very angry and punches Bob, injuring him; Frank threatens John in such a way to make him very frightened. When he goes back into the shop one of his assistants reports that they suspect a woman of shoplifting. Frank, in haste, asks the wrong woman, Mrs Green, to go into his office. He locks her in to attend to the problems outside and then calles the police, who arrive an hour later; unfortunately for Frank the woman who has been locked in for over an hour is able to prove her innocence.

In this situation we have three examples of trespass to person for which Frank could well be sued. Trespass to person can take one of three forms:

1 Assault – which means threatening someone in such a way that they genuinely believe they are going to be physically hurt.
2 Battery – the actual application of force.
3 False imprisonment.

It is easy to see that John has been assaulted (note the word 'assault' has a different meaning than when it is used in criminal law); he really feared the threat. Bob has suffered a battery, and Mrs Green has been falsely imprisoned.

Assault and battery are civil offences which often occur together, i.e. the threat followed by the force.

There are several defences which a defendant might use if he is being sued for trespass to person:

1 He could say he was acting in self-defence, i.e. he was being attacked.
2 He could say he was preventing a 'greater' evil, i.e. someone else was being attacked and he was assisting them.
3 A parent who punishes his child could say he has the right to do this – the defence is parent authority – though the law protects children

against excessive and unreasonable punishment.

4 In some instances the defendant may have consented, i.e. it is hardly likely that a boxer could sue his opponent for battery.

5 Finally there are instances where it is legal to arrest someone, and even though the person in question subsequently proves his/her innocence, provided the defendant had reasonable grounds for his/her suspicion then it is unlikely that he/she would pay damages. An offence must, however, have been committed. This is known as a citizen's arrest. The police have wider powers of arrest than an ordinary citizen.

Exercise 9

1 List the three types of trespass to person.

2 Study the following and say with reasons whether you think the plaintiff in italics might be successful in sueing for trespass to person.

(a) Ray Ellis goes to the aid of an old woman who is being mugged and injures *Mike Edwards* the assailant, in giving this aid.

(b) *Mrs Smythe* beats her thirteen-year-old son with a strap because he comes in after 10.30 p.m. one night.

(c) Fearing for his own safety John Duffy, site foreman, punches one of *his employees* who is threatening him.

(d) *Nick Smart* is acting suspiciously outside the premises of Peak Engineering Ltd. The security man, Phil Goodwin, arrests him and locks him in a storeroom and calls the police.

(e) Having asked him to leave the shop because he has been causing a disturbance, the manager punches *Michael* and pushes him out.

(f) *Jack Phillips* plays rugby for his local club and after one game threatens to sue one of his opposite number for a painful injury he received after a tackle.

Trespass – Trespass to Goods

Plant Hire Ltd hires out heavy earth-moving equipment. As part of this business it hires to a local builder, Westons & Co. (Builders), a large earth remover for one week. The hire charge is paid in advance but Westons refuse to return the equipment or pay for a further week's hire.

Plant Hire could sue Westons either for the return of the equipment or if it was damaged beyond repair for damages to cover the loss. Plant Hire would sue for trespass to goods and because Westons & Co. are denying Plant Hire their goods this is known as conversion. (Conversion could arise also where a person buying goods on hire purchase tried to sell them without permission of the owner - see Chapter 5.)

Trespass to goods can also arise where goods are removed from someone's premises or damaged in some way. If for example someone's car was wilfully damaged by a neighbour then he could sue for trespass to goods. You will note that the word 'wilfully' has been used, because if it was an accident then the action would be one for negligence, as we saw in the previous section.

Exercise 10

Read the following, explaining the legal situation involved.

1 While Graham is reversing out of his drive he accidentally collides with his neighbour's car. The neighbour decides to sue Graham for trespass to goods.
2 Mary borrows some very expensive books from her firm's library. Being short of money, Mary decides to sell them for £100.

Nuisance

In the last section when we considered trespass to land we defined it as unlawful direct interference with the land of another. In this section we will be considering indirect interference which may result in an action for nuisance. The following example will help to explain this.

Western Printing Supplies Ltd is a fairly small company which specialises in the production of inks and dyestuffs for the printing industry. The managing director, Simon Beckford, has discovered a new process which involves loud banging every hour and the emission of quite a distasteful smell. Mr and Mrs Ogden who have lived next door to the factory for the last ten years complain about this but the company does nothing, so they decide to sue.

As we can see, this involves indirect interference with Mr and Mrs Ogden's enjoyment of their property and would be termed private nuisance. Private nuisance, which is a tort, can take many forms such as noise, smoke, smells, vibration, fumes, the blocking of a right of way.

In Mr and Mrs Ogden's case they would argue that the noise and the smells were unreasonable. In coming to a decision the court would try to balance the company's need to produce at lower cost and Mr and Mrs Ogden's convenience. In nuisance cases it is this delicate balance which the court tries to find, i.e. an owner of land can do what he wishes provided this does not interfere unduly with others. The court would take into account such factors as frequency and duration of the alleged nuisance. If in our situation Western Printing Supplies Ltd allowed the bang and the smell to occur only once per week then this might be allowed; or if the hour-interval bangs and smell only lasted one week in a year this might be allowed. The court will also take into account the locality, e.g. you may have to put up with more in an industrial area than in a residential area.

Two points need to be stressed in nuisance:

1 It is no defence for a defendant to say that the plaintiff came to the nuisance. If the Ogdens moved and other people bought their house the fact that they came to a nuisance will not carry any weight in the court. The new occupants could still sue for nuisance.
2 A defendant may not plead that it is a necessity. In some cases doctors who have to make night emergency calls have been sued successfully for nuisance by neighbours disturbed by their departure. A plea of necessity is not acceptable by the court.

Having taken all these matters into account, if the court held that the Ogdens were in fact suffering a nuisance then it could award damages; however, the most likely possibility is the granting of an injunction ordering Western Printing Supplies to refrain from this process.

Generally nuisance is a tort and action is taken in the civil court, usually the County Court but where large sections of the public are affected it can be termed a public nuisance and therefore a crime. In this case action is taken in the criminal courts; for example:

Eastern Haulage Ltd have a large depot in Ashford. Lorry drivers awaiting check-in often park the lorries on a road leading to the depot, and residents and other vehicle users are subject to long delays because of this.

This would be an example of Eastern Haulage committing a public nuisance. A Magistrates' Court, if it found the company guilty, could order it to refrain from parking lorries in this way.

Exercise 11

1 What is the difference between a public and a private nuisance?

2 Study the following examples and say whether you think the party in italics would have a case in nuisance.

(a) Michael lives next door to *two old-age pensioners*. Michael is very quiet but he always has a birthday party each year with music, etc. The two pensioners threaten to sue him.

(b) *Frances* has just come to live near a restaurant. The smell and noise from the restaurant are, she feels, excessive. The restaurant owner argues that it has always been like this and that Frances' predecessors had never complained.

(c) *John* lives next door to a vet who sometimes has to make emergency calls. John claims he is disturbed by the noise of the vet going out late at night. The vet claims that his visits are essential.

Defamation

Timeright Ltd produces a range of watches. One of its sections specialises in the production of expensive ladies' quartz watches. Despite what the company had regarded as very good security systems it appears that a member of the workforce is taking watches out. The management order a close investigation and suspicion falls on one of the supervisors, Mrs Patricia Pryce. The personnel manager decides to take immediate action and pins a notice to the staff noticeboard which reads:

> We have reason to believe that Mrs Patricia Pryce has abused her position of trust with the company and is responsible for the spate of thefts recently. I should be grateful if Mrs Pryce could report to my office immediately.
>
> J. Jackson,
> Personnel Manager
> Timeright Ltd

Mrs Pryce, who is in fact quite innocent, is very angry and decides to take the company to court saying she believes this is a defamation of her character. (In any event most people would agree that pinning a notice up of this sort was not a very sensible thing to do.)

In order to be successful in a defamation action it is necessary for the plaintiff, i.e. Pat in this instance, to prove three things:

1 Did the statement refer to Pat by name or innuendo? In this instance she was named, though it is possible for a person to be referred to by a nickname or described in such a way that no one is in any doubt that the statement referred to him or her.

2 Was the statement communicated to a third party or parties? There is no doubt it was communicated; in fact all the workforce had the opportunity to see it.

3 Was the statement capable of lowering a person's reputation in the eyes of right-thinking members of society? In other words was it likely that the person about whom the statement was made might be regarded with ridicule, contempt or even hatred? It would seem that dishonesty of the sort alleged against Pat is something which causes her reputation to be lowered.

Because the answer is 'yes' to all three questions as far as Pat is concerned she would have a case in defamation. Defamation is in two forms: libel, permanent and usually the written form; and slander, temporary and usually the spoken form. Statements made on television or the radio would be termed libel because although spoken they are more permanent. Pat would sue for libel. The case would come before the High Court because the tort of defamation can never be heard in the County Court. The reason for this rule is so that frivolous actions are discouraged. High Court actions are of course very expensive.

Exercise 12

1 Defamation may be in two forms: (a) which is the written form and (b) which is the spoken form.
2 Name the three things which must be proved in an action for defamation.
3 Study the following case and say whether the person italicised has a case in defamation, and if not why not.

Paddy Byrne works for a firm manufacturing cigarettes. He and six friends have organised a system whereby they are stealing from the company to the tune of about £50 per week. The management decide to tighten up security and it becomes impossible to do this any longer. The friends think Paddy has informed management, which in fact is not the case. One friend pins a notice to the staff noticeboard which contains the lines:

'He who gave the game away let him *byrne* in hell and rue the day.'

Defences in Defamation

There are a number of defences a defendant might use in a defamation action.

If a defendant who is being sued for defamation can prove the truth of a statement then there can be no defamation, because if we think about it there is no reputation to spoil. If in our first example Pat Pryce had been stealing watches and the defendant could prove it then Pat would not be successful. However, it is important to note that a defendant would only use this defence if he was absolutely sure he could prove the true of the statement. If he was not sure then his attempt might cost him additional damages because a court will take the view that a plaintiff who has been defamed is suffering greater indignity as a result of an unsuccessful attempt at proof in the court.

On some occasions statements are given absolute protection or privilege from defamation action. Statements made in Parliament or in court proceedings are given this protection. This means that for example a judge can say anything he likes without fear of any legal action.

Some statements are given what is called qualified protection or privilege, which means that action can only be taken if it can be shown that the statement was made maliciously. The best example is in references – if an employer is asked to give a reference to another exployer. Generally the employer giving the reference is protected from defamation actions unless it can be shown that he maliciously made the statement about his employee.

If a newspaper unintentionally publishes a defamatory article, e.g. if in reporting a case it gets the defendant's name wrong, then it can offer as a defence (a) the statement was made unintentionally, (b) an offer of amends is made to the person named, (c) an offer of a printed apology is made; for example:

Michael Street picks up his local newspaper and reads that Michael John Street of 14 Winchester Way, Basingstoke has been convicted in the Crown Court of rape. He is surprised and annoyed because this is his address. The convicted person was Martin James Street of 14 Warwick Street, Basingstoke. Michael rings the Hampshire Gazette *and the editor offers him £250 and prints an apology which reads: 'We wish to point out that Michael John Street of 14 Winchester Way, Basingstoke, was not the person convicted of rape on 14 March 1981 and we apologise for any inconvenience or embarrassment caused by our error.'*

If Michael refused the £250 and decided to sue then the Hampshire Gazette *could use this as a defence.*

This particular defence is quite a complex one and a newspaper could still be sued successfully even if it did make an offer of amends.

Finally certain people in public life or perhaps sportsmen can expect that they will be criticised. If, therefore, a newspaper writes of a footballer following a poor performance that 'he must have been burning the candle at both ends recently', he would not be successful in an action of defamation though if the newspaper went on to comment on his private life this might be different. This defence is sometimes known as fair comment.

Exercise 13

Examine the following and say whether you think the defendant might have a defence in a defamation action.

1 Mary Moore, an accountant with Associated Metal Products, applies for a post as chief accountant with a firm of TV rentals. In the reference which Associated Metal Products writes to the TV rental firm Mary is described as incompetent and disloyal. Mary sees the reference and threatens to sue her firm.

2 Mr Green MP in a speech in Parliament makes a serious allegation against the chairman of one of the nationalised industries.
3 Roger Lewis is a reporter with the *Bristol Times*. He has always had a grudge against his neighbour Phil Brayshaw, and following a conviction for theft against a Philip Bagshaw Roger maliciously reports that it was Philip Brayshaw and this is printed. When his neighbour complains to the editor, the editor offers amends of £300 and a printed apology.
4 Jennie Rogers, who has been convicted of shoplifting, decides to sue the *Kent Times* for printing details of the case.

Exercise 14

1 What are the three elements necessary to prove negligence?
2 What are the three elements necessary to prove defamation?
3 Name one situation where a statement is protected absolutely and one where a statement is given qualified protection.
4 Name the three types of trespass.
5 Why is the notice 'trespassers will be prosecuted' usually misleading?

This chapter has only been able to deal with the law relating to torts in outline.

At the end of the book you will find details for further reading on this area of the law.

CHAPTER 8

SAFETY AT WORK

Bert Ogden is an apprentice electrician employed at a large paper mill in the South of England, International Paper Products Ltd. Bert has nearly finished his apprenticeship and in fact has just come back from his last block release course at the local technical college. Part of the electrical equipment in relation to one of the pulp machines has developed a slight fault and Bert is asked by his foreman, Mick Mason, to examine the problem. Company rules lay down quite clearly that all electrical equipment must be isolated before it is examined. However the managing director has issued a statement to his employees that they must in all circumstances make every effort to keep production going.

Accordingly Bert, encouraged by Mick, looks at the equipment while it is still operational. While examining the equipment Bert receives an electric shock which causes him to fall against the pulp-making machinery and he is very badly injured.

When the trade union hears about the accident the steward. Eric Disdale, decides to notify the Health and Safety Executive and urges a full inspection. Four Health and Safety Inspectors visit the mill and they are not happy with what they find. Their report makes a number of recommendations to the management including a prohibition order and an improvement order. The inspectors promise that they will make another visit in fourteen days' time. At the same time they decide to charge International Paper Products Ltd with having committed a criminal offence under the Health and Safety at Work Act.

8.1 HEALTH AND SAFETY AT WORK ACT 1974

It seems that International Paper Products Ltd are running a mill which is not very safe. Health and safety at work questions are regulated by the Health and Safety at Work Act 1974, and in this chapter we will be dealing with the operation of this Act and also the remedies available to an injured employee following injuries at work.

The Health and Safety at Work Act 1974 was passed with a view to bringing under one Act the various health and safety legislation which had been passed. It does not replace the Factories Act 1961 but gradually the Factories Act will be replaced by regulations under the Health and Safety at Work Act. The Health and Safety at Work Act is what is known as an enabling Act; that is, it allows a Minister of State to issue regulations which have the force of law. It is hoped that before long most health and safety rules will be covered by the Act. You will remember in Chapter 1 we gave an example of a regulation issued in respect of First Aid in 1981.

The Health and Safety at Work Act imposes certain duties on the employer:

1 To provide and maintain plant and systems of work which are as far as practicable safe and without risk to health.
2 To make arrangements for the safe use, handling, storage and transport of articles and substances.
3 To provide information, training and supervision to ensure as far as is practicable the health and safety at work of the employees.
4 To provide a safe place of work including safe means of access and egress (entry and exit).
5 To provide a working environment that is as far as practicable safe and consistent with the welfare of the employees.

These duties to employees are supplemented by a general duty to non-employees who may be at the particular place of work. This means that visitors are protected by the Act.

If we examine for a moment Bert Ogden's case then it is quite clear that International Paper Products are at fault. It is obviously unsafe to work on electrical equipment which is live; although a company rule was that electrical equipment had to be isolated this was rather confused by their request that production must go on. You will remember that Bert was encouraged by the foreman to work on the equipment without turning it off. Another question we might ask ourselves is, Was Bert aware of the company rules concerning isolation of electrical equipment? Under the Health and Safety at Work Act companies must issue for their employees a statement outlining the company's safety policy.

Activity

If you are employed see if you can find the statement of your firm's safety policy. It may be on a noticeboard or may have been given to you personally.

Because International Paper Products are in breach of the Health and Safety at Work Act they are liable to a fine of up to £2000. The case would be laid before a Magistrates' Court. Health and Safety Inspectors have a right to inspect places of work and normally make recommendations. In serious situations, as clearly found at International Paper Products, they can issue:

1 a Prohibition Order which prohibits (stops) the use of a particular part of a process. It is possible for a prohibition order to stop the whole factory; and/or
2 an Improvement Order which says improve this situation within a certain time.

It is important to note that inspectors are more anxious to establish by persuasion safe practices in places of work, and usually reports which they issue are persuasive rather than mandatory; in other words, they recommend rather than order. It is possible in more serious breaches for cases to come to the Crown Court, and of course heavier fines are possible.

Exercise 1

1 The Health and Safety at Work Act 1974 introduces a new range of civil offences. *true/false*?
2 Explain the term 'enabling Act' as it applies to the Health and Safety Act.
3 Explain the meaning of an Improvement Order.
4 What is the maximum fine for an offence under the Health and Safety Act?

The Health and Safety at Work Act also imposes duties on any employee. Employees have a duty while at work to:

1 take reasonable care for the health and safety of himself and other persons who may be affected by his acts or omissions;
2 cooperate with the employer in matters of health and safety;
3 not to intentionally or recklessly interfere with anything provided in the interest, safety or welfare of employees.

It does seem that the foreman Mick Mason in our example has breached the first of these duties in allowing Bert to do this job. The Act provides that not only the employer (International Paper Products) but also the employee (Mich Mason) can be fined for breaches of the Act.

The following examples will help to explain the duties of employees.

Dave Stewart, a foreman at a heavy engineering works, encourages his men to engage in heavy lifting without using the regulation lifting gear. One of the employees suffers a severe back injury.

Jackie Redstone works in a busy insurance office. She is aware that the electrical connection for some office machinery is faulty but she decides it is none of her business. She does not make a report and one of her colleagues is seriously injured. She admits to the manager that she had known for a long time that this fault existed.

Terence Clapham is a waiter in a busy hotel with a reputation as a practical joker. He decides to change the signs on the IN/OUT doors. One of his colleagues carrying hot food is badly burned as a result.

In all three cases the employee in question could be fined under the Health and Safety at Work Act. Dave Stewart for 'not taking reasonable care of other persons who may be affected by his acts or omissions', Jackie for 'not cooperating with the employer', and Terence for 'recklessly interfering with something provided for health and safety'.

Exercise 2

In the following examples say what might be the legal position under the Health and Safety at Work Act 1974.

1 Ten employees have suffered serious accidents in the last five weeks while operating a piece of machinery at London Road Engineering Co.
2 An injury of a chef at the Hotel Regal reveals that he has never been instructed in the use of new infra-red ovens.
3 Two apprentices at a firm of electrical engineers have been warned about skylarking while at work. As a result of another incident of this kind one of them, John Hartley, is badly injured.
4 Because of extreme humidity the environment at Victoria Laundry is very unhealthy and the floors have become like ice rinks. A complaint is made to the Health and Safety Executive.

8.2 CIVIL ACTION AVAILABLE TO EMPLOYEES INJURED AT WORK

Although the Health and Safety at Work Act 1974 has done a great deal to improve health and safety in workplaces, as we have seen breaches result in criminal action. In our example relating to Bert Ogden and International Paper Products, Bert would not be compensated as a result of criminal action. We have, however (in Chapter 7), seen that it is possible for persons to sue for negligence, and in fact Bert could do this as long as he was able to show the existence of three elements.

Exercise 3

See if you can remember the three elements necessary to prove negligence.

It would then be necessary for the plaintiff (i.e. Bert Ogden) to prove the existence of these three elements. There is no doubt that International Paper Products owed Bert a duty of care. This duty of care had been breached by allowing Bert to work on electrical equipment which had not been isolated. Bert suffered injuries as a result of the breach and thus he could claim damages. The duty of care is sometimes known as a common law duty of care. International Paper Products could point to the existence of their rules that no electrical equipment should be worked upon unless it was isolated, and indeed it was Bert's foreman Mick Mason who had authorised the work. However, this would be no defence because the law provides that employers can be vicariously (indirectly) liable for the torts of their employees. International Paper Products would therefore be liable for Mick Mason's action. In fact even where a company forbids a course of action then the company still could be held liable if an employee engages in it.

For example, *Hudson* v. *Ridge Manufacturing Co. Ltd* (1957): A plaintiff's wrist was broken when he was tripped by a fellow worker who was skylarking. The firm was held to be liable vicariously for the tort of its employee even though the company had expressly forbidden this sort of behaviour.

International Paper Products could argue in their defence that the fault in the electrical appliance was not their concern since it had been supplied by another firm, Associated Electrical Products Ltd. Therefore it was to this firm that Bert's claim ought to lie. If this sort of defence was possible then plaintiffs would have considerable trouble in ever making a successful claim because companies would blame suppliers who in turn might blame other suppliers. The Employers' Liability (Defective Equipment) Act 1969 now enables a worker to sue the employer in these circumstances and the employer may then claim from his supplier. Thus Bert would sue International Paper Products, who may in turn sue Associated Electrical Products.

Exercise 4

Read the following cases and say whether you think the plaintiff in italics would have a case in negligence.

1 *Ben Bennett* is a lathe operator with Peakdale Engineering Co.

The lathe has developed a fault which has been reported. Ben is injured while using the lathe.

2 *Fred Wingfield* is a bricklayer working on a large office block. His firm is very strict about safety regulations especially the standards of scaffolding. The site foreman is less careful and, in an effort to keep in front of the schedule, he orders scaffolding to be erected which is not up to standard. Fred, who is working on the third floor, falls following a collapse of the scaffolding and is very badly injured. The firm, North West Builders Ltd, claim that the foreman was not acting under instructions and refuse to pay out any compensation to Fred.

3 The Hotel Sceptre has just installed new infra-red ovens. One of these ovens is faulty, and a chef, *Adam Cranston*, is injured quite badly. The hotel disclaim responsibility saying Adam has a claim against the supplier, Midland Catering Equipment Ltd.

We have seen then that employees injured in accidents may sue their employers in negligence. It is necessary for them to prove the existence of the three necessary elements. In addition to sueing for a breach of common law duty it is also possible for an injured employee to sue for a breach of statutory duty. This means that an employee can sue because he can claim a breach of the Factories Act 1961. (We learned in Chapter 1 that Acts of Parliament are called statutes and this gives rise to the term 'statutory'.) In practice, workers will often be advised to sue for both negligence and breach of statutory duty in the hope of succeeding in one or the other. If he succeeds in both he will of course not obtain double damages, but only damages sufficient to cover his loss or compensate him for injury.

The following example will help to explain how breaches of statutory duty will apply.

David Stanley has just completed his apprenticeship as a craft engineer. He is employed by Burlow Engineering Co. While operating a grinding wheel which has not been properly guarded he so badly injures his thumb that it has to be amputated.

David goes to his lawyer who advises him to sue Burlow Engineering for a breach of statutory duty. In order to do this David would have to show that the Factories Act applied to this situation. This would clearly be the case because the Factories Act 1961 applies to workshops of this kind, and there is a definite duty to fence such machinery. David would have to show that the duty to fence the machinery applied to his employer and was owed to him. Neither of these two elements would be difficult. David would then have to show that the statutory duty had been broken, and Burlow Engineering Co.'s failure to fence machinery indicates this clearly. Finally, David would have to show that he was injured as a result of the breach of the statutory duty, and again this was the case.

As you can see, proving a breach of a statutory duty is not very different from proving negligence - the difference in this case is that the statute in question, the Factories Act 1961, applies to workers, whereas negligence can apply to any situation.

A plaintiff wishing to sue under the Factories Act must therefore show, as David Stanley needed to show:

1 that the Act applied to the situation;
2 that the defendant owed a duty of care;
3 that the defendant was entitled to benefit from that duty.

The following case sums up the situation in respect of the Factory Act very well. In *John Summers & Sons Ltd* v. *Frost* (1955), the respondent injured his thumb on a revolving grinding wheel which had only been partly guarded. It was held that the duty to fence dangerous machinery was strict and that it was no defence that fencing would make it impossible or impracticable to operate the machine.

Many workers who are injured at work will not go to court to prove negligence or breach of statutory duty. It is sometimes difficult to prove negligence or breach of statutory duty and often workers do not have sufficient knowledge of the law or perhaps they lack any initiative to take action; even if they do, the possible cost of a lost case proves to be a powerful deterrent. The Social Security Act 1975 provides that an injured employee can gain industrial benefit irrespective of whether his injuries arose from negligence or breach of statutory duty. Benefits are payable by the state provided that:

1 personal injury was caused by an accident which arose out of and in the course of employment; or
2 the employee has suffered an illness not as a result of an accident but as a result of working on a process. The regulations which govern claims for industrial illnesses are the Social Security (Industrial Injuries) (Prescribed Diseases) Regulations 1980.

If, for example, an employee claims that he has suffered from a skin disease as a result of working with particular materials he may be able to claim industrial benefit.

The present regulations for industrial benefit include provisions for a disablement pension, a dependant's allowance and a death benefit.

Exercise 5

1 If an injured employee decided to sue his employer for breach of statutory duty under which Act of Parliament would he sue?
2 If an injured employee cannot prove his employer was at fault he will get no compensation for his injuries. *true/false*?

3 Linda Brazier, who works in an office, is injured in the works canteen when she slips on a patch of grease on the floor. The company proves it has done everything reasonable to keep the floor clean. Can Linda obtain any compensation?
4 The duty of care in negligence is sometimes known as a

Exercise 6

In the following examples explain the legal principles involved. If after checking your answers you find that you do not understand a particular aspect of the law as it relates to safety at work, read this chapter again paying particular attention to that aspect.

1 David Hogg, a supervisor in a chemical plant, fails to do the safety checks which the company has laid down; as a result a serious explosion occurs.
2 John Adams, one of her Majesty's Health and Safety Inspectors, is refused permission to enter a factory premises but he decides despite this refusal to go in and make an inspection. He orders one particular process to be discontinued. John is threatened with civil action for trespass.
3 Philip Brown is a fork-lift driver. As a result of a serious fault in a new fork-lift truck he is driving Philip sustains a serious head injury. The company say that the supplier of the truck is to blame.
4 Maureen Williams is an operative at a firm using a process involving asbestos. She finds as a result of a hospital examination that she is suffering from cancer, which she claims is due to the process she works on. Her company employ a leading lawyer to prove that the process is not responsible.
5 John Harris injures his back carrying heavy loads for his company, who claim that he was not acting under the company's instructions for handling heavy equipment.
6 Despite company rules to the contrary, Bob Bown the foreman orders one of his apprentices to work on an unfenced machine. The apprentice is injured. The company deny liability, blaming the foreman.

CHAPTER 9

TYPES OF BUSINESS ORGANISATION

9.1 SOLE TRADER AND PARTNERSHIP

Rino Rinaldi is an Italian waiter working in a large restaurant in London. It has always been his ambition to run his own restaurant and he feels that a restaurant concentrating on relatively cheap meals but with emphasis upon good quality service will do well. As a result of a lucky pools win of £160 000 Rino is able to achieve his ambition and he buys a restaurant in Maidstone which he names Italiano, *specialising in steak and wine. The business does well and Rino decides to expand his business to other towns in Kent but unfortunately he lacks the capital. He decides on a partnership and his wife Wendy uses £60 000 of her savings, and two ex-colleagues, Stuart Conway and John Drew, decide to provide £120 000. This together with money from his present business allows the partnership to buy another two restaurants, one in Ashford and the other in Sittingbourne The emphasis upon good service, Italian wine and well-chosen steaks is obviously very effective and the three restaurants do very well indeed. Rino and his partners decide to form a company and Rino, John, Stuart and Wendy each are given shares in the company. A number of other shareholders are interested and their money buys two additional restaurants in Horsham and Tunbridge Wells. Italiano Steaks & Wine Co. Ltd, as the new company is called, clearly is a success story; Rino and Stuart Conway, the two directors, decide that they must expand and 'go public', i.e. form a public company: £1 million ordinary shares are offered to the public. This allows branches all over the South of England to be opened.* Italiano, *from such small beginnings, has become a prosperous and well-known company.*

This very successful venture has resulted in four different types of business organisation being formed, and in this chapter we will use this example to explain the legal difference existing between the various types of business.

Sole Trader

Rino started his business as a sole trader, which means that he was the only owner. He may have employed people full-time or part-time to work at the restaurant but he was the only person who had money in the business. There are of course many one-man businesses in this country, perhaps more than any other kind Just like any individual, Rino can be sued, can sue and can be prosecuted for anything he might do in the course of his business. Thus, for example, if customers in the restaurant were injured as a result of Rino's or his staff s negligence then Rino could face action in the civil courts.

One of the problems of running a business in this way is that the owner has what is called unlimited liability. To explain what this means, remember that Rino started his business with £160 000. In fact the business flourished but let us assume for a moment that the venture was a complete failure and after a year Rino was faced with debts amounting to £180 000. Rino s liability for debts is not confined to the original £160 000 but is unlimited and in court action by creditors to recover the money Rino could find that he could lose his own personal property, e.g. his house or car, which the court could order to be sold to pay his debts. This is what is meant by unlimited liability; sole traders' liability is not limited to the amount of their initial investment.

Exercise 1

John Craven invests £50 000 in a small lock up shop which he runs himself. John is not really cut out for shop work and the business runs heavily into debt. John finds to his horror that his creditors are asking the court to order him to sell his own private house to meet his debts. Is this a risk which John might face?

You will also have noticed that Rino has decided to call his restaurant *Italiano*. Until 26 February 1982 it was necessary for any business operating under a name other than the name of the owner to register the name with the Registrar of Business Names. The Companies Act 1981 abolished this requirement. However, the new requirement regulated now by the Business Names Act 1985 is that a business operating under a name other than its owner(s) must:

1 display the name(s) and address(es) of the owner(s);
2 show this information on business letters, written orders, invoices, receipts and written demands for payment of debts.

Activity

Have a look for examples of this. You will find examples of names displayed in any business or shop which is trading under a name which is not the name of the owner(s). You may still find certificates relating to the old regulations under the Registration of Business Names Act 1916, which has now been replaced.

Failure to comply with the regulations regarding business names can lead to a fine but, perhaps what is more serious, contracts entered into by Rino using the name *Italiano* cannot be enforced against another party.

If, for example, Rino gave credit to a company for senior executives to have meals at his restaurant, then if he had not complied with the registration requirements as far as the business name was concerned he would not be able to enforce the contract against the company if it refused to pay the bills in respect of their staff.

Partnership

Rino's business flourished and after some time he decided to expand to buy two additional restaurants, but to do this he formed a partnership with four partners, namely himself, Wendy Rinaldi, John Drew and Stuart Conway. A partnership is defined by the Partnership Act 1980 as 'the relation which subsists between persons carrying on business in common with a view to profit'. The Companies Act 1985 lays down that there should be a maximum of twenty in a partnership. Rino's partnership seems to satisfy both rules:

1 It has been set up with a view to profit.
2 It has four partners and therefore has not exceeded the legal maximum of twenty partners.

As with a sole owner the partners will not enjoy limited liability, which means that Wendy, Stuart and John could risk losing much more than their original investment of £60 000, £120 000 and £120 000 respectively. Also it would be necessary for the partnership to comply with the business name requirements of the Companies Act 1981.

It is most likely that before entering into partnership with each other the four persons involved would have drawn up an agreement which defined clearly their rights and obligations. It is likely that such an agreement, sometimes known as a partnership deed, would include such matters as:

1 The involvement of the partners in the business: it may be that Rino's wife is designated a 'sleeping' partner, which means that although she

has invested £60 000 and will receive a percentage share of the profits she will not take any part in the running of the business. The agreement may also lay down the duties of the other three partners.

2 The agreement will lay down probably how the profit is to be shared and define clearly the precise amount of money Rino has invested, because you will remember Rino formed the partnership from an existing business.

3 Each partner will have agreed not to start any competing business and to give the other partners full information about any dealings in respect of *Italiano*.

It is possible for partnerships to be formed without an agreement and in this case the Partnership Act 1890 lays down clearly the relationship between the partners. It is important for partners to trust each other because each partner can make the other liable for his acts. If, therefore, one of the partners ordered expensive equipment for the firm's use then the other partners would equally be liable in contract. If as a result of John's negligence a customer is hurt then all the partners would be sued. It is possible for a partner who has retired from the partnership to remain liable for debts. Thus if John retired from the partnership and the partnership incurs a debt with a company then he could be liable unless he has expressly told the company in question that he has retired or he publishes the fact that he has retired in the *London Gazette.*

Exercise 2

1 Define the expression 'sleeping partner'.
2 Explain the expression 'unlimited liability'.
3 Name two acts which regulate partnerships.
4 If a partner wishes to retire he can avoid being liable for partnership debts by taking two possible courses of action. What are these?
5 Linda Brasier and Christine Benton form a partnership and open a shop known as Canterbury Fashions, selling women's fashion clothes. Unknown to Linda, Christine orders very large stocks from SE Clothing Products Ltd and the partnership falls heavily into debt. SE Clothing Products Ltd have not been paid and sue the partnership, Canterbury Fashions, but Linda refuses to be held liable, saying she did not agree to the order from SE Clothing Products. Is Linda liable?

Dissolution of a partnership (ending of a partnership). Partnerships may be brought to an end by order of the court where a partner applies. There are certain conditions under which a court may issue a decree dissolving (bringing to an end) a partnership, e.g. if one of the partners had been declared a patient under the Mental Health Act 1983, or if the partnership could only be carried on at a loss. It is of course possible for partnerships to be dissolved by the partners themselves. It is likely that in any partnership deed drawn up between Rino, John, Wendy and Stuart the methods of dissolution will have been laid down.

The precise methods by which the capital resulting from the sale of *Italiano* would be shared out would be included in the partnership agreement.

Exercise 3

1 Explain the meaning of the phrase 'dissolution of a partnership'.
2 Explain the two main ways partnerships may be dissolved.

9.2 FORMATION OF A COMPANY

We have now considered two types of business organisation, namely the sole trader type and the partnership. You will remember, however, that Rino because he wanted to obtain further finance decided to form a company and the existing partners were given shares in the new company, Italiano Steak & Wine Co. Ltd. Also shares were sold to several new investors. At first a private company was formed and as you will remember later this became a public company. The major differences between a public and a private company are:

1. A private company may not offer or advertise shares to the public but a public company may offer or advertise its shares to the public. In fact, this is the reason for the word 'public', i.e. the company's shares are available to the public. A private company's shares, however, are only available privately.
2. In its memorandum of association, which is one of the legal documents setting it up, a public company must state that it is a public company.
3. A public company must have a minimum share capital of £50 000. (This amount can be altered by the Secretary of State.)

Activity

In many newspapers you can find examples of companies advertising their shares. Look out for some examples. All these companies will public companies because they are selling their shares to the public.

A company, whether public or private, is quite different legally from a partnership. In order for a company to be formed certain important requirements have to be met. These requirements are laid down by the Companies Acts 1985 and they are called therefore statutory requirements.

Exercise 4

What does 'statutory' mean?

To illustrate the method by which companies are formed let us return to the restaurant business Italiano. You will remember that it was decided to form a private company to be called Italiano Steak & Wine Co. Ltd. It would be necessary for the promoters, i.e. Rino, Stuart and John, to deposit with the Registar of Companies two documents: The memorandum of association and the articles of association.

Memorandum of association. This document must contain certain information and we shall illustrate this by reference to Italiano's application:

1 The name of the company with the word Limited, i.e. Italiano Steak & Wine Co. Ltd.
2 The address of the registered office, which in this case is 14 Canterbury Road, Maidstone, UK; this in fact is an office over the very first restaurant which Rino bought.
3 The objects of the company or in other words why the company is being set up. Italiano Steak & Wine Co. Ltd is being set up 'with the object of providing food and drink in restaurants to the public'. It is important that the promoters get the objects correct and it contains exactly what they wish to do, because as we will see there are difficulties when a company tries to engage in activities outside the range of its objects. There are provisions to vary the objects within certain laid-down guidelines.
4 The promoters would have to make a statement under this clause that the shareholders of the new company would have limited liability. This means that they could only lose what they put in, e.g. if Christine Benton decided to buy 5000 £1 shares from the newly formed company Italiano Steak & Wine Co. Ltd, then this is all she could lose. This then explains the word 'limited'. Each shareholder is limited in liability to the amount of his shareholding.
5 The promoters have to state the nominal amount of capital the company will start trading with and it is likely that Italiano Steak & Wine Co. Ltd would start with about £600 000. The promoters also have to state how this is to be divided, i.e. 600 000 £1 ordinary shares is a possible and likely division.

6 Finally, for a company at least two people must sign the association clause. We will assume that Stuart, Rino and John are the three signatories in this case and they also have to indicate their own shareholding. Thus John may indicate 140 000 £1 shares. This document, known as the memorandum of association, is really a document setting out the relationship of the company Italiano Wine & Steak Co. Ltd with the outside world.

Exercise 5

1 Name two differences between a public and a private company.
2 When you see Motor Supplies Company Limited what does the term 'limited' mean?
3 In addition to the memorandum of association, name the other document which must be provided to the Registrar of Companies before a company can be formed.
4 In the memorandum of association what do you understand by the 'objects' of a company?

Articles of association. Just as the memorandum of association regulates the external affairs of a company, the articles of association are concerned with the internal running of the company. It is likely that Italiano Steak & Wine Co. Ltd would have included in their articles of association such matters as:

1 how shares would be transferred;
2 the powers of the company to borrow money;
3 how meetings are to be arranged and their frequency;
4 voting rights of shareholders.

The articles must be signed by the same people who signed the memorandum, i.e. in the case of Italiano Steak & Wine Co. Ltd, it would have been Rino, Stuart and John.

The two documents, the memorandum and the articles, are sent to the Registrar; one of the directors and the company secretary must sign what is called a statutory declaration. This is merely a form which states that all the requirements of the Companies Acts have been complied with. Once the Registrar is satisfied he will issue the applicant company with a 'certificate of incorporation' and this means in the case of a private company it can begin trading right away.

It is important to understand what incorporation means. You will remember in the first section of this chapter we pointed out that partners in partnerships could be sued or be prosecuted for matters relating to the partnership. In a company the shareholders will not be sued or prosecuted for illegal acts of the company. This is because by incorporation the company takes on a legal status and becomes as far as the law is concerned a 'legal person'. Thus a company has a legal existence quite separate from its shareholders; if Italiano Steak & Wine Co. Ltd were in breach of contract for non-payment of orders they had made the company would be taken to court. This is a very important legal principle and it is what distinguishes companies from the other two types of business organisation. A company just like an individual person can sue, be sued, prosecute or be prosecuted.

A famous case *Saloman* v. *Saloman Co. Ltd* (1897) laid down that 'a limited company is an artificial legal person with a separate and distinct existence apart from its members'.

You will remember that when explaining the memorandum of association mention was made of nominal capital. This is the amount of money that the company thinks it may raise. The sum of £600 000 was mentioned for Italiano Steak & Wine Co. Ltd. A separate statement of this amount must be given, for companies are taxed on this amount. A company need not issue the full amount and so Italiano might issue £500 000 and keep £100 000 aside. Thus a distinction is made between nominal capital of £600 000, i.e. that amount which the company is authorised to raise, and the issued capital of £500 000, which it has actually raised.

Another clause of the memorandum which needs to be explained more fully is the objects clause. This sets out the purpose for which the company is operating. For Italiano Steak & Wine Co. Ltd the object was 'to provide food and drink in restaurants to the public'.

> *It is quite apparent that Rino has a good business head on his shoulders and it has not escaped his notice that a restaurant which they have acquired on the outskirts of Canterbury has quite extensive grounds with some very large outbuildings. Rino persuades his fellow directors and the shareholders that for a modest outlay these buildings can be converted into large vehicle repair shops and he hits on the idea of advertising MOT and servicing 'while you eat'. This proves very successful but unfortunately for the company the repair, servicing and testing of vehicles is not part of the company's objects.*

Italiano Steak & Wine Co. Ltd runs a serious risk because if several of its customers refused to pay the servicing or repair bills that money could not be recovered because the contract between the company and the customers would be *ultra vires*, beyond the company's powers as laid down in the memorandum. Any agreement entered into by a company which is beyond its powers is void and cannot be enforced against the other party.

Ashbury Railway Carriage Co. v. *Riche* (1875) is a case which illustrates that any Act outside the objects is *ultra vires* and therefore void. The company in its object was authorised to make railway carriages but entered into an arrangement to finance a railway line. This was adjudged to be *ultra vires*.

If, however, Italiano Steak & Wine Co. Ltd had ordered £5000 worth of spares for its motor trade, could it avoid payment saying that it was *ultra vires*, beyond the powers of the company? This would be very unfair on the firm supplying the spares, but until the UK became a member of the EEC this very unfair rule applied. The following example was, as you can see, before the time when the UK became a member of the EEC. In *Introductions Ltd* v. *National Provincial Bank Ltd* (1969), a company formed in 1951 with the objects of promoting tourism was not bound by contracts made when it went into pig farming many years later. However, because it is necessary for our commercial rules to coincide with our partners in Europe, the law now is that if a company deals with another in good faith, i.e not knowing that the other was acting beyond its powers, then a contract can be enforced against the other company. Thus, provided the £5000 of spares was supplied by a company which did not know that Italiano was acting *ultra vires* then the £5000 could be enforced despite what is technically a void contract. Section 9 of the European Communities Act 1972 would allow the supplier to enforce the contract against Italiano Steak & Wine Co. Ltd.

Exercise 6

1 A company in its memorandum states that it will raise £1m but only decides to sell 500 000 £1 shares. What is the company's (a) nominal capital, (b) issued capital?

2 Explain the legal positions in each of the following.

(a) Unicorn Motor Supplies Co. Ltd owe Ford plc £500 000. Ford plc decide to take the managing director, Bill Boyle, to court for breach of contract.

(b) SE Touring Co. Ltd was set up to provide tours of the South East of England to foreign visitors. The managing director decides to develop a road haulage sideline and orders two wagons for £60 000 from Heavy Vehicle Supplies Ltd. The vehicles are delivered but the £60 000 is never paid. SE Touring Co. Ltd claim the contract is void because it is *ultra vires*.

(c) Palatine Publishing Co. Ltd decide to extend their business into sports shops and open up three shops in the North of England. A football club orders £2000 of equipment from them but does not settle the bill. The football club chairman is a solicitor and he knows that supply of sports equipment is not included in Palatine Publishing Co. Ltd objects.

We have already explained the differences between a private and a public company. A public company unlike a private company cannot begin trading when it gets a certificate of incorporation; it must await the issue of a certificate of trading. Thus, when Italiano Steak & Wine Co. Ltd decided to go public it needed to apply to the Registrar with details of its proposals for issuing shares. Public companies must include Public Limited Company in their title or the abbreviation plc.

Legal bodies. Finally, besides private and public companies which have separate legal status, County Councils such as Kent or Derbyshire will be legal bodies with the right to sue or prosecute and able to be sued and prosecuted. Other local authorities such as county and metropolitan districts, e.g. High Peak Borough in Derbyshire and Wolverhampton in the West Midlands, are all legal bodies existing separately from the councillors. The powers of these local authorities are provided by the Local Government Act 1972 and, like companies, local authorities must not exceed the powers given them under this Act because if they do, like companies, they will be acting *ultra vires*. As the following case shows. In *London Borough of Bromley* v. *Greater London Council* (1982), it was held *ultra vires* and unlawful for the GLC to subsidise public transport out of rates in the way in which it had done so.

In addition to local authorities, there are also what are called nationalised corporations which have been set up by Act of Parliament, e.g. National Coal, the British Rail, the South East Electricity Board are just a few of the many nationalised bodies which all have legal status and all have powers laid down under the Act of Parliament which set them up. The National Coal Board like any other nationalised body may not exceed its powers, i.e. act *ultra vires*.

Exercise 7

Try to answer the following questions which all relate to types of business organisation. Check your answers and if there is anything you do not understand then refer to the chapter again.

1 John Hartley decides to set up business as market gardener; he calls his business *Garden Produce*. He contracts to sell £1000 of produce to a local restaurant, who refuse to pay the bill claiming that John has not complied with the need to display the name *Garden Produce*. Would John be able to claim his money?

2 Name the Act which regulates partnerships in this country.

3 What is the minimum and maximum number of partners allowed in a partnership?

4 David Stuart, managing director of Smalldale Engineering Co. Ltd, is sued in the courts for recovery of debts incurred by the company. Advise David as to whether he would need to pay.

5 A company has legal status separate from its members. Name two other types of organisation which have similar legal status.
6 Name the certificate which brings a company into existence.

BANKRUPTCY AND LIQUIDATION

10.1 BANKRUPTCY

John Smith has been employed as a garage mechanic for about ten years with a large motor company in Exeter. He has always wanted to go into business and an opportunity presents itself when a small garage with showroom and petrol pumps becomes available on the outskirts of Exeter. John set up business operating under the name of Merton (Motors). John has no real experience in running his own business and after about a year of trading he finds that he is quite heavily in debt. With trade particularly poor in all aspects of his business, i.e. in petrol sales, servicing and second-hand cars, he cannot see any prospect of settling the following outstanding debts:

£353	*to the local authority for rates*
£1500	*to Associated Motors for spares*
£8500	*to Quality Cars Ltd for three second-hand cars*
£3000	*to United Motor Equipment Ltd for garage equipment, tools, testing gear, etc.*
£5300	*to a leading petrol company for petrol*
£120	*to Allcock & Sons Ltd, a local builder, for building repairs*

John is very anxious about these debts and would like an opportunity to get rid of the embarrassment and to make a fresh start. The creditors, i.e. the firms, etc. to which John owes money are anxious that they get some payment. Obviously whatever is available ought to be shared out by some fair method.

Dealing with such problems is the object of bankruptcy. In the last chapter we considered the various types of business organisation. Sole traders and partnerships can go bankrupt, but companies can only be liquidated. In this section we will be considering the law of bankruptcy and liquidation.

John Smith is a sole trader and therefore can be made bankrupt. We will use this example to explain the law of bankruptcy. The law relating to bankruptcy is laid down in the Bankruptcy Act 1986. In order for proceedings in bankruptcy to be commenced it is necessary to show that the debtor (i.e. John Smith) has committed an act of bankruptcy. There are a number of different acts of bankruptcy but it will be sufficient to define the most common act of bankruptcy as where 'The debtor gives notice to any of his creditors that he has suspended or that he is about to suspend payment of his debts.'

The notice to the creditors may take a number of forms and it is sufficient that the notice is inferred (assumed) by the debtor's behaviour. Thus John would either indicate to his creditors that he cannot pay his debts or show by his failure to respond to demands from his creditors that he cannot pay. If John received a number of letters from Associated Motors demanding settlement of the £1500 and he did not reply then it would be treated as though he had committed an act of bankruptcy, as though he had sent the notice. A creditor may only petition if the debt is £750 or more. Associated Motors are well above this minimum.

Exercise 1

1 A company may be declared bankrupt. *true/false*?
2 What are the two main objects of bankruptcy?
3 Give one example of an act of bankruptcy.

The Petition

When an act of bankruptcy has been committed either the debtor (John) or one or more of the creditors can present a petition. As we have seen, only creditors who have £750 or more owed can present a petition, though two creditors such as the local authority and Allcock & Sons may combine to present a petition.

We will assume that Associated Motors, who have a debt of £1500 owed to them, decide to present the petition. The petition is really a request to the court, i.e. the County Court in that area where the debtor resides, to make a receiving order against John. The petitioner (Associated Motors) must prove three things:

1 that a debt existed, i.e. that they had supplied spares to John's business and had not been paid;
2 that John had committed an act of bankruptcy, i.e. that he had not paid his debt despite requests;
3 that the petition had been presented.

A Receiving Order

If we assume that Associated Motors can prove these three things to the court then the court, if satisfied with the facts set out, will make a receiving order against the debtor. Under this order an Official Receiver is appointed who has legal rights over all John's property. Nothing can happen to John's property without the permission of the Official Receiver.

1 The receiving order is published in the *London Gazette* and a local newspaper.
2 If it is felt that John's business is still a going concern then the Official Receiver will put in a manager to run the business on his behalf.
3 The fact of a possible bankruptcy will be registered against John's name at the Land Charges Registry so that if John tried to sell his house he would be effectively prevented from doing so because no solicitor would advise a client to buy a house from John in these circumstances. Solicitors acting for a purchaser of a house will always check the Land Charges Registry for bankruptcy.

Exercise 2

1 What three things must be proved by a petitioner in bankruptcy proceedings?
2 Who is appointed as a result of a receiving order?
3 In which two publications must receiving orders be advertised?
4 Why is it difficult for a person facing bankruptcy proceedings to sell his own private house?

Seven days after the presentation of the petition John will be required to submit a statement of his affairs to the Official Receiver. This statement, which must be a sworn statement, usually before a solicitor, must contain:

1 Full particulars of John's assets (all that he owns) and liabilities (all that he owes).
2 The names and addresses of the creditors. Any creditor can examine this statement.

Creditors' Meeting

Within fourteen days of the receiving order a meeting of creditors is called. At this meeting John has an opportunity to present a scheme of arrangement or composition in which he could say how he proposed to meet his debts. If this is not acceptable to the creditors or where John does not present a scheme then the creditors will petition the court that John be declared bankrupt.

Public Examination

John will be asked to attend a public examination where his conduct, dealings and property will be examined. He will be examined on oath and must answer any questions. If John fails to attend he could be arrested. It is likely that John will be adjudged (declared) bankrupt by the court, in which case a trustee to look after his affairs will be appointed; the effect of this is that John has certain disqualifications:

1 He cannot become a Member of Parliament.
2 He cannot become a Justice of the Peace (magistrate).
3 He cannot become a local authority councillor.
4 He cannot obtain credit.

The trustee will then arrange for John's property to be disposed of so that his creditors can be paid. Creditors must prove the existence of debts. From the money available the trustee must pay the costs of the proceedings, the Official Receiver's fee, take any fees owing to himself, and pay employees if necessary. Rates are regarded as a preferential debt so that these are paid before any other debts. If any money is left over this will be shared out among the creditors.Thus for example 25p in the £ may be declared by the trustee and in this case Associated Motors would receive £375.00, i.e. £1500 ÷ 4.

Discharge of a Bankrupt

John may apply to the court for a discharge and the application is heard in open court. The court may if satisfied grant John:

1 an absolute discharge, so that he is no longer a bankrupt;
2 a conditional discharge, which means that John will get a discharge if he has satisfied certain conditions, e.g. made certain payments;
3 the court may refuse a discharge.

There are certain circumstances in which a court will never give an absolute discharge; some of these are:

1 if John brought about his bankruptcy by gambling or by unjustifiable extravagance or neglect of his business;
2 if after the receiving order he gave preference to a creditor, e.g. he paid United Motor Equipment in full thereby leaving the other creditors less;
3 if he had not within three years of the bankruptcy kept accounts.

If John does get a discharge then he is released from all his debts, except debts to the Crown. He will not be released, for example, from a tax debt.

Exercise 3

1 What might John do to avoid bankruptcy at the creditors' meeting which must take place within fourteen days of the receiving order?
2 What four types of disqualifications might a bankrupt suffer?
3 Before creditors are paid from a bankrupt's assets name three other costs which must be paid.
4 Name three circumstances in which a court will never discharge a bankrupt.

10.2 LIQUIDATION

Fortray Coach Tours Co. Ltd is a private company operating in the South West of England. In the past the company has been very successful in promoting coach tours to some of the best parts of Devon and Cornwall. However, due to escalating operational costs and the twin effect of the poor weather and recession the company has a disastrous year and finds that it is unable to meet four very heavy bills:

1. *A petrol account with a local garage, Torbay Garage Ltd, amounting to £2400*
2. *A repair bill with another garage Exeter Road Garage Ltd, of £3000.*
3. *Rent for its main booking office in Torquay to Atlantic Properties Co. Ltd, amounting to £5600.*
4. *Hire charges to another coach firm of £9000.*

This is very similar to the situation in which John found himself in the previous section, but in this case because Fortray Coach Tours Co. Ltd is a company it cannot be declared bankrupt. In fact the only way this situation can be dealt with is by liquidation. The law as it relates to liquidation will be dealt with in this section. You will remember from the last chapter that a company is regarded as a 'legal person' and because of this its existence can only be terminated by a legal process, the legal process known as liquidation or winding up. Liquidation means to make the company's assets liquid, or in other words to turn the assets into money. Winding up, which means bringing to a conclusion the company's existence, is part of the same process.

There are three ways in which a company may be liquidated or wound up

Compulsory Winding Up

Fortray Coach Tours Co. Ltd may be wound up by the court compulsorily under the following circumstances:

1 It is unable to pay its debts.
2 It fails to hold a meeting as laid down in the Companies Acts, i.e. a statutory meeting.
3 It does not commence business within a year of its formation or it suspends business for a year or more.
4 The number of members/shareholders falls below the statutory minimum, which you will remember is two.

In Fortray Coach Tours' case it is the company's inability to pay its debts which is the problem; usually it is one of the creditors who petitions the court for a winding up order.

Exercise 4

1 Explain the terms 'liquidation' and 'winding up'.
2 Under what circumstances may a court make a compulsory winding up order?

Let us then assume that Torquay Garage Ltd who are owed £2400 request the court for a winding up order. If the court is satisfied that the company cannot pay its debts it will order that Fortray Coach Tours Co. Ltd be wound up. The Official Receiver is appointed as liquidator and he will ask Fortray Coach Tours Co. Ltd's directors to prepare a statement of affairs which will list Fortray's assets, i.e. two coaches, second-hand value £5000 each equals £10 000; office equipment £1500; bank account £500; total £12 000. Liabilities - the bills amounting to £20 000. There is then a deficit of £8000 and the Official Receiver will present this information to the court giving some explanation for the company's failure.

The Official Receiver's task is to realise the company's assets and distribute them to the creditors. We have seen that by selling the company's assets £12 000 will be realised. The Receiver will then prepare two lists - list A the present shareholders, and list B, any shareholder who has held shares with the company in the year before liquidation.

As we have seen, shareholders are only liable to the extent of their shareholding but companies sometimes only require shareholders to pay a proportion of the share, e.g 75p in the £1 share; therefore there is 25p unpaid. If still the company debts cannot be paid list B may be called upon and these former shareholders may be liable for the extent of their former holdings of shares.

Let us assume that all shareholders are fully paid up in Fortray and there is no list B, then the Official Receiver declares a dividend to the creditors of 60p in the £1 because he can only meet 60 per cent (12 000) of the debt of £20 000.

> **Exercise 5**
>
> If the liquidator declares a dividend of 60p in the £ how much will Torquay Garage Ltd get?

Each creditor must prove to the Official Receiver the existence of the debt.

Voluntary Winding Up

Compulsory winding up usually arises as a result of the action of a creditor petitioning the court but the company can decide to wind itself up because it wishes to discontinue business or amalgamate with another company. If the directors of the company declare that it can meet its debts then the members (shareholders) of the company wind it up; but if the company is insolvent i.e. cannot meet its debts, then it is the creditors who wind it up.

In both cases a liquidator is appointed who takes over from the directors. He converts the assests of the company into money and uses the money to pay off any debts, paying any balance to the shareholders.

The liquidator then sends a return to the Registrar of Companies. This return is registered and three months following the registration the company is deemed to have been dissolved.

Winding Up Under the Court's Supervision

There are certain circumstances where even though a company is being wound up voluntarily it is felt that it would be better done under the supervision of the court and the court appoints an additional liquidator to make sure everything is done fairly.

> **Exercise 6**
>
> **1** Name the three ways in which a company may be wound up.
> **2** Peter White a local printer is owed £250 for printing done for Chapel Engineering Co. Ltd. The company is wound up and a dividend of 30p is declared. How much will Peter get?
> **3** United Meat Company is sued by a creditor three months after it has been voluntarily wound up. Advise the creditor.

Exercise 7

Answer the following questions which are based upon Sections 10.1 and 10.2 of this chapter. If when checking your answers you find that you have not understood any particular part go over that part again.

1 Sterndale Engineering Co. is owed a sum of £950 for machine repairs by Fraser Bros, a small partnership. Fraser Bros are heavily in debt and cannot pay this bill. How can Sterndale Engineering Co. obtain all or some of its money?
2 What is a receiving order?
3 Who is appointed when a person is adjudged bankrupt?
4 Ashford Machine Tool Co. Ltd is facing compulsory winding up. Its liabilities are £40 000 in unpaid debts. Its assets are £20 000 for buildings, 16 000 £1 shares (unpaid portion 25p), 200 shareholders who have left the company within a year with shareholdings of £4000, other equipment £2000. Calculate the dividend payable to the creditors.

CHAPTER 11

BUSINESS PROPERTY

11.1 BUYING A BUSINESS

Reg Pullin has been employed for a number of years as a sales clerk in a large company producing cardboard containers. As a result of a down-turn in trade the company decide to try to shed staff by a voluntary redundancy policy Reg has been for a long time interested in running his own business and he sees the following advert in a newspaper:

> Village Newsagent/General Stores and Sub-Post Office in pleasant area in the Peak District. Attractive detached property with 4 bed-rooms, 2 reception rooms, modern bathroom and 2 w.c.s. Full gas fired central heating. Lawned garden. Takings: £2400 per week, plus Post Office salary £12 000. Price: £108 000.

Reg is very interested and he and his wife Lynne are even more keen when they view the property. He decides to sell his own house for £68 000 and to use his redundancy money of £20 000 to purchase the post office/newsagents. He decides to see his bank manager, who agrees to advance him the remaining £20 000 over fifteen years.

Reg makes an offer of £108 000, which is accepted 'subject to contract' by the sellers, Mr and Mrs Reaney.

The £108 000 which Reg has agreed to pay really is made up of two elements:

1 the property, let us say £70 000; and
2 the business itself, i.e. what is sometimes called the goodwill, £38 000.

In this section we will be seeing how a business can be acquired; the difference between acquiring a freehold in a business and acquiring just the business, i.e. a tenancy. It would have been possible for Mr and Mrs Reaney to have kept the property and just sold the business for £38 000 for perhaps a twenty-year lease, in which case they could have charged Reg a rent of let us say £6000 per annum.

However, as we have seen the Reaneys are selling the property freehold which means that on completion Reg will own the property and the business. The Reaneys are selling two things: the property at £70 000 and the business at £38 000.

How then can the property and the business pass from the ownership of Mr and Mrs Reaney to Reg? It is most likely that both parties will employ the services of a solicitor and although the property and the business will be sold simultaneously, for simplicity's sake it might be better if we dealt with the two transactions separately.

Property

This is being sold for £70 000 and Reg's solicitor would first raise what are called 'preliminary enquiries'; these are just questions to the solicitor acting for Mr and Mrs Reaney about the property in question, which we will describe as 24 Edale Road, Bakewell, Derbyshire. At the same time Reg's solicitor would make what are called local searches with the local authority. These local authority searches are an attempt to ensure that no plans are being made by the local authority which might affect the property, e.g. the building of a road.

When satisfactory replies are received from both the seller's (vendor's) solicitor and the local authority, Reg's solicitor will ask Reg to sign the contract which has been sent to him by the vendor's solicitor. Reg's solicitor will send the signed contract with a 10 per cent deposit, i.e. £7000, to Mr and Mrs Reaney's solicitor, and he should receive back an identical contract signed by Paul and Anne Reaney. This process is known as 'exchange of contracts' and this means that Reg is legally bound to buy and Paul and Anne must sell. Until an exchange of contracts is made either buyer (Reg) or seller (Paul and Anne) may pull out of the deal. Once contracts are exchanged then both buyer and seller are legally bound.

If the buyer (Reg) decided not to proceed following exchange of contracts, then he would lose his deposit. If Paul and Anne decided against completing the sale even though they have exchanged contracts, then they would be sued for damages and in some circumstances, the court may award 'specific performance', i.e. make Paul and Anne complete their side of the agreement. An example of a contract was shown on page 58.

Exchange of contracts to completion. Reg's solicitor must now do four things.

1 He must satisfy himself that Paul and Anne Reaney really own the land they are selling and he will do this by closely examining copies of all the documents relating to the property. The copies will have been supplied to him by the solicitor acting for the Reaneys.
2 He must also make searches at the Land Charges Office in Plymouth. (Derbyshire is not an area of compulsory registration. In many parts of

the country properties are registered and searches are made at the nearest land registry.) These searches will reveal the existence of any problems in respect of Mr and Mrs Reaney. For example, as we learned in Chapter 10, if the Reaneys were bankrupt, and therefore not entitled to sell 24 Edale Road, this would be revealed. It is most likely that a certificate will come back to Reg's solicitor in respect of Paul and Anne Reaney marked 'no subsisting entry', which means that there are no problems in respect of the vendors.

3 You will remember that Reg is buying the property with the aid of a mortgage of £20 000 and it will be necessary for Reg's solicitor to draw up a mortgage deed, which is a document which creates a mortgage and means that the bank advancing the money has a right to the property should Reg default in his monthly payments.

4 Finally, Reg's solicitor would draw up a conveyance, which is a document signed, sealed and delivered; when signed by both parties, i.e. Paul and Anne Reaney, the vendors, and Reg, the purchaser, the conveyance transfers the property. 'Sealed' means attaching a seal against each signature. Each signature must be witnessed, e.g.:

Signed Sealed and Delivered
in the presence of

(Signature of Witness)

Reg now owns the property, which is mortgaged to a bank, and he will have to pay monthly instalments to the bank for fifteen years. Reg is known as the mortgagor and the bank the mortgagee.

Exercise 1

1 The vendor is not legally obliged to sell property until contracts are exchanged. *true/false*?
2 Name one reason why the purchaser's solicitor makes a search in the Land Registry.
3 Name the document which transfers ownership of land.
4 If the document transferring land is not signed sealed and delivered it has no legal significance. *true/false*?
5 Name the mortgagor and the mortgagee in the following circumstances: Colin Elderson buys a DIY shop with the aid of a mortgage from Commercial Credit Co. Ltd.

The property known as 24 Edale Road, Bakewell, is now owned by Reg though in the transfer he would have had to pay a government tax known as stamp duty. On £70 000 the current rate is 1 per cent, which means Reg would have paid £700. To show that this has been paid the conveyance, which will remain with the mortgagee until Reg has paid off the loan, will be stamped with an official government stamp.

In this example, the legal document transferring ownership was a conveyance. This was because as we have seen the area of Derbyshire in question is not an area of compulsory registration. Many areas in the country are areas of compulsory registration. In Chapter 2 we looked at the transfer of a property in Kent. This was registered property and the process was slightly different. One difference was that instead of a conveyance, a transfer was used.

Activity

Try to find out if the area you live in is an area of compulsory registration.

The Business

At the same time as the property is transferred the Reaneys would sell the business. The cost of this was £38 000. This really is the price put on the business by the Reaneys and of course will depend upon how successful the business is. Reg's solicitor would draw up a document known as an 'assignment' which when signed, sealed and delivered would transfer (assign) the business from Paul and Anne Reaney to Reg. What is being sold is sometimes known as the goodwill of the business. Again the government charge a stamp duty on an assignment which on £38 000 is at present 1 per cent, i.e. £380. The evidence of the payment is stamped on the assignment. Reg now owns both property and the business and usually at the same time he buys the stock at cost. Many commercial properties are transferred on a Monday so that the vendor and purchaser can spend the weekend stocktaking. This will allow them to calculate a price for the stock, let us say £10 000. This is a normal sale and does not carry any stamp duty.

Reg is anxious that Mr and Mrs Reaney do not sell the business to him and then start up again nearby because this could seriously affect the business. It is usual, therefore for the purchaser of a business to require the vendor to sign a covenant that the vendor will not open up a similar business for three years within a three-mile radius of the business they have sold. Courts will if they regard such a clause as reasonable enforce it against the vendor. If, however, a purchaser inserts a clause which is too restrictive, e.g. not to start a business for ten years in Derbyshire, then this would not be enforced; since it could not be enforced the vendors Mr and Mrs Reaney could open up a similar business next door. It is important that a buyer of a business seeks legal advice before drawing up a covenant of this type to make sure it is not too wide. This particular aspect was dealt with more fully in Chapter 2.

Exercise 2

1 How can one check that stamp duty has been paid?
2 Name the document which transfers ownership of a business.
3 The value of stock sold at completion carries stamp duty. *true/false*?
4 Lewis Williams buys a milk round from Unicorn Dairies Ltd. He requires the sellers to sign a document that they will not deliver milk within a forty-mile radius for ten years. Unicorn sign this but then start competing with Lewis directly. Lewis seeks your advice.

Tenancy of Business Property

Instead of selling the property, Mr and Mrs Reaney could lease (let) the property and sell the business. The selling of the business would be the same as described above. An assignment would be drawn up transferring the business for £38 000. The property could be leased at a rental, let us say £6000 per annum for a period of twenty years. The lease would be granted to Reg by means of a document known as a lease which again would need to be signed, sealed and delivered. The property would still be owned by Paul and Anne Reaney and if Reg subsequently decided to sell the business he would:

1 sell the business by means of an assignment;
2 provided Paul and Anne were in agreement he could assign the lease to the buyer.

One of the problems in taking out a lease is that if the lessee, as Reg would be called, built up a successful business Paul and Anne Reaney may not renew the lease when it expired in twenty years. This would be clearly unfair to someone like Reg who had worked hard to develop a good business. Fortunately tenants such as Reg are given protection by the Landlord and Tenant Act 1954 which allows tenants who are operating businesses to seek a renewal of their lease, and the courts will often assist in setting the terms of the renewed lease. Landlords (Paul and Anne) can get tenants out only under strictly prescribed conditions. All the following three conditions must exist:

1 where the tenant has been unsuitable;
2 where a landlord has owned the property for the last five years at least and wants the property for himself;
3 where the landlord wishes to make an extensive redevelopment of the property in question.

Generally, however, the Landlord and Tenant Act gives good protection to a business tenant wishing to renew his lease.

Exercise 3

Answer the following questions, which are based upon this section. If you have any difficulty with any of the questions read the section again.

1 Susan Rownes (a hair stylist) buys a hairdressing salon from a firm owned by June Greatorex. Susan obtains a covenant in which the vendor (June) agrees not to work as a hairdresser within a two-mile radius of the shop and for three years. After a year the vendor states a hairdressing business down the road. Can Susan do anything about this?

2 If a business tenant wished to sell his business he would transfer the lease by means of a document known as

3 Name the Act which protects a business tenant from eviction at the end of the lease.

4 Elizabeth Moore is a wealthy landlord who has owned four shops for about three years which are on lease. One of the shops is run by Franklin Welch, who has a thriving small self-service store. The lease has only six months to run and Elizabeth gives Franklin notice that she wishes the shop for herself and that she has bought adjoining property and wishes to make an extensive development. Is Franklin at risk?

11.2 PATENTS AND COPYRIGHTS

Patents

John Paget works for a small partnership of central heating engineers. John has had little training but is very able and he discovers a simple device which seems to have great potential for fuel saving. In fact, simple tests suggest that using the device the same heat output can be achieved at 20 per cent less cost. The two partners, Roy Peckham and Dave Bennett, realise that this is a most valuable invention and suggest that john becomes a partner in the firm and that he gets his invention patented.

It seems fair that if someone makes an invention they ought to get some financial benefit from it. The patent law which is contained in the Patents Act 1977 gives an inventor twenty years of monopoly, in other words only he can develop the invention in question. In this section we will be examining the law of patent. Because John has become a partner it will be necessary for him to apply for a patent with his two other partners, Roy and Dave.

The application is in a number of stages:

1 The applicants, i.e. the three partners, send in an application form to the Patents Office in Southampton Buildings, London. Accompanying this application will be a specification which gives full details of the invention together with appropriate drawings.
2 The application is examined in detail. Because of the pressure of work at the Patents Office often it will be twelve months before this examination takes place.
3 The Patents Office will search their records to make sure that no other invention exists of this sort. If the invention has already been published then the application may be refused.
4 The specification is then published and a period of three months is given during which anyone can give notice that they oppose the grant of a patent and a procedure is laid down to hear the basis on which there is opposition.
5 If there is no opposition or if the opposition is not upheld then the Patents Office will grant a patent to the partnership in question, which would give to John, Roy and Dave a monopoly in the production of this device for twenty years. This process of granting a patent is known sometimes as sealing a patent.

The law relating to patents is designed so that inventors can obtain the benefit of inventions and it is designed to promote inventions and developments. John instead of becoming a partner could have assigned his rights in the invention to Roy and Dave. Once someone has been granted a patent he may if he wishes assign this to someone else who then will become the patent holder with the resultant benefits.

Exercise 4

1 How long do rights under a patent last?
2 An inventor can give up his rights by means of
3 What is the period following publication allowed for opposition to patents?

Copyright

As we have just seen, it is possible for an individual or a business to hold a patent, the effect of which is to give twenty years' protection to develop the particular invention which is the subject of the patent. The law of patents is designed to encourage inventions because it allows the inventor or someone to whom he has assigned his rights the chance to enjoy the financial benefits which might result. In a similar way individuals and businesses can enjoy copyright in connection with their work. Copyright can apply to works of art, music, drama and writing. The following example will help to illustrate the law relating to copyright as laid down in the Copyright Act 1956 and various amendments in 1982 and 1983.

New Music Discovery Co. Ltd is a small but very prosperous and expanding company which has concentrated upon recording new music groups, often giving them a chance with their first recording. A number of top stars have been launched with the New Discovery label. The two directors of the company Bob Bown and Toby Edwards, are well versed in the copyright law and they get each group or singer to sign an agreement which gives them a set commission on sales. Attracted by the success of the company, one of the employees, David Pryce, forms a partnership known as David Pryce Associates (Musical). David continues to work for New Music Discovery Ltd but takes home taped recordings which he records and makes his own records which he sells under his own label. This proves a very lucrative business and begins to threaten New Music Discovery Co. Ltd's sales and profits.

The legal position is quite straightforward. When New Music Discovery Co. Ltd negotiated with the singers and obtained signed agreements providing for commission on sales, usually 6¼ per cent, the copyright which originally belongs to the performer became vested in the launch of the maker, i.e. New Music Discovery Co. Ltd. Copyright under the Copyright Act 1956 lasts for fifty years from the end of the calendar year in which the record was made. The only way in which David Pryce Associates could lawfully produce a record is where New Music Discovery Co. Ltd. had given the firm a licence to do this. Clearly this is not the case and therefore David Pryce Associates have infringed the copyright belonging to New Music Discovery Co. Ltd.

New Music Discovery Co. Ltd could sue David Pryce and his partners in the High Court and possibly obtain damages for lost profits and also an injunction – an order saying that David Pryce and his associates should cease copying material belonging to New Music Discovery Co. Ltd.

Copyright for fifty years is also available for literary and dramatic works in addition to musical work. Thus it is an infringement of copyright to:

1 reproduce the work;
2 publish the work;
3 perform the work in public;
4 broadcast the work;
5 make any form of adaptation of the work;
6 allow it to be recorded for transmission to subscribers, e.g. through a video recording service.

Painters also can gain protection for their work through copyright and for artistic work it is an infringement of copyright to:

1 reproduce the work;
2 publish the work;
3 include the work in a TV broadcast.

A good deal of work is covered by copyright and before anyone attempts to copy or reproduce someone else's work it is always wise to see whether copyright is being infringed. Copying BBC material would certainly be an infringement because the British Broadcasting Corporation is entitled to fifty years' copyright on any television or sound broadcast. Copyright laws do not extend to a person's home and it is quite safe to reproduce material at home for home consumption. If this were not the case then people with video recorders would be breaking the law every time they made a recording of any television programme. However, if these recordings are made available to the public then copyright has been infringed. There are certain other exemptions possible but recently educational establishments have been shown that their activities are not beyond copyright. Oakham School in Leicestershire has had to pay extensive damages for copying sheet music which was covered by copyright.

Activity

Look at records or books to see if you can find statements expressing the copyright which exists.

A common form used in books is as follows: 'All rights reserved. No part of this publication may be reproduced or transmitted in any form or by any means including photocopying and recording without the written permission of the copyright holder application for which should be addressed to the publisher. Such written permission must be obtained before any part of this publication is stored in a retrieval system of any nature.' If you look at the front of this book you will find a notice to this effect which protects the publisher. By the Copyright (Computer Software) Amendment Act 1985 copyright has been extended to computer software. It is also important to note that unlike patents copyright need not be registered but arises automatically at publication.

Exercise 5

Answer the following questions which relate to copyright.

1 How long does copyright last?
2 What remedies, and in which court, exist for a person or business if their copyright has been infringed?
3 Is it legal to copy material produced by the BBC?
4 Examine the following and say whether you think the person

in italics has infringed copyright.

(a) *Mrs Linda Brazier* works until 7.30 each night and always records the nightly episode of *Eastenders* so that she can see it when she gets home.

(b) *Wellings (Publications) Ltd* have produced a book of contemporary art and many of the photographs have been taken from various art exhibitions around the country.

(c) *Dr John Hartley* is writing a scientific article and he writes to a publisher asking if he can reproduce a diagram from a book. The publisher gives him written permission.

11.3 OWNERSHIP OF A COMPANY

In Section 1 we learned how a business could be acquired. You will remember that Reg and his wife bought a shop. It is possible for individuals to own companies by holding shares, though in many cases the shareholders do not have anything to do with running the company. In this section we are concerned with ownership of companies, considering the different forms of shareholding.

Dr Michael Harper has set up in business producing scientific instruments. A very successful start results in a company being established known as Harper (Scientific Instruments) Co. Ltd. A number of very lucrative contracts with overseas educational organisations result in a need for expansion, and the firm becomes a public company. The following indicates the company's capital structure:

£1 million in £1 ordinary shares
£250 000 in £1 8 per cent preference shares
£150 000 in £1 8 per cent debenture stock

The capital is made up in three different ways but only those people holding shares are owners of the company, i.e. the first two categories. In this section we will be examining the rights and obligations which go with company shareholdings and also we will be considering the position of those who hold debentures.

Ordinary Shareholders

In our example there are one million £1 ordinary shares.

Each share carries one vote in the annual meeting of the company. There is no limit to the number of shares one person has, so if Michael Harper holds 250 000 then he will have 250 000 votes.

Ordinary shares are sometimes known as equity shares because each shareholder has one vote for every share he holds.

A shareholder is entitled to a share of the company's profit (known as a dividend – a dividing of the profit). The amount of dividend will depend upon:

1 the company's profit position; and
2 the proportion of the company's profits which the directors wish to distribute to shareholders. Many companies will use a proportion of the profits for the company, they will in other words 'plough back' the profits. The government will often give a tax incentive to firms if they plough back their profits in investment.

Dividends will often be declared as so much in the £, e.g. 10p in the £, which is equivalent to 10 per cent profit.

While ordinary shareholders have a chance to benefit from high profits, by the same token they may lose from low profits because when profits are being distributed they come after preference shareholders and debenture holders; e.g. if Harper (Scientific Instruments) made only £32 000 profit in a particular year by the time it had paid 250 000 × 8 per cent to the preference shareholders (£20 000) and 150 000 × 8 per cent to debenture holders (£12 000) there would be nothing to distribute to the ordinary shareholders.

If Harper (Scientific Instruments) after poor sales, resulting in an inability to pay its debts, should have to be liquidated, shareholders could only lose what they had invested. Thus if David Hogg had 100 £1 shares in the company then this £100 is the total amount he could lose. This is because the company is limited: each shareholder's liability for the company's debts is limited to the extent of his holding.

It is often the case that not all the £1 shares are called up (i.e. paid), so for example shareholders may have 20 per cent (20p) unpaid. The directors can call up the unpaid proportion at any time and if a company is going into liquidation the unpaid-up portion must be paid to meet the company's debts.

Finally, when a company has been liquidated and there is money left over after all the debts have been paid, the preference shareholders get first right to the money outstanding and only when they have been paid (given preference) will ordinary shareholders be paid. If there is any money left they may be given perhaps 50 per cent of their holding, i.e. 50p for each £1 share.

These aspects of liquidation were dealt with, as you remember, in the last chapter.

Exercise 6

Answer the following questions.

1 Each shareholder in a company is given one vote. *true/false*?
2 What are the two factors which determine an ordinary share-

holder's dividend?
3 An ordinary shareholder with a holding of £250 000 in a company might have to sell his own house to pay the company's debts. *true/false*?
4 Explain what you understand by the term preference shares.

Preference Shareholders

Harper (Scientific Instruments) Co. Ltd has 250 000 £1 8 per cent preference shareholders. A preference shareholder differs from an ordinary shareholder in the following ways. A preference shareholder has no vote in the company's annual meeting. A preference shareholder is entitled to a fixed interest, i.e. 8p in the £ or 8 per cent. This 8 per cent will never vary unless of course the company makes insufficient profit to pay out.

The preference shareholder will take preference over the ordinary shareholder (1) if the company is being liquidated, (2) when the profits of the company are being distributed the preference shareholder will always get his 8 per cent first.

Like an ordinary shareholder a preference shareholder enjoys limited liability and can lose only what he has put into the company. However, if the preference shareholder has a proportion of his share still to be paid up then this unpaid proportion can be demanded.

Debenture Holders

Harper (Scientific Instruments) has issued 150 000 £1 debentures at 8 per cent. A debenture holder is not a shareholder and has no rights of ownership. A debenture holder is a creditor, i.e. the company owes him money. Thus if the company is being liquidated the debenture holder like any other creditor will have to be paid before the shareholders are paid.

The debenture holder will receive a fixed interest of 8 per cent, i.e. 8p for every £1, and if this is not paid then just like any other creditor a debenture holder in certain circumstances has the right to appoint a receiver or present a petition to wind up the company.

There are two types of debentures:

1 A debenture secured by way of a fixed charge – this means that the debenture is tied to a fixed asset of the company, e.g. it may have been raised to buy a particular piece of machinery. In this case where the company defaults (fails to pay) in payment of interest to the debenture holder then the debenture holder has the right to bring an action in the courts to force the company to sell the machine to pay its debts.
2 Debentures may be secured by a floating charge, which means the

debenture is not tied to any particular asset and is related to the company's assets as a whole. A holder of a debenture secured by a floating charge cannot bring an action to sell any specific assets.

Exercise 7

1 Name three ways in which a preference shareholder differs from an ordinary shareholder in relation to the company in question.
2 A debenture holder is an owner of a company. *true/false*?
3 A debenture tied to a particular asset is known as a floating charge. *true/false*?
4 Disdale Administrative and Secretarial Services Co. Ltd make a profit after tax of £50 000. The directors decide plough back £17 500. The company has 10 000 £1 debenture holders at 5 per cent and 20 000 £1 preference shareholders at 10 per cent. How much in the £ will be dividend to the 60 000 shareholders?

Exercise 8

Answer the following questions which all relate to Chapter 11. Check your answers and if you have any difficulty read the particular section again.

1 Frank Harris (Funeral Services) sells a lucrative business to George Giles. Frank is asked to sign an agreement that he will not start up a funeral business for twenty years within a 100-mile radius. Two years later Frank starts a funeral business next door to George. George decides to sue Frank. Advise George.
2 Susan McCarthy has just bought the freehold in a business which is leased to Mark Stacey who runs a turf accountant business. Mark is anxious to renew the lease but Susan decides she wants the business for herself. Advise Mark.
3 Dave Stuart has patented a new revolutionary typewriter. A rival firm has somehow got the plans and is producing this typewriter. Advise Dave.
4 Janet Brown uses her video recorder to tape BBC documentaries which she sells to an overseas customer at enormous profit. The BBC decide to sue Janet. Advise Janet.
5 Dave Ogden has £100 worth of debentures in a company known as Murgia Italian Ware Co. Ltd. Dave goes along to the annual general meeting and demands 100 votes for each of his £1 debentures. Advise Dave.
6 Joyce Whitehead has 50 000 £1 shares but only 80p in the £ has

been paid up. The company in which Joyce has got her shares is badly in debt and following liquidation Joyce is asked to pay £10 000 and she refuses. Advise Joyce.

CHAPTER 12

CHEQUES

A cheque is a very common method of payment and, besides being used increasingly by individuals, it is also used extensively in business transactions. In this chapter, we are going to look at the law as it relates to cheques.

Let us assume for a moment that a small furniture firm, owned by two partners, R. and M. Spencer, trading under the name of Brassingtons, wishes to pay one of its suppliers Conquest (Furniture) Co. Ltd, the sum of £5430 by means of a cheque. R. and M. Spencer have their account at the Midland Bank and therefore the cheque will carry the Midland Bank Ltd name and symbol. The cheque is dated 28 December 1988.

The legal definition of cheque as defined in the Bill of Exchange Act 1882 is 'A Bill of Exchange drawn on a banker payable on demand'.

The Bill of Exchange Act defines a bill of exchange which also includes cheques as 'an unconditional order in writing addressed by one person to another, signed by the person giving it, requiring the person to whom it is addressed to pay on demand, or at a fixed or determinable future time, a sum certain in money to or to the order of a specified person or bearer.' This definition is very important. Notice particularly the following points:

1 The order must be unconditional; a mere request to pay is not enough.
2 The order must be in writing; no special form is needed. In practice banks supply their customers with ready-printed cheque forms which are convenient and help both to identify customers and to prevent fraud. However there are no legal rules on the particular form required.
3 The order must be signed by the person making the order, known as the drawer.
4 The order must be addressed by one person to another, known as the drawee. Where a specific person is named the bill is known as an order bill. If the bill is made payable to bearer it is known as a bearer bill. Where the drawer draws a bill on his own account for payment to himself he is both drawer and payee, the person to whom payment is to be made.

5 The order must be payable on demand or at a fixed or determinable future time. If no time is specified, the bill is a demand bill payable immediately. If a special date was given or a determinable future time was specified, e.g. twenty days after date, the bill is a 'time' bill. A demand bill becomes overdue if not presented within a reasonable time. There is no specific limit for this; banking practice is to treat cheques as overdue if not presented within six months. A 'time' bill is overdue if not presented on the date given or within three days.

In any cheque transaction there are always three parties:

1 The payee – the person in whose favour the cheque is drawn, i.e. Conquest (Furniture) Co. Ltd.
2 The drawer, the person ordering the payment. In this case there are two drawers, R. Spencer and M. Spencer, the two partners in the firm known as Brassingtons. The particular arrangement of this partnership is that there should be two signatories on cheques drawn on Brassingtons' account.
3 The drawee, i.e. the bank on which the cheque is drawn, in our case Midland Bank Ltd.

Exercise 1

Name the drawer, drawee and payee in the following transactions:

J. Fraser, who has an account with Barclays, pays £15.20 to Rock Base (Garage) Ltd, whose account is with National Westminster.

Cheques must always be payable on demand; this implies that a cheque can be presented to the bank for payment at any time. In fact, however, if a cheque is more than six months old, e.g. if Conquest Co. Ltd presented it on 1 August 1989, it would not be paid.

Cheques are usually written thus:

Pay Conquest (Furniture) Ltd or order.

'Or order' means that the Spencers have given instructions to their bank to pay Conquest or anyone else to whom Conquest transfers the cheque. Conquest may transfer the cheque to someone to pay one of its own debts.

If the payee (Conquest Co. Ltd) of a cheque wishes to pass it to someone else then he merely endorses it, i.e. he signs his name of the back.

In the situation relating to Conquest and R. and M. Spencer, Midland Bank is the banker with whom R. and M. Spencer have their account. The relationship which exists between banker and customer is that of debtor and creditor. The bank (the Midland) is the debtor because it owes money to the Spencers, who are therefore creditors.

When the partnership known as Brassingtons, i.e. R. and M. Spencer, opened an account with the Midland a *contract* was formed between the two parties: the Midland offered banking services which R. and M. Spencer will pay for by means of bank charges. This contract has certain implied conditions. First, that Midland will preserve confidentiality in respect of the Spencers' account. This means that the Midland will never disclose information about the account to anyone but the holders unless of course they are ordered to do so by a court.

The second duty imposed upon the bank is that it must honour (i.e. pay out on) any cheque drawn on the Spencers' account provided the account is:

1 in credit (there is enough money to meet the cheque in the Spencers' account, i.e. £5430) or
2 arrangements have been made for it to be overdrawn.

If the bank refuses to pay out (dishonours) a cheque and there were sufficient funds to meet it on the account on which it was drawn, then:

1 The bank might have to pay damages to the account holder. The damages would be for breach of contract because the bank has broken one of the implied conditions.
2 Where the cheque is returned to the payee (i.e. Conquest Co. Ltd) with 'Refer to Drawer' (R/D) printed on it the bank (the Midland) could be sued by the Spencers for libel. If a cheque is returned in this way this means that it has not been honoured and it can imply that the drawer (the Spencers) have not sufficient money in their account to pay the bill outstanding. This would be a suggestion of libel because:
   (a) It was communicated to a third party, Conquest.
   (b) It named the Spencers by implication since they were the drawers.
   (c) The statement R/D which carries an innuendo that the business has no money is capable of lowering 'the reputation of the Spencers in the eyes of right-thinking members of society'.

Where business is involved as in this case then damages could be substantial. In the case of a private individual damages would be nominal, i.e. of little value but designed to make the point that the defendant (the bank) was in the wrong.

Exercise 2

1 Name the two implied duties existing between a bank and its customer.
2 For what could a bank be sued if it failed to keep one or both of the two duties?

3 If Wendy Palmer had an account with National Westminster, who would be the debtor and who the creditor?
4 What does 'refer to drawer' usually mean?
5 When a cheque is not paid by the drawee bank it is said to be
6 In the contract between a bank and its customer, what is the consideration?

A bank's authority to pay cheques may be terminated (ended) in four ways. In each of these circumstances the bank will 'stop' the cheque, which means in effect when it is presented itis not paid. The following example will help to illustrate this.

Janet Davison runs a small secretarial agency. She has a bank account with Barclays. Janet pays for an electronic typewriter with a cheque for £1430.29 which she pays to IBL (Office Equipment) Ltd. Barclays' authority to pay this £1430.29 will be terminated in the following ways.

1 If Janet noticed a serious fault in the new typewriter on the day of delivery and on the day she paid the cheque to IBL she could if she wished 'stop' the cheque by instructing the bank in writing or orally that she did not wish them to pay out. Provided notice had been given before the cheque had been cleared (usually three days is the period for clearance) then the bank will not be entitled to debit Janet's account. In fact, if the bank does debit Janet's account by £1430.29 even though the notice has been given then the bank would be liable. It is quite clear that this should be so because the creditor (Janet) can instruct the debtor (the bank) to deal with her money as she wishes and the bank must follow her instructions. It must be remembered, however, that if the cheque is cleared (IBL has already been paid) then Janet could not 'stop' the cheque.
2 If the bank (Barclays) receives notification of Janet's death then it will immediately 'freeze' her account; any cheques which have not been cleared will not be paid out on, i.e. they will be stopped.
3 If a petition for a receiving order has been made then the account of the person against whom the petition has been made will be 'frozen' and all cheques still uncleared will be stopped.
4 If a receiving order has been made against the drawer (Janet) then the bank must stop all cheques. This is because as you will remember the Official Receiver becomes responsible for all Janet's financial affairs and therefore for her account.

Exercise 3

1 Explain the meaning of a 'stopped' cheque.
2 If a drawer wishes to prevent a cheque being paid how can he do it?
3 Name the four ways in which a cheque may be stopped.
4 Read the following example and advise the drawer:

Celia Bennett buys a tape recorder from Delta Music Store for £256. She pays this by cheque drawn on Lloyds. Celia feels she shouldn't have spent the £256 and the next day takes the tape recorder back to the shop and demands a money refund. The shop refuses and Celia writes to the bank telling them to 'stop' the cheque. The bank does not act upon this and Celia's account is debited.

We have already seen that in the contractual relationship existing between the bank and the customer the bank owes to the customer certain implied duties.

Exercise 4

Try to remember the two duties.

The customer also owes the bank certain duties which the following examples will illustrate.

Jane Smith works as a chief clerk for a firm of accountants. The firm owes her £45 for expenses she has incurred on the firm's behalf. Jane is told to prepare a cheque for this amount and she completes the figures but not the words, as shown below:

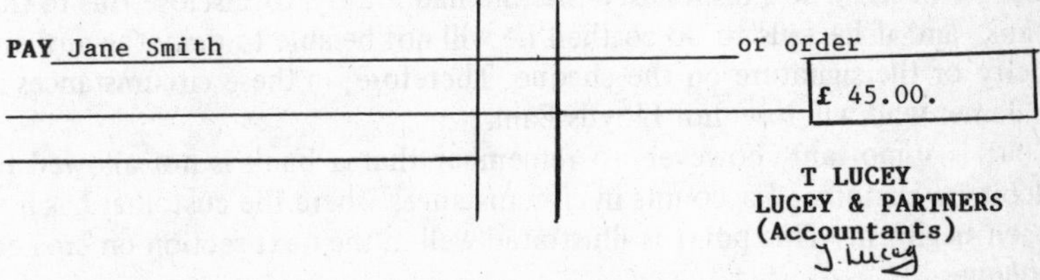

PAY Jane Smith or order

£ 45.00.

T LUCEY
LUCEY & PARTNERS
(Accountants)
J. Lucey

The senior partner, Terry Lucey, signs the cheque and Jane fills in the words as 'two hundred and forty-five' and she puts a 2 in front of the figures £45. She then cashes the cheque. Mr Lucey is very angry and sacks Jane and tells the bank that they ought to meet the loss, because after all the bank had paid out the money. However, a duty owed by a customer is that 'he must indemnify the bank against authorised payments made on his behalf'. Terry had been negligent in not insisting that the words be completed; he had through his negligence facilitated the forgery; therefore he, not the bank, is liable. Terry or the partnership must 'indemnify' the bank and therefore the partnership account will be debited by £245.

The first duty owed by the customer, then, is that he must meet the loss if cheques are drawn on his authority when he has perhaps been negligent.

A customer owes a duty to his banker when drawing cheques to take care. Where he does not the bank is not liable for money wrongly paid out. This is well illustrated by a decided case *London Joint Stock Bank* v. *Macmillan and Arthur* (1918).

In this case Macmillan signed a bearer cheque leaving the space to enter the amount in words blank, and entering £2 in the space for figures. Someone found the cheque which Macmillan had carelessly left lying around and wrote in the words 'one hundred and twenty pounds' and altered the figures accordingly. He presented the cheque and the bank cashed it. The bank was held entitled to debit Macmillan's account because of his negligence.

James Smith has an account with Lloyds and on several occasions his wife had forged his signature on a cheque and obtained cash from his account. She had admitted this to James but he decided to overlook it. Some months later, however, Mrs Smith decided to forge her husband's signature again on a cheque and she drew £250 from his account.

When Janes discovered this he rang the bank to say that since they had allowed payment on a forged signature then the bank should stand to lose.

However, the second duty owed by a customer to his bank is that he must take reasonable care when operating his account; if he has in the past known of his wife's dishonesty then he had a duty to disclose this to the bank, and if he fails to do so then he will not be able to deny the authenticity of the signature on the cheque. Therefore, in these circumstances it is James who will lose, not Lloyds Bank.

It is important, however, to remember that a bank is not allowed to debit its customers' accounts in circumstances where the customer has not been negligent. This point is illustrated well in the next section on crossed cheques.

Crossed Cheques

If you have a bank account you will probably find that the cheques you have been issued have a crossing in the middle of them usually, for example:

The meaning of a crossing is that the cheque cannot be cashed across the counter but must be paid into an account. Thus if Fred Wingfield received a cheque from David Willis for £50 which was crossed, Fred could either pay it into his account or ask someone who had an account to pay him £50. Fred would need to endorse the cheque on the back and then the person receiving it for £50 could pay it into his account.

Sometimes, however, a cheque will be crossed with the words 'Account Payee Only':

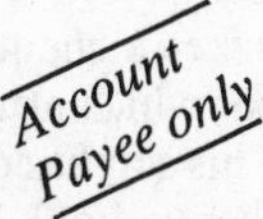

This means that the cheque can only be paid into the account of the payee; for example:

> *Wendy Thomas (Fashions) Ltd, with an account at the Midland, receives a cheque for £75 from a customer marked 'account/payee only'. One of Wendy's employees, Brenda, pays the cheque into her own account and her account at X Bank is credited to the tune of £75. When Wendy finds out about this she sacks Brenda on the spot and tries to recover the £75 from X Bank.*

In fact X Bank is in the wrong because it did not have an account in the name of Wendy Thomas (Fashions) Ltd, and therefore it is liable to Wendy for £75.

Negotiable Instruments

A cheque is normally regarded as a negotiable instrument. This means that unless it is crossed 'Account Payee Only' it can be transferred from person to person provided that it is endorsed in turn by each person transferring it. The person receiving the cheque finally can pay it in knowing that he has good title to it, that is he has a right to it. However, cheques sometimes are marked 'Not Negotiable' and if this is the case it means that anyone who accepts it other than the payee takes a risk. If the drawer refuses to honour the cheque then there is nothing the holder can do because it has been marked 'not negotiable'; for example:

Frank Brown pays a cheque to Edith Owen for £200 marked 'Not Negotiable'. Edith leaves the cheque lying around and it is stolen; the thief gives it to John Smith in settlement of a debt but when John pays it in he finds that the bank refuses to pay out and although he accepted it in good faith there is nothing John can do.

Exercise 5

Read the following and explain the legal position of the person whose name is in italics.

1 *Michael Beresford* is a partner in a firm of wholesalers with an account with Barclays. He is late for an appointment and he signs five blank cheques to be completed by one of his clerks. The clerk, who is short of money, makes a cheque payable to herself for £150 and pays it in to her account which after three days is credited.

2 *Jim Hough* knows that his son has on several occasions forged his signature. Jim leaves his cheque book lying around and his son completes a cheque made payable to himself and forges Jim's signature. The cheque is for £95 and Jim decides to sue his bank, Lloyds, for cashing the cheque.

3 *Ian Creedland* receives a cheque for £100 from his firm marked 'Account Payee Only'. Ian's account is with National Westminster, but the cheque is stolen and is paid into another bank by the thief, John Green. The other bank cashes the cheque in favour of John.

4 *Roy Goldstraw*, a sub-postmaster, is asked to cash a cheque for £100 marked 'Not Negotiable'. Roy agrees to do this but when he presents the cheque it is not honoured because it has in fact been stolen.

Protection Against Forged Endorsements

Let us return to our original example in which R. and M. Spencer, operating as Brassingtons, made out a cheque for £5430 in favour of Conquest (Furniture) Co. Ltd. As you will remember the cheque was drawn on the Midland Bank, known as the drawee or the paying banker. It is known as the paying banker because the £5430 will be paid from an account held with the bank. A paying banker is protected by the Bills of exchange Act 1882 and the Cheques Act 1952.

The protection given to the paying bank is in connection with forged endorsements. You will remember that unless a cheque is marked 'Account

Payee Only' the payee can pass the cheque to someone else by signing his name on the back. It would be clearly unfair if the bank was made liable for forged endorsements because it would have no way of knowing whether the signature was valid or not. The law therefore provides that where the bank pays the cheque in good faith and in the 'ordinary course of business' then it cannot be made to meet the loss in respect of a stolen cheque and forged endorsement.

'In good faith' means without knowing that it was forged and in the ordinary course of business means during normal banking hours.

A bank can however be held liable where the drawer's name is forged and thus if R. and M. Spencer's signatures were forged and the bank paid out on the cheque then it would stand to lose unless the bank could show that the account holders had been negligent.

In our example Conquest has an account with Barclays and Barclays would be known as the collecting bankers. It happens sometimes that cheques which are stolen are paid into a bank. The bank will sometimes in good faith accept the cheque and pay it into the person's account and then collect from the paying banker. The Cheques Act 1957 protects the collecting banker provided he has not been negligent. Negligence could be assumed if:

1 the bank opened an account without taking up references;
2 cheques are collected from a customer but the cheque is drawn in favour of the customer's employer. Thus a bank collecting this cheque drawn in favour of Conquest Co. Ltd and paying it into an employee's account would not be protected;
3 a cheque marked 'Account Payee Only' had been paid into an account other than that of the payee.

Exercise 6

Explain the legal position of the bank concerned in the following cases.

1 Michael Field pays one of his employees, Bob Price, by means of a cheque for £150 drawn on the Midland. Bob puts the cheque into his wallet which is subsequently stolen. The thief endorses the cheque and presents it for payment. The cheque is honoured by the Midland.

2 Barclays pays out on four cheques despite the fact that the signature of the drawer has been forged.

3 National Westminster opens an account for Robert Davies without taking up references. Robert is in fact engaged in fraud and pays twenty cheques which he has stolen into his account. The drawers of the cheques in question decide to sue the bank.

Exercise 7

Answer the following questions, which are based upon this chapter. Check your answers and if you have not understood any aspects of this chapter read over that part of the chapter again.

1 A cheque dated 6 June 1987 presented on 30 January 1988 will be paid. *true/false*?

2 Name the two duties owed by a bank to its customers.

3 If a cheque is not honoured by a bank and sent back to the payee marked 'refer to drawer', the drawer could sue the bank in two respects. Name these.

4 If a bank pays out a cheque which has been stopped by the drawer it may be liable for the money paid. *true/false*?

5 If a drawer is negligent in handling his account and an employee misuses a cheque the bank is liable. *true/false*?

6 A crossed cheque marked 'Account Payee Only' can be endorsed and paid into any account. *true/false*?

7 If Bill Brown unknowingly receives a stolen cheque which is negotiable and pays it into his own account, he receives no good title to the cheque and the payee can claim on it. *true/false*?

8 Explain (a) the protection afforded to a paying bank, (b) the protection afforded to a collecting bank.

AGENCY

Edward Burch runs a successful export business. He often has to make trips overseas in furtherance of his business. One one particular occasion he has to travel to West Africa and telephones a local travel agent to book him flights to Ghana, Nigeria and Ivory Coast, and hotel accommodation for the period of his 10-day trip in various towns including Accra, Lagos, Kano and Abidjan. Edward gives precise details of his requirements and the travel agent, known as Ajax Tours, books flights with KLM and Swiss Air, and the hotels.

This is not a particularly unusual occurrence but it introduces an important aspect of law, i.e. the law of agency. In this case, the principal, as he is called, instructs his agent to make a contract on his behalf. Edward Burch is the principal and Ajax Tours is the agent. There are, of course, numerous examples of where a person uses an agent to deal for him. Many people these days use estate agents to sell their houses. In these instances, the estate agent as the name implies, is the agent and the seller is the principal. In our example, Edward Burch in his work as an exporter could well act himself as an agent for a company wishing to export goods abroad. When we discussed partnership in Chapter 9, you will remember that one partner can bind others by his actions. He is acting as their agent.

A manager of a company will act as the agent of his company when making decisions. A headmaster of a school or principal of a college often can act as agent of his local authority when entering into contracts of employment.

Exercise 1

In the following examples, identify the principal and the agent:

1 Alex Ferguson, manager of Manchester United Football Club, signs a player from another club for an agreed fee.

2 Janet Baker (Fashions) Ltd instructs Business Property Services to acquire property for her in Brighton.
3 Derek Butterfield, a wealthy businessman, phones his stockbroker to arrange for him to buy shares in a particular company.

13.1 CONTRACT OF AGENCY

Contract of Agency

Agency is really a contract whereby the principal contracts with his agents for particular services. Thus a client could ask an insurance broker to arrange insurance for him. The contract of insurance will be between the principal (the client) and the insurance company. The broker will receive his consideration, i.e. a commission for arranging the insurance, though, in practice, the commission is often paid by the insurance company.

There are, in agency arrangements, two contracts as the following example shows.

Bev Dewar wants to sell a shop, and he instructs an estate agent to act on his behalf. The estate agent finds a buyer and when the sale goes through, he sends his account to Bev. There are two contracts:

1 Bev (the vendor) and the purchaser
2 Bev (principal) and the estate agent (agent).

Agencies may be set up in a number of ways.

Express Authorisation by the Principal

This is where a principal, orally or in writing, instructs an agent to act on his behalf. You will remember that some contracts must be made by deed, e.g. transfer of land. If a principal wants an agent to act for him in a transfer, then the agency must be made by deed. This is only where the agent (possibly a solicitor) signs the transfer deed when, for example, the vendor or purchaser is out of the country.

By Implication

Often it is assumed that an agent has authority to act for his principal. A manager of a large shop will order goods on behalf of his company and it will be assumed that he has that authority. A principal becomes liable for any debts incurred because the law implies authority where such authority is usual in the position the agent is in.

In a decided case *Watteau* v. *Fenwick* (1893) the manager and licensee of a pub ordered cigars from a salesman. His principal tried to avoid payment, saying he had expressly forbidden such purchases. However, the court held that the principal was liable because the manager had, despite the principal's instructions, made a contract on behalf of the principal. The salesman could not possibly have known that this was the case. You will appreciate that managers/licensees are usually assumed to have this authority.

By Statute

The Partnership Act 1890 lays down quite clearly that partners in a partnership act as agents for each other. You will remember from Chapter 9 that partners bind each other by their actions.

By Apparent Authority

The following example will help to explain this.

John Harris has been an assistant solicitor with his firm for four years and he is asked if he would like to be a partner. John agrees and is given the task of sorting out the firm's computing and word processing requirements. He sees a number of salesmen and they have reason to believe he is able to act on behalf of the firm. He orders a computer for £2500 but the partners decided not to ratify John as a partner, and seek to avoid the contract with Computer Power plc. The court would find for the computer firm because agency, on the part of John, would be assumed by apparent authority. The rule is that a principal cannot hold out a person or his agent then deny his authority.

The situation is well summed up in a case *Freeman & Lockyer* v. *Buckhurst Park Properties Ltd* (1964) where BPP had allowed a director to act as managing director and then sought to avoid contracts made by him saying he had not been expressly appointed.

By Ratification

This applies where someone acts for another without authority but his action is then ratified and he becomes an agent, e.g. Janet Davidson is a secretary to a managing director. She is visiting an exhibition of typewriting and word processing equipment. She is offered a typewriter at a bargain price and she accepts on behalf of her company. The managing director could reject this and he would not be bound or he could ratify, as it were, Janet's agency and the contract could be effective from the time the contract was made.

Ratification is possible where:

1 The agent acted as agent and not in his/her own name. Janet, in this situation, bought the equipment for her firm.

2 The principal must have had contractual capacity, i.e. in the case of a company to buy equipment must be within its powers.

By Necessity

There are circumstances where an agent acts for his principal out of necessity. The following example will help to explain this.

Bob Dash works as a caretaker for a firm of civil engineers and lives above the offices. Fire damages one of the offices and, not able to contact any of the partners who were all abroad, Bob contacts a builder to do some necessary work to preserve the fabric of the building pending major reconstruction. It would be held that an agency of necessity had been established provided that it could be shown:

1 Bob was in control of the property;
2 there was a genuine emergency;
3 he could not contact the principal/s;
4 he acted in good faith.

Exercise 2

Name the five ways in which agency can be created.

13.2 DUTIES OF PRINCIPAL AND AGENT

Joyce Richards owns a number of properties in London which she lets out as flats, offices and for other uses. She decides to appoint a property manager, Philip Cheetham, to deal with these matters and, of course, in this situation Joyce is the principal and Philip is the agent. Let us take this example to identify the duties of principal and agent to each other.

Duties of a Principal to an Agent

1 Joyce has a duty to pay Philip for his duties.
2 She will need to reimburse him for all expenses incurred, e.g. any travelling involved.

Duties of an Agent to a Principal

1 Philip must obey Joyce's instructions; if she said she does not want 12 Green Park let as offices but only as residences, then Philip has to obey.
2 Philip must perform his services personally, not in any way sub-contract his agency.

3 He must use reasonable care and skill, e.g. if he let an expensive Chelsea flat for £500 per year, this might not be an indication of his skill.
4 He must act in good faith to his principal, e.g. he must never make any secret profit from his dealings.

In *Hippisley* v. *Knee Bros* (1905), an advertising agent obtained discounts from printers with whom he regularly dealt. It was held that the discounts had to be passed on to the principal. On the other hand, the agent had not been fraudulent, and was still entitled to his commission.

You will note that this list is not very different from the list of duties owed by an employee to his/her employer.

We must remember that in an agency, arrangements such as the one we have described between Joyce and Philip - that the agent is merely the go-between - the contract is between the principal and the other party. In any contract entered into by Philip on behalf of Joyce, then Joyce is liable provided the agency is effective. If the agency is not effective then Philip would be liable.

13.3 HOW AGENCY IS BROUGHT TO AN END

There are basically two ways by which an agency may be brought to an end:

1 *By law*
   (a) where either party dies, i.e. principal or agent;
   (b) the insanity of either party;
   (c) lapse of time, i.e. where an agent has been appointed for a period of time;
   (d) performance where an agent has been appointed to do a particular job, e.g. a house agent appointed to sell a house then his agency comes to an end when the house is sold.
2 *By agreement*
   (a) by agreement between the parties;
   (b) by the principal withdrawing his authority, i.e. by terminating the agency. You see from time to time notices in the newspaper such as:

> *F. Davies Co Ltd wishes to point out that John Evans, formerly sales manager, no longer is employed by the company and therefore the company accepts no liability for any arrangement entered into by John Evans on its behalf.*

   This really is a protection to be company so that it is not liable for the former agent's actions.
   (c) by the agent resigning his duties.

Exercise 3

1 List the four duties owed by an agent to his principal.
2 How might an agency be brought to an end?

Exercise 4

Answer the following questions which are all based upon agency. Check your answers against those given and if you are unclear about any aspect of this topic, read the chapter again.

1 Advise the party in the following situation, identifying two separate contracts.

Geoff Thomas, a wealthy antique dealer, employs Sheila Prince to go to Manchester to purchase regency furniture at a large antique sale. Sheila buys three pieces of furniture from NW Antiques plc for £9500. When Geoff sees the furniture, he is angry and refuses to pay the balance outstanding of £8500 (a deposit of £1000 has already been paid by Sheila).

2 Peter May is the manager of a Sports Shop owned by Kent Sports plc. Despite the managing director's instructioms that they wanted to run down their stock of cricket gear, Peter buys twenty cricket bats carrying the name of Ian Botham from International Sports Equipment plc. Kent Sports plc refuse to pay the bill.
Advise Sports Equipment plc.

3 Realising that the price of a particular share was likely to rise considerably, Greenfield (Stockholders) Ltd buys £500 000 of shares on behalf of one of their wealthy clients, Sir Roger Beckwith. Roger refuses to accept these saying he had given no instructions and Greenfield could have easily contacted him.
Advise Greenfield (Stockbrokers) Ltd.

4 Following the death of his principal, Sir Adrian Evans, John Martin agrees to sell a property for a good price feeling it might benefit Adrian's beneficiaries.
Advise John.

CHAPTER 14

REVIEW

We have now covered a number of important business law topics. However, in an introductory book of this sort it is not possible to deal with these topics in any great detail. You may be interested in learning more about business law or you may be interested in learning more about one or two particular topics. There are many excellent business law books available and at the end of this chapter there is a list of books which cover the topics more thoroughly.

This chapter is tended as a review of the various business law topics that have been dealt with in other chapters. It consists of a number of review exercises. Try to do these exercises without looking back at the relevant chapter or section. If you find you do have difficulty with any of them, then refer to the book. At the end of each set of review exercises there is the chapter number which indicates the part of the book which deals with the topic which is the subject of the exercises in question.

Exercise 1

1 For each of the examples outlined below say: (a) whether it is civil or criminal law; (b) what court is likely to hear the case.
(i) Mrs Gardener has been convicted by magistrates on a charge of drinking and driving; she decides to appeal.
(ii) Michael Pavey refuses to sell his house, value £100 000, to a buyer despite the fact that contracts have been exchanged.
(iii) Jean Mitchell is injured while coming down the stairs of the college where she works. Her solicitor advises her to claim £100 damages.
(iv) The Inland Revenue has successfully prosecuted a wealthy business man for tax evasion. Such, however, is the importance of the case that it is heard on appeal in the highest court in the land.
2 Name four civil courts.
3 Name four different sources of law.

4 When a judge, in his summing up, gives his reasons for coming to a decision this is known by the Latin phrase
5 Imran Shah is told by his employer that due to his colour, he cannot apply for a post of promotion in his firm. Imran decides to take the matter to court. Which court would deal with the situation?
6 In a civil case, what three documents are known as pleadings?

Reference: Chapter 1

Exercise 2

1 Why are the following *not* legally binding contracts? In each case state the element which is missing.
(a) David Stuart is writing a book and he offers his wife £50 if she will do the typing for him.
(b) Michael agrees to buy a suit from Easiwear priced at only £12.50; the salesman, who has priced it wrongly, refuses to sell.
(c) Tony Bendrey accepts a post as foreman motor mechanic with Super Motors Ltd but demands £150 per week not the advertised wage of £120.
(d) Andrew Martin (aged fourteen) signs a complicated hire purchase agreement to purchase a new cycle.
(e) Under threat of violence Mrs Ward sells her seventeenth-century house worth £250 000 for £55 000.
(f) Brian Webster agrees to work as hard as possible if he gets a rise of £30 per week.
2 If an offeror agrees to keep an offer open to an offeree for three days then he (the offeror) is bound by his promise. *true/false*?
3 Name three ways in which an offer can come to an end.
4 Under what circumstances will a promise of a gift be enforced?
5 Name the five rules of consideration.
6 A boy of sixteen has, in English law, full contractual capacity. *true/false*?
7 Stanley Oldham enters into a verbal credit agreement with a garage to buy a motorcar for £6500. Stanley defaults on payment and the garage decides to sue him. Does the garage have a good case?
8 Explain the three circumstances where *consensus ad idem* may not exist.

Reference: Chapter 2

Exercise 3

1 Give an example of an Act of Parliament which provides for implied terms in a contract of sale.

2 Terms and conditions which are written are known as implied terms. *true/false*?
3 Explain the difference between a condition and a warranty in a contract.
4 Do you think the following contract is breached?

Computer Power Ltd agree to deliver a mini computer together with various software packages to Safe Sure Insurance Co. on 31 August 1988. The delivery takes place on time but one item of software is delivered three days late on 3 September 1988.

5 Explain to the proprietor the significance of the notice below:

M. & G. (Groceries) Ltd cannot accept liability for loss or damage to customers' property while they are shopping in this store. Nor can the company be liable for personal injury to customers.

6 Name four ways in which contracts may be discharged.
7 Specific performance is always available to a plaintiff in a breach of contract case. *true/false*? *Reference:* Chapter 3

Exercise 4

1 Contracts of employment must always be in writing to make them valid. *true/false*?
2 The Employment Protection (Consolidation) Act 1978 lays down that a statement must be given to an employee within weeks of his employment.
3 Is the following situation legal and if not why not?

Kanwar Singh applies for a job as a driver with United Haulage Co. but is turned down because company policy does not allow the employment of foreigners.

4 List the four conditions which are implied in a contract of employment in respect of the employee.
5 List three of the four conditions which exist in a contract of employment in respect of the employer.
6 Explain the legal position of Dual Accounting Services Ltd in the following situation:

Alex Hall is an accountant with Dual Accounting Services Ltd. He has a poor record both in terms of attendance and the accuracy of his work. He applies for a job as chief accountant with an engineering firm and on the strength of a good reference from Dual Accounting Services who are anxious to get rid of him he obtains the post, but three months later he involves his new company in heavy losses as a result of unsound financial and accounting practice.

7 Tony Bendrey (48) has been a motor mechanic with Bowdens (Bristol) for ten years at a wage of £150 per week. Due to a heavy fall in trade Tony is given a week's notice and a £250 bonus. Is Tony entitled to more than this and if so how much?

8 James Street has been employed at a firm of motor suppliers for ten years. Following a firm audit it is discovered that James has been stealing from the firm to the tune of about £2500. James is dismissed instantly and he decides:
(a) to appeal against unfair dismissal;
(b) to claim redundancy;
(c) to claim the statutory notice period or money in lieu.
Do you think James would be successful in any of the above?

Reference: Chapter 4

Exercise 5

1 In each of the following cases advise the party in italics of his/her position in law.
(a) *Peggy Kerr* buys an antique for £500 from Disdale Bros in a small antique shop. A few weeks later the police call at Peggy's house saying the antique has been stolen and it is handed back to its rightful owner. Eric Disdale, the owner of Disdale Bros, tells Peggy he did not know it was stolen and says that unfortunately it is Peggy's loss.
(b) Richard Partridge buys a stereo record player for £350 from *Good Bargain Radio Supplies Ltd*. He finds that after a few weeks the stereo develops a fault which can only be put right at a charge of £150. Richard demands his money back.
(c) *John Martin* buys a Christmas cake from United Bakeries for £10.50. He selects from a range of cakes displayed. He is given a cake already packed but when he unpacks he discovers it is completely unlike the one he chose. He demands his £10.50 back.

2 (a) Which Act of Parliament makes it illegal for shops to wrongly describe goods?
(b) Double pricing is a criminal office. *true/false*?

3 When a person buys an article on hire purchase he/she owns the car on payment of the first instalment. *true/false*?

4 Examine the following cases and advise the party italicised:
(a) *Jeff Evans* buys a car for £6500 on hire purchase. Although he signs a form at the car showroom he never receives a copy and refuses to pay the last five instalments.

(b) *Susan Murgatroyd* signs an agreement to buy a washing machine. She signs the agreement at her house but the following day changes her mind and notifies the firm *Household Supplies Ltd*. The firm threatens her with legal action. *Reference:* Chapter 5

Exercise 6

1 Which of the following risks are non-insurable? Fire, theft, failure to make profit.
2 Insurance companies take on large numbers of risks at quite modest premiums. This is known as
3 In the following situations advise the party in italics and say what insurance principle is involved.
(a) Michael Jones' hobby is stunt motorcycling. In an insurance against accidents he omits to mention this. Michael is injured while stunt riding and the *Star Insurance Company* refuses to pay out.
(b) *Surety Insurance Ltd* refuse to pay out any compensation to Michael Hunter, who has taken out insurance on his friend's house which is destroyed by fire.
(c) *Frank Brown* insures his car (value £5000) with two separate companies. Following an accident which completely wrecks his car Frank claims a total of £10 000. *Reference:* Chapter 6

Exercise 7

1 Name the three elements which must be proved in any negligence action.
2 A duty of care is never owed to a trespasser. *true/false*?
3 State four defences that might be used by a defendant in a negligence action.
4 Name the three kinds of trespass.
5 Libel is the written form of defamation. *true/false*?
6 Do you think the party italicised would have a good case in defamation? Give your reasons.

When she comes to work *Marlene Wardle*, the office supervisor, sees a notice on the noticeboard which reads:

'It is strictly against company policy to use the firm's telephone for making private calls and this includes Mrs M. W.'s calls to New Zealand. Signed F. Jones, Managing Director.

Reference: Chapter 7

Exercise 8

1 The Health and Safety at Work Act 1974 has introduced a new range of criminal offices. *true/false*?
2 Under the Health and Safety at Work Act, what is a Prohibition Order?
3 State three duties imposed upon employees by the Health and Safety at Work Act.
4 Employees injured at work can sue for negligence or for breach of statutory duty. To what Act of Parliament does this statutory duty apply?
5 If an injured employee cannot prove negligence or breach of statutory duty, can he still get compensation?
6 Explain what 'vicarious liability' means.

Reference: Chapter 8

Exercise 9

1 Brian Webb and Fred Hutchinson buy a small grocery shop, and they trade under the name Spider Webb. The two partners do not register the name and they decide to sue a customer for non-payment of a £250 bill. Explain why the court will probably award damages despite the fact that the name has not been registered.
2 In a partnership what is a sleeping partner?
3 Name three types of business organisation which have legal status.
4 A company which acts outside the powers laid down in its memorandum of association is said to be acting
5 What does the word 'limited' imply for a shareholder in a company?
6 What is the maximum and minimum number of partners allowed in a partnership?

Reference: Chapter 9

Exercise 10

1 If a person is adjudged bankrupt what disqualification does he have?
2 Companies may be declared bankrupt. *true/false*?
3 If a company goes into liquidation with debts of £10 000 but only £6000 in assets, what might the Official Receiver do?
4 What three things must a petitioner for bankruptcy prove?

Reference: Chapter 10

Exercise 11

1 A buyer of a business property is not legally bound to buy until there is an exchange of contracts. *true/false*?
2 If a business such as a shop is sold but not the property, what is being sold is known sometimes as
3 Fred Bellamy is selling a lucrative restaurant. He signs a contract with the purchaser that he will not operate a restaurant for twenty years in the UK. Within a year Fred has opened a restaurant in the same street. Could the purchaser do anything to stop him?
4 A landlord who owns the property from which a business operates can evict the tenant at any time. *true/false*?
5 If an inventor wants to get the benefit of his invention he would be wise to take out a
6 If Heather Brooks video-tapes a television programme for home use she is in breach of the copyright law. *true/false*?
7 Ordinary shareholders have a vote at the company's annual general meeting. *true/false*?
8 Company X is liquidated and after paying its creditors and other outstanding accounts it has £100 000 left over. The company has 100 000 £1 ordinary shareholders and 50 000 £1 preference shareholders. How much will the ordinary shareholders get and how much will the preference shareholders get? *Reference:* Chapter 11

Exercise 12

1 In a cheque transaction who is the drawer, the drawee and the payee?
2 State the two duties owed by a bank to its customer.
3 If a receiving order is made against a businessman all cheques drawn by him will be stopped by the bank. *true/false*?
4 How can a cheque be drawn so that it can only be paid into the account of the person in whose favour it is made?
5 In respect of cheques what does 'negotiability' mean?
6 State two circumstances where a bank might stop a cheque.
Reference: Chapter 12

Exercise 13

1 Identify the principal and agent in the following:
(a) Kenny Dalglish signs a player from a 2nd division club for £200 000. The player signs for Liverpool FC.

(b) Ward & Co buys machinery on behalf of Kent Engineers plc.
(c) Mr Y contracts for a famous pop group to appear in a pop festival in Sheffield.

2 List three ways in which an agency is created.

3 List two duties owed by a principal to his/her agent.

4 All partners in a partnership are agents for each other. *true/false*?

5 Contracts entered into by agents for their principals are always avoided by the other party. *true/false*? *Reference:* Chapter 13

ANSWERS

CHAPTER 1

Exercise 1

1 Criminal law could be defined as being concerned with conduct of which the state so strongly disapproves that it will punish the wrong-doer.
2 Civil law could be defined as being concerned with settling disputes between individuals and providing a remedy to the person wronged.
3 (a) The other party in a criminal case is known as Regina or Queen and in some cases the police.
3 (b) The other party in a civil case is known as the plaintiff.

Exercise 2

1 This is a dispute between Brenda and the shop and would be a civil case.
2 This is a dispute between David and the garage and would be a civil case.
3 Deborah has committed a minor wrong but one of which the state disapproves. It would be a criminal case.
4 This is a good example of a crime and would be a criminal case.

Exercise 3

1 This would be a good example of an appeal 'on a case stated' and would be heard by the Divisional Court of the Queen's Bench Division.
2 Michael would be tried for this minor driving offence in the Magistrates' Court.
3 John would be tried in the Crown Court.
4 Jennifer's appeal would go to the Court of Appeal (Criminal Division).
5 Because of its legal importance James Johnson's further appeal would go to the House of Lords.
6 Syd's appeal against sentence would go from the Magistrates' to the Crown Court.

Exercise 4

1 Peak Building Supplies is the plaintiff and Woodruffe Renovations is the defendant.
2 A default summons is issued by the plaintiff for the recovery of money whereas an ordinary summons relates to other types of claims.
3 There are many examples you could have mentioned, e.g. recovery of money, claims for compensation for injury, bankruptcies, undefended divorces, disputes relating to housing.

Exercise 5

The three divisions are the Queen's Bench Division, the Chancery Division, the Family Division.

The Queen's Bench Division deals with contract and negligence.

The Chancery Division deals with bankruptcies, mortgages, company affairs.

The Family Division deals with divorces, and family matters.

Exercise 6

1 The first case is a civil case and because the compensation claimed is below the £5000 limit it will be heard in the County Court.
2 This is again a civil case but because the amount of compensation is likely to be considerably more than £5000 it will be heard in the Queen's Bench Division of the High Court.
3 This would be a criminal case heard in the Crown Court originally but with the appeal being heard in the Court of Appeal (Criminal Division).
4 This is a criminal case heard orginally in the Magistrates' Court and therefore the appeal against sentence would be in the Crown Court.
5 This is a very serious criminal case which would be heard in the Crown Court.
6 This is a civil case. It provides a good example of 'leapfrogging'. The case has gone to the highest court in the land, i.e. the House of Lords, and missed out (leaped over) the Court of Appeal Civil Division.
7 Jenny would have a case which would go to the Industrial Tribunal.
8 Provided it was allowed for in the business contract, then the dispute could be settled by arbitration.

Exercise 7

1 The two main sources are legislation and precedent.
2 The three stages are House of Commons, House of Lords, Royal Assent.
3 It is important that a reason is given because the decision of one judge may be followed by other judges in similar cases.
4 The decisions of the House of Lords are binding on all other courts.
5 Ministers, local authorities (district councils), nationalised industries.

6 Orders in Council.
7 Regulations of the EEC made by the European Commission and the Council of Ministers.

Exercise 8

1 Statement of Claim; Counterclaim; A Defence to a Counterclaim.
2 Discovery.
3 Writ.
4 Court of Appeal (Civil Division) or in some cases the House of Lords.

Exercise 9

1 *British Railways Board* v. *Herrington* (1972).
2 Three judges hear the appeal by taking account of the notes from the previous judgement. They can hear barristers arguing their case. In this instance, the Appeal Court reversed the decision of the Queen's Bench Division.
3 The term means 'reason for the decision' and the case *Donogue* v. *Stevenson* (1931) illustrates what is meant by neighbourhood principle.
4 This is an interpretation of an Act of Parliament where the literal rule would lead to a ridiculous conclusion.
5 It means beyond the powers.
6 A solicitor takes advice (counsel) from a barrister and then will prepare a case (brief).

CHAPTER 2

Exercise 1

1 False – although some contracts are made with the help of a solicitor this is not usually the case.
2 False. In fact more contracts are verbal than in writing.
3 A suitable definition would be 'an agreement which the law will recognise'.

Exercise 2

Alan is the offeree because the offer is being made to him. Ian is the offeror because he is making the offer.

Exercise 3

Since the radio is displayed with a view to 'invite customers to make an offer' and since an offeree can also reject an offer the shopkeeper (the offeree) can legally refuse to accept an offer of £5.

Exercise 4

There would be no contract between Frank and his employee because as we have learned consideration must be two-way. A gift is only a one-way consideration. Frank is supplying consideration but the employees are not. Except in rather special circumstances a court of law will never enforce the promise of a gift.

Exercise 5

John is the offeror; Good Deal Motors is the offeree; consideration is the Rover 2.6 and the £5250.

Exercise 6

The list should have included offer, acceptance, two-way consideration, capacity and legality.

Exercise 7

A clause which contains words such as 'binding in honour only' is likely.

Exercise 8

You should have in your list: offer, acceptance, consideration, capacity, legality, *consensus ad idem* (meeting of the minds), legal intent and form.

Exercise 9

1 This agreement is lacking in the essential element of legal intent. It is a domestic arrangement and it is assumed that there is no legal intent unless there is a specific statement to the contrary.
2 All hire purchase agreements must be in writing. The agreement between Keith and the garage is not in the required form and is not therefore legally binding.
3 All contracts need to be supported by two-way consideration.
In this case the customer is giving no consideration and therefore it is only one-way consideration.
4 Since Michael is unaware of the reward there is no offer to him and since all legally binding agreements must start with an offer this is the element lacking here.
5 Although John and his wife have written to book a room this is only an offer which the hotel has not accepted. There is no acceptance and therefore no contract. In a situation such as this John should have contacted the hotel before he and his wife set off.
6 There is no 'meeting of the minds' between Douglas Pochin's company and Low Peak Co. Ltd. Douglas has persuaded Low Peak to buy by misleading them; therefore there is no contract.

7 Young people below the age of eighteen have limited contractual capacity. They have no capacity in respect of credit agreements. This agreement lacks capacity in respect of Carol.

8 Courts will never enforce agreements which are based upon an illegal act. This agreement is not legally binding by reason of illegality. John could never recover the £2000 through the courts because there has been no breach of contract because no contract exists.

Exercise 10

1 Acceptance and withdrawal or recovation.
2 Acceptance.
3 By the offeree paying a sum of money to the offeror.

Exercise 11

1 Acceptance, withdrawal, rejection, lapse.
2 (a) A counter-offer (b) Roger would be the offeror.
3 Expiry of time and death of offeree.

Exercise 12

1 True - acceptance must match the offer completely.
2 False - postal acceptance takes place when the letter is posted.
3 False - the offeree must accept in the manner suggested by the offeror.
4 False - it must be communicated directly.

Exercise 13

Commercial Supplies Ltd are supplying consideration in the form of a typewriter and Highgate Televisions Ltd are supplying consideration in the form of £450.

Exercise 14

If you examine this situation carefully you will see that there are two separate agreements:

1 East Credit Ltd lend Mary £400. Mary agrees to pay this back + 20 per cent over twelve months. Therefore there is two-way consideration.
2 East Credit Ltd agree to give up the interest. Mary, however, only agrees to fulfil an existing obligation and therefore no consideration exists.

Since only the first agreement is supported by two-way consideration it is the only one legally binding and therefore East Credit Ltd could sue for recovery of the £80.

Exercise 15

1 Consideration must be two-way.
2 Consideration may be future or present but cannot be past.
3 Consideration cannot be an existing obligation.
4 The courts are not concerned with the adequacy of considerations.

Exercise 16

1 Marchant Machine Tools must keep the offer open to Sterndale Engineering Co. because they have received the £1500 consideration. Sterndale could sue Marchant Machine Tools for damages.
2 Deepdale Cash Registers Ltd have made an agreement with the Palace which became effective when the letter was sent, provided the letter was prepaid and correctly addressed.
3 The promise of the gift cannot be enforced against Harpur Builders Ltd because it is an agreement based upon one-way consideration. A written statement is not sufficient. Only a deed will make the agreement legally binding.
4 You will have noted the word 'past'. Paul's offer of a week at his cottage is merely an offer of a gift since the solicitor's consideration is past, and past consideration is not consideration.
5 Reg could not recover the car. Although £2000 is far too low a price, provided the agreement had been entered into freely it is legally binding. This comes from the rule that the courts are not concerned with the adequacy of consideration.
6 Julian could recover as a result of the Road Traffic Act 1972.

Exercise 17

1 Contracts for necessaries.
2 Contracts for employment, apprenticeships and education.

Exercise 18

1 Agreements relating to necessaries, apprenticeships, education and employment.
2 Agreements relating to non-necessaries, credit.
3 Agreements in respect of leases, partnerships and shares.

Exercise 19

1 False, because some agreements take out this legal intent, e.g. football coupons.
2 False - the sender could not sue in the court because no contract exists between him and the Post Office because the legal intent has been removed by Act of Parliament.

3 True - domestic agreements because they are usually binding in honour only are not legally enforceable.

Exercise 20

1 (a) Misrepresentation, (b) duress, (c) undue influence.
2 (a) Agreement to commit a criminal act, (b) agreements involving sexual immorality, (c) agreements affecting public safety, (d) agreements to defraud the inland revenue, (e) agreements tending to the corruption of public life.
3 Where an agreement is made to sell the goods of only one supplier and if it is unreasonable.

Exercise 21

It means that the house is sold but the agreement to buy and sell cannot be enforced until a written contract is drawn up - sold, therefore, subject to a written contract being drawn up.

Exercise 22

1 This is a document signed, sealed and delivered.
2 Leases of three years or more; conveyances or transfers of land; agreements supported by one-way consideration.
3 Agreements to buy company shares; agreements to buy certain goods by instalments; agreements to insure ships.
4 Agreements to buy a house.

Exercise 23

1 You should have: acceptance; revocation (withdrawal); rejection; lapse.
2 Acceptance takes place at the time of posting; therefore if Alan withdrew his offer after the letter was posted this is too late for offers cannot be withdrawn after they have been accepted.
3 (a) False - consideration can never be past.
(b) False - courts are not concerned with adequacy.
(c) True - a promise to fulfil an existing obligation is never consideration.
4 Bob need not worry because this is a credit arrangement and since Bob is not yet eighteen he has no capacity to enter into this sort of arrrangement.
5 Misrepresentation; duress; undue influence.
6 (a) True.
(b) Because they are regarded as being 'in honour only' and therefore there is no legal intent.

CHAPTER 3

Exercise 1

False – expressed terms must be stated (expressed) in some way but this can be verbally or in writing.

Exercise 2

1 The most likely term to be regarded as a condition is term 4, which stipulates that the ownership of the goods in question pass to the buyer. Any attempt by the board to interfere with the buyers' ownership would be regarded as a breach of condition and would affect the very basis of the agreement.
2 (a) A warranty is a term which is not so important as to go to the heart of the contract.
(b) The plaintiff could sue for breach of warranty not breach of contract.

Exercise 3

If you have applied the test 'does the breach go to the heart of the con-contract?' then it is clear that:

1 John is in breach of warranty – his failure to attend one practice does not fundamentally affect the contract. Note the connection between this and *Bettini* v. *Gye*.
2 Michael is in breach of a condition since playing for the team is the essential part of the agreement. To miss six games is very serious indeed. Remember *Poussan* v. *Spires & Pond* (1870).
3 Although the absence of a programme will cause Michael some inconvenience it is not so essential and Michael could sue for breach of warranty.
4 It would seem that the tipping facility is something which goes to the heart of the contract. Indeed this is why H. & G. ordered the vehicle. Certainly the manufacturer is in breach of a condition and therefore in breach of contract.

Exercise 4

1 Rachel could sue because the new motorcar is not of 'merchantable quality'.
2 Precision Engineering could sue because there is an implied term that the lathe will be suitable.
3 Mr and Mrs Goldstraw would recover the £150.50 because being rat-infested suggests that the premises are not fit for human habitation. Real Estates is therefore in breach of an implied term.

Exercise 5

1 An exclusion clause is also known as an indemnity clause or disclaimer clause.

2 False - an exclusion clause may be relied upon if it is brought to the attention of the other party by means of a prominently displayed notice.
3 False - they must be introduced at the time the contract is made.

Exercise 6

1 Veronica would be successful because the exclusion clause must be introduced at the time the contract is made. If it is introduced during the flight it gives Veronica little chance to disagree with the terms and change her mind.
2 Francis could sue because the Unfair Contract Terms Act prevents businesses from excluding liability for personal injury arising from negligence.
3 It is unlikely that Electrical Components would be successful. They have agreed to the exclusion clause which is in respect of loss or damage of equipment. Though the court would look at the charges imposed by County Store Ltd if the charges were high the exclusion might be regarded as unreasonable.

Exercise 7

1 Discharge can take place by: (a) performance; (b) agreement; (c) frustration; (d) breach.
2 Law Reform (Frustrated Contracts) Act 1943.
3 *Krell* v. *Henry* (1903).

Exercise 8

1 Since Nigel cannot play football as a result of the unfortunate accident the contract is discharged by frustration. The very basis of the contract has been destroyed.
2 Provided that Timber Supplies Ltd agree to release Stanley's firm from the contract then the contract is discharged by agreement.
3 Both sides, Precision Engineering Ltd and Western Machines Ltd, have fulfilled their respective sides of the bargain and the contract has been discharged by performance.
4 Leather Supplies Ltd are clearly in breach of contract since they have failed to deliver the goods in time or reasonably near the time. The contract is discharged by breach.

Exercise 9

1 The court could never adequately supervise an employee to see if he was fulfilling his agreement.
2 It would not make sense to force an unwilling person to work somewhere he did not want to.

Exercise 10

1 Damages, specific performance, injunction.
2 False – specific performance orders will never be awarded for contracts of a personal nature and employment is of a personal nature.
3 An injunction is an order requiring someone **not** to do something.
4 This means that the court can award an injunction or a specific performance order if it wishes, it is not compulsory.

Exercise 11

1 In the first case John Bennett would receive damages but not for £6500. He would receive £500 so that he would be in the same position as before the contract was breached.
2 It is possible that the court would grant an injunction preventing Chris from playing for the second club. Remember *Warner Bros* v. *Nelson*.
3 Since the furniture is rare Tony would not really want damages and it is likely that the court would grant a specific performance order ordering United Antique Dealers Ltd to sell the furniture at the agreed price to Tony.
4 It is unlikely that Mr and Mrs Disdale would obtain a specific performance order. More likely they would receive damages of £3000 so that they could buy a similar property or to compensate them if they had bought the property from another company.

CHAPTER 4

Exercise 1

1 A legally binding contract has not come into existence because there is an absence of two-way consideration. Only Matthew is giving consideration. It could also be argued that this is a domestic agreement and therefore the assumption in the courts will be that it will lack legal intent.
2 No offer has been made to Vic and, therefore, there is no acceptance. Since these two elements are lacking there is no legally binding contract.
3 It would appear here that Keith has no authority to bind his company to an agreement with Roy Spencer. Keith does not possess the capacity to make this contract and, therefore, it is not legally binding.
4 There is no doubt that the purpose for which Michelle entered into this agreement was illegal. Therefore, it is not legally binding.
5 A contract of employment, like any other contract, must be based upon reality of consent. Therefore, if one party was persuaded to reach agreement because it based its decision on false information provided by the other party, then the party misled has a right to avoid the contract.

The possession of an HGV licence is essential and, therefore, the agreement is not legally binding.

6 Even though there has been nothing in writing between Pamela and Trenchard Industrial Holdings, nevertheless a legally binding contract is in existence and Pamela could be sued for breach of contract.

Exercise 2

1 Stephen could not treat this contract as breached because the absence of these particulars does not affect the validity of the contract. Indeed, the firm could sue Stephen if he left without giving the minimum notice agreed.

2 In this case, the written particulars supplied to Audrey by Boston Furnishings Ltd do have the weight of law because they have been endorsed by an industrial tribunal and, therefore, Audrey can challenge the firm because of the change in her conditions of employment.

3 The law states quite clearly that under the Race Relations Act 1976 no discrimination must exist in arrangements made for selection; and since here discrimination does exist, Vivian has a case to take to an industrial tribunal.

4 The Sex Discrimination Act 1975 makes it illegal to discriminate on grounds of sex or marital status and Anne could take this case to an industrial tribunal.

Exercise 3

1 The need to obey lawful and reasonable instructions.
2 The need to work competently and carefully.
3 The need to conduct himself/herself in the interest of his employer.
4 The need to show good faith to his/her employer.

Exercise 4

1 To provide a safe system of work.
2 Not to discriminate on grounds of sex, race or union membership.
3 To reimburse employees for any expenses incurred while they are on the firm's business.
4 To deduct PAYE and national insurance contributions.
5 To provide reasonable management.

The following case is a good illustration of this implied duty. In *Donovan* v. *Invicta Airways Ltd* (1970), a pilot was, three times in rapid succession, put under pressure by management to take abnormal risks on flights. On two occasions, there were passengers aboard. He refused each time. Relations with management deteriorated, and he left the company. Although the decion to leave was his, he was held to have been dismissed, and received £900 damages for breach of contact. This promotes a good example of constructive dismissal.

Exercise 5

1 Burlow Road Building Supplies are clearly in breach of what was probably an express condition of their office manager's contract of employment.
2 Michael is not in breach of an implied condition to obey reasonable and lawful orders. It is not reasonable to expect a development engineer to engage in painting and decorating.
3 Margaret is in breach of faith in respect of her employers since her position demands that she does not discuss this sort of information.
4 An implied condition is that an employee must not misconduct himself. Stealing from the firm is a clear case of misconduct and John is in breach.
5 Since a contract of employment requires that employees work competently it would appear that Philip is in breach.
6 It is an implied duty resting upon an employer that an employee is reimbursed for expenses incurred. Therefore, Midland Dairy Food in refusing Richard's claim are in breach of this implied condition. Provided Richard can show that the money was spent in the course of his work, then Midland Dairy Food are in breach.
7 Fashion Textiles were clearly in breach for the implied condition that requires employers to provide a safe system of work.
8 Unfortunately for Reginald it is not an implied condition of employment that an employer provides a reference, and TV Rentals Ltd are not therefore in breach.
9 £951 – i.e. $\frac{9}{10} \times 100 \times 6 = £540$
and $34.25 \times 12 = £411$.

Exercise 6

1 Reg would be entitled to twelve weeks' notice or £1800 in lieu of notice.
2 Carol would be entitled to one week's notice or £80 in lieu of notice.
3 Ken would not be entitled to any notice under the Act because he has only been in employment for three weeks.
4 Tracey would be entitled to two weeks' notice or £170 in lieu of notice.

Exercise 7

1 Frederick is not entitled to redundancy because he is a government employee, which is one of the categories not entitled.
2 Bob is entitled to two years' at 1 week × £110, i.e. £220, plus four years at ½ week × £110, i.e. £220 – a total of £440. He is not entitled to anything for the first two years of his employment because the scheme only starts at eighteen.
3 Frank unfortunately is not entitled because he has reached retirement age.

4 Rita is entitled to twenty years' service.
9 years at 1½ × £150 = £2025
11 years at 1 wk × £150 = £1650

A total of £3675

5 Susan is not entitled because she is a part-time worker and does not work the necessary sixteen hours a week to qualify.

Exercise 8

1 The loss of status for Dr Morris is so considerable as to make the alternative offer unsuitable. Dr Morris could justifiably refuse this and still claim redundancy.
2 This would seem a suitable offer; Deborah is offered the same post only ten miles away. She could not really refuse this and still claim redundancy.
3 This would not be regarded as a suitable offer. A move from York to Torquay for a married man with a family is a big move and Fred could justifiably turn down and still claim redundancy.

Exercise 9

1 The three stages are as follows: (a) complaint to the industrial tribunal; (b) a copy of the complaint to ACAS; (c) hearing before an industrial tribunal.
2 (a) Basic award; (b) compensatory award and (c) additional award.
3 52 weeks, but for a small firm with less than twenty employees 104 weeks.
4 (a) Adam would be unlikely to be successful because of the serious nature of his misconduct.
(b) Jane would be successful even though she has only been with the firm for two weeks because being a member of a union is not a fair reason for dismissal and if an employee is dismissed for joining a union he does not need to have the 52 weeks' qualifying service to appeal against unfair dismissal.
(c) Roy would be successful because the Codes of Practice would have required that he be given a warning. In fact a poor month on top of two years success would not probably be regarded as a sign of incompetence.
5 104 × 175 = £18 200.

Exercise 10

1 False – contracts of employment need not be in writing.
2 True – apprenticeship contracts must always be in writing.
3 Written particulars must be provided within thirteen weeks.
4 An employer has no legal duty to provide a reference.
5 An employee with fifteen years' service is entitled to twelve weeks' notice.

6 The employee is entitled to £1250, i.e. 5 years at 1½ weeks and 5 years at 1 week.
7 False - employees may turn down offers if they are not considered suitable and still claim redundancy.
8 52 weeks or 104 weeks in the case of a firm employing less than twenty employees.
9 Provided Mary gives notice of her intention to leave at least twenty one days before leaving, she is entitled to return within twenty-nine weeks of her confinement.
10 Until 1987 Michael had no rights in this respect, but now he must be given the information within forty days.

CHAPTER 5

Exercise 1

1 Leisure Supplies Ltd, sale of a music centre to Philip is a consumer sale.
2 Since John is reselling the furniture this is not a consumer sale. Also it is not for his private use.
3 Although United Food Ltd are selling in the course of business the grocery chain is buying with a view to resale and not for private consumption, therefore this is not a consumer sale.
4 Malcolm is not selling in the course of business therefore it is not a consumer sale.

Exercise 2

A car of two years old costing £4650 would not be considered of merchantable quality if so early on it needed a new gear box and it is likely that Rachel could claim a full money refund because Associated Motor Sales has breached an essential condition.

Exercise 3

1 That the buyer has the right to sell.
2 That the goods are of merchantable quality.
3 Goods sold by description must correspond to it.
4 Goods sold by sample must correspond to it.
5 Goods supplied must be fit for the purpose.

Exercise 4

1 David could sue because the racquet is apparently not of 'merchantable quality'.

2 Brian could possibly sue despite the twelve months' warranty, which can only add to his rights. A £7500 car should not need such attention after only fourteen months.

3 Muriel could sue because the goods do not correspond with the sample.

4 Caroline could sue because the car she has purchased does not correspond with the description.

5 Philip relied upon advice and he could sue because the goods supplied are not fit for the purpose.

6 David could sue because of the implied condition that the seller had the right to sell them.

Exercise 5

1 False – the Trade Descriptions Act 1968 created criminal offences and contravention could lead to prosecution.

2 (a) False description of goods; (b) double pricing; (c) false description of services, accommodation and facilities; (d) importation of goods bearing a false indication of origin.

Exercise 6

1 Alan Harrison has imported goods bearing a false indication of their origin. West Germany is certainly not regarded as a Third World country.

2 Torbay Holiday Flats Ltd have made a false description in respect of accommodation and therefore broken the law.

3 The answer would hinge on whether the full price was charged for a 28-day period during the last six months.

4 Country Kitchen Bakery have falsely described the goods as being 'home-made', which is not the case.

Exercise 7

1 A secured loan is one where the creditor regains some interest in property of the person seeking the loan. In an unsecured loan no such interest exists.

2 False – the goods become the property of the debtor immediately.

3 False – the goods remain the property of the creditor until the last instalment is paid.

Exercise 8

1 This agreement is not regulated because it is made with a company.

2 Loans to buy houses are exempt and in any event this exceeds the £5000 limit.

3 This would be a regulated agreement.

4 This would not be regulated because it exceeds the maximum limit which at present is £15 000.

Exercise 9

1 Secure Finance Ltd could face criminal prosecution and a court may not enforce the agreement against Jane because the company is *not* licensed.
2 All agreements of this sort must be in writing to be enforceable. John will never be forced to pay.
3 Ian can withdraw because this is a 'cancellable' agreement. His so-called 'cooling off' period lasts for five days after receipt of his copyof the agreement.
4 50 per cent is an 'extortionate' rate of interest and the court would require John to repay the loan but could change the agreement to reduce the interest.

Exercise 10

1 True – the hirer is also the debtor.
2 The maximum proportion of the hire purchase price payable on termination is one half.
3 The finance company has broken the law since it needs a court order to 'snatch back' the goods. In this instance two thirds of the hire purchase price has been paid and, as we have seen, the goods are protected.

Exercise 11

1 Unfortunately, since this is a private sale Bob can do very little unless his friend misrepresented the condition of the machine.
2 Deborah could sue under the Sale of Goods Act 1979 because the goods she obtained did not correspond with the description.
3 Wainwrights (Domestic) Ltd are contravening the Trade Descriptions Act 1968 and could be prosecuted.
4 Again this is an example of a contravention of the Trade Descriptions Act 1968. The Magistrates' Court has the power to award compensation to the parties affected by the false description and Mr and Mrs Taylor may get some money back.
5 This agreement can never be enforced in the court because the debtor must receive a copy of her agreement.
6 Audrey is allowed a five-day 'cooling off' period from the receipt of the copy of the agreement; since the agreement was signed away from the business premises. Whether she could cancel depends upon when she received the copy agreement.

CHAPTER 6

Exercise 1

1 A proposal form.
2 Insurance companies cannot estimate the number of claims for this sort of risk.
3 Pooling of risks.

Exercise 2

1 Hang-gliding is apparently a very dangerous hobby and it is essential that in any life insurance this hobby is mentioned. James's widow could not really recover the £20 000 from Security Insurance.
2 It is vitally important for the company to assess the risk that Brian mentions, both the past burglaries and his rather irregular practice with the back window. The insurance company could refuse to pay out.

Exercise 3

1 Michael could not really claim an interest in the boat despite the fact that he has borrowed it occasionally. Michael could take out insurance for the period when he was using the boat because he might be liable if the boat was damaged.
2 Mrs Yeomans does have an interest in her husband's life.
3 Victor could claim an insurable interest in what is his own car.
4 Sheila could under no circumstances claim an interest in her best friend's life in the sense that she would suffer no financial loss as a result of her friend's death.

Exercise 4

1 Indemnity means that the insured will be indemnified (compensated) for his loss.
2 Because no one can measure the value of life.
3 Over-insurance exists where the insurance cover is more than the value of the property. Under-insurance exists where the insurance cover is less than the value of the property.

Exercise 5

1 Carole cannot get double compensation because of the principles of indemnity and contribution.
2 (b) Subrogation.

Exercise 6

1 John could find that the insurance company in the event of a claim could refuse to pay out. This fact of epilepsy is most relevant. Remember insurance contracts rely upon utmost good faith.
2 Again Bob should have disclosed this very important fact.
3 The money Michael gets from the sale of the carpets legally belongs to the insurance company because they have paid out in full for his loss.
4 In the event of loss Pat could only claim up to £65 000, i.e. the value of the cottage.
5 Anne has no insurable interest in her neighbour's life.
6 Bob is liable to pay back the value of one claim and the two companies would share the cost of the other.

CHAPTER 7

Exercise 1

1 'Wrong' - from the French.
2 Sheila as plaintiff.
3 False; negligence is civil.

Exercise 2

1 Richard Huyton would be the defendant in this instance and David Pritchard the plaintiff.
2 Drivers of vehicles on the public highway owe a duty of care to all pedestrians and other road users who might be affected by their acts or omissions, thus Richard clearly owed David a duty of care.
3 The clue as to whether the duty of care had been broken lies in the phrases 'in a hurry' and 'far too fast'. It would suggest that the standard of care exercised by Richard was not that of a reasonable person.

Exercise 3

1 The three elements are: (a) duty of care; (b) breach of duty; (c) loss arising from the breach.
2 £400 plus an assessment of the amount to compensate George for pain and discomfort.

Exercise 4

1 Buxted Engineering Co. owe no duty of care to Michael because he is a trespasser and Michael would be unsuccessful.
2 Low Peak District Council owe a duty of care to all lawful visitors. Mary is a lawful visitor. Low Peak have breached their duty and Mary is injured. She would be successful.

3 Alan clearly owes Rachel a duty of care but Alan is a careful driver and has maintained this high standard during his journey down the main street. Alan has not broken this duty and Rachel would therefore not be successful. He can explain the skid.
4 Although the hospital owed Margaret a duty of care which had clearly been broken by the existence of loose floor covering, it is likely that Margaret would have died anyway and her death probably did not arise from the breach. It is unlikely John would be successful.
5 Michael would not be successful, for although there was a duty of care which had been broken, there was no loss because Michael did not suffer any injury.
6 Although Andrew is a trespasser, because of his age Easibuild Co. Ltd would owe him a duty of care which has been breached and injury has resulted. David Knowles would be successful.

Exercise 5

1 The defendant may claim: (a) no duty of care existed; (b) no breach; (c) no loss or injury arising from the breach; (d) consent; (e) contributory negligence.
2 False. Since the passing of the Unfair Contract Terms Act it is no longer possible to use as a defence a disclaimer notice disclaiming liability for death or personal injury.

Exercise 6

If we apply our three essential elements then there is little doubt that the hotel was negligent. Having a member of staff with a known police record who has access to guests' rooms is very questionable. The notice in the room could not be used as a defence because it has been introduced too late. To be relied upon by the hotel it needs to be shown to guests at the time they book in, i.e. at reception. The hotel, however, could argue that Alan should not have kept such valuable equipment in his room but should have left it at Reception. It is possible that full compensation would not be awarded and that Alan would bear some of the cost. You may have remembered the case *Olley* v. *Marlborough Court Hotel.*

Exercise 7

An injunction is an order saying 'don't do something'. In this instance it would be an order saying to Rachel and Doreen, 'Do not continue to walk through the timber yard.'

Exercise 8

1 Burlow Motors could not prosecute because trespass is a civil offence.
2 Provided Marc used a minimum of force to eject the man then Weavings could not be sued.

3 Although probably unwelcome visitors, the Health Inspectors would be considered lawful visitors and therefore could not be trespassers.
4 Bill started as a lawful visitor but has clearly acted in a way which makes his presence unwelcome. After being asked to leave he becomes a trespasser and the fact that he has paid for his ticket is really immaterial.

Exercise 9

1 The three types of trespass to person are: (a) assault; (b) battery; (c) false imprisonment.
2 (a) Ray could rightfully claim he was preventing a greater evil and Mike would have little chance in a trespass case.
(b) This is more difficult and it would be for the court to determine if this comes within the normal interpretation of parental authority.
(c) Probably John could use as his defence that he was acting in self-defence.
(d) If no offence had been committed at this time either by Nick or someone else then Phil could be sued for trespass to person, i.e. false imprisonment.
(e) It is within one's rights to use minimum force to eject a trespasser provided he has been requested to leave. This might be regarded, however, as excessive use of force in which case Michael might be successful.
(f) Jack really could not sue successfully because he has consented by implication to be battered by taking part in games such as rugby where injuries are a distinct possibility.

Exercise 10

1 Graham has been negligent since this was an accident. Trespass to goods must be wilful. The neighbour could sue in negligence.
2 The firm could sue Mary for conversion since Mary is denying the firm's ownership of the books by trying to sell them.

Exercise 11

1 Public nuisance is a crime and it is something which affects a number of people. Private nuisance is a tort and is concerned usually with on individual or family.
2 (a) The pensioners would have little chance because once a year would not be regarded as unreasonable.
(b) If the noise and smells are excessive then Frances would be successful; it is no defence to say it has always been the same.
(c) John might be successful; necessity as claimed by the vet is no defence.

Exercise 12

1 (a) Libel; (b) slander.
2 (a) The statement must refer to the plaintiff; (b) the statement must be

communicated to a third party; (c) the statement must be capable of lowering the plaintiff's reputation in the eyes of right-thinking members of society.
3 If we apply our three rules; (a) the statement has been communicated to a third party; (b) Paddy was named by inference; note the spelling of the word 'byrne'; (c) But Paddy's reputation is not lowered in the eyes of right-thinking members of society because to give the game away is, despite his friends' view, the right thing to do. Therefore he would have no case in defamation.

Exercise 13

1 Mary would be unsuccessful, because provided Associated Metals did not write the reference with malice then the firm has protection.
2 Mr Green is privileged, i.e. absolutely protected against a defamation action. If he repeated the allegation outside Parliament then this would be quite a different matter.
3 The *Bristol Times* could not use as a defence the offer of amends and the printed apology because the statement about Brayshaw had been printed intentionally.
4 Jennie would have little chance because the statement was in fact true and the fact of the conviction would make it easy for the *Kent Times* to prove it. The newspaper also has a defence in that it has privilege in respect of fair, accurate and contemporaneous reporting of court proceedings.

Exercise 14

1 The three elements are (a) was there a duty of care? (b) was the duty broken? (c) did injury or loss come from the breaking of the duty?
2 (a) The plaintiff was referred to. (b) The statement was made to a third party. (c) The statement lowered the plaintiff's reputation in the eyes of right-thinking members of society.
3 Absolute protection is given for statements in court or Parliament. Qualified protection is given for references.
4 Trespass to land; trespass to person; trespass to goods.
5 Because trespass is usually a tort and not a crime.

CHAPTER 8

Exercise 1

1 False – the Act introduces a new range of criminal offences.
2 'Enabling Act' means that ministers can add to the Act by issuing regulations which have the force of law.
3 Work places must make improvements within a certain period of time.
4 The maximum fine at present is £2000.

Exercise 2

1 There is little doubt that such a sad accident record would lead to a Prohibition Order taking this particular piece of machinery out of action.
2 The Hotel Regal could face criminal action because it has not provided sufficient 'information, instruction, training or supervision' in the use of these new stoves.
3 This constant skylarkying makes it debatable whether a safe system of work is being provided. If the company cannot deal with it then they must, in the interest of safety, terminate the employment of the two apprentices. Both of the employees involved could face legal action because they are 'not cooperating with the management in the interests of safety'.
4 It is a duty of the employer to provide a safe and healthy environment. Victoria Laundry clearly is not doing this and the inspectors will either simply recommend or perhaps issue an Improvement Order.

Exercise 3

(a) The existence of a duty of care.
(b) The breach of that duty of care.
(c) Injury or loss as a result of the breach.

Exercise 4

1 Ben has a good case; Peakdale Engineering Co. owe him a duty of care, this has been broken and Ben is injured.
2 North West Builders are liable to Fred despite their claim to the contrary. Employes are vicariously liable for the torts of their employees. Therefore North West Builders are liable for the tort of the site foreman.
3 It is no defence for Hotel Sceptre to blame the supplier. The Employers' Liability (Defective Equipment) Act provides that an employee such as Adam can sue his employer even though the fault may lie with the supplier.

Exercise 5

1 Factories Act 1961.
2 False - he/she may be compensated by the state for industrial injuries.
3 Linda would not be successful in negligence but the industrial benefit scheme has defined employment as anything arising out of an employee's presence at work. The works canteen would come within this category.
4 Common law duty.

Exercise 6

1 David Hogg is liable for prosecution under the Health and Safety at Work Act 1974 because he is under a duty to take care for the health and safety of himself and fellow employees, and also to cooperate with his employer in health and safety matters.

2 John can inspect the factory and will be termed a lawful visitor and therefore not a trespasser. If he is of the opinion that a particular process is dangerous he can issue a prohibition order ordering it to be discontinued.
3 Philip could sue his company in negligence and as we have seen the Employers' Liability (Defective Equipment) Act 1969 prevents the employer denying liability or trying to shift liability to someone else.
4 Maureen could apply for industrial injuries benefit because this is likely to be one of the prescribed diseases in the 1980 regulations. She might be successful in a negligence action.
5 John may not be able to claim in negligence against his company but he could claim industrial injuries benefit.
6 The apprentice could sue for a breach of statutory duty which makes it necessary for machines to be fenced. The company could not deny liability by blaming Bob Brown because as we have learned companies can be vicariously (indirectly) liable for their employees' actions.

CHAPTER 9

Exercise 1

John could lose his house because his liability is not limited to the £50 000 of his original investment.

Exercise 2

1 A sleeping partner is one who has invested money but takes no part in the running of the business.
2 Unlimited liability means that a partner may be liable for debts over and above his/her initial investment.
3 Partnership Act 1890; Companies Act 1985.
4 By expressly informing firms that he has retired and/or by publishing his retirement in the *London Gazette*.
5 Unfortunately Linda cannot plead ignorance; she is bound by any agreement made by her partner, Christine.

Exercise 3

1 'Dissolution of a partnership' means bringing it to an end.
2 Partnerships may be dissolved (a) by order of the court; (b) by the partners themselves according to the agreement, or if no agreement exists by methods laid down in the Partnership Act 1890.

Exercise 4

Statutory refers to anything which has been laid down by statute, that is, Act of Parliament.

Exercise 5

1 The two differences are: (a) a public company must have a minimum share capital; (b) only public companies can sell their shares to the public.
2 That the shareholders in the company have their liability limited by the amount of their total shareholding.
3 Articles of association.
4 The objects are the reason why the company is operating.

Exercise 6

1 (a) Nominal capital is £1 million; (b) issued capital is £500 000.
2 (a) Unicorn Motor Supplies Co. Ltd has full legal status and it is the company not the managing director who will be sued.
(b) SE Touring Co. Ltd can no longer claim this because our laws in this respect have been brought into line with EEC regulations.
(c) Unfortunately for Palatine the football club could refuse payment and payment could not be enforced because supply of sports equipment is outside its objects.

Exercise 7

1 John could stand to lose the £1000 because it is a legal requirement that anyone trading under a name other than his own needs to display this.
2 Partnership Act 1890.
3 Minimum two, maximum twenty.
4 David could not be made to pay. The company, not David, would be sued.
5 A local authority and a nationalised industry.
6 Certificate of incorporation.

CHAPTER 10

Exercise 1

1 False – companies go into liquidation; they can never become bankrupt.
2 (a) To save the debtor from embarrassment; (b) to share the assets of the debtor as fairly as possible amongst the creditors.
3 A debtor giving notice that he cannot pay his debts. The notice may be inferred (assumed) by the debtor's refusal to pay his debts.

Exercise 2

1 (a) An act of bankruptcy has been committed; (b) that the petition has been presented; and (c) that a debt did in fact exist.
2 An Official Receiver.
3 In the *London Gazette* and the local newspaper.

4 Because details of the bankruptcy will be entered in the Land Charges Registry which will be inspected by a purchaser's solicitor.

Exercise 3

1 John could present a scheme of arrangement which if acceptable to the creditors would avoid bankruptcy.
2 He cannot become a JP, an MP, or a local authority councillor or get credit.
3 The Official Receiver's fees, the cost of the proceedings, the salary and expenses of the trustee.
4 The three circumstances in which no court will discharge are: (a) the bankrupt had never kept accounts; (b) the bankruptcy was brought about by gambling; (c) after the receiving order the debtor had paid one of his creditors in full.

Exercise 4

1 Liquidation – to turn the company's assets into money. Winding up – to bring the affairs of the company to an end.
2 (a) The company cannot pay its debts; (b) the membership falls below the legal minimum; (c) the company does not hold the statutory meeting; (d) the company has not operated within a year of its setting up or has suspended business for a year or more.

Exercise 5

£2400 × 60p = £1440.

Exercise 6

1 (a) Compulsorily; (b) voluntarily; (c) under the court's supervision.
2 £75
3 The creditor cannot sue the company because it no longer exists.

Exercise 7

1 Sterndale can petition the court to get a receiving order against Fraser Bros which may lead to bankruptcy.
2 An Official Receiver is appointed to look after the affairs of the business.
3 A trustee.
4 The company's assets are as follows:

Buldings	£20 000
Equipment	£ 2000
Unpaid-up shares	£ 4000
List B	£ 4000
Total	£32 000

Therefore liabilities £40 000; assets £30 000; dividend 80p.

CHAPTER 11

Exercise 1

1 True – a vendor is only legally obliged to sell after exchange of contracts.
2 To make sure that the seller is not bankrupt because if he is he would have no right to sell.
3 Conveyance or transfer.
4 True – this is an example of a contract which must be in deed form, i.e. signed, sealed and delivered, before it can be legally binding.
5 Colin is the mortgagor. Commercial Credit Co. is the mortgagee.

Exercise 2

1 It is stamped on the conveyance, transfer or assignment document.
2 An assignment.
3 False – stock sales are not affected by stamp duty.
4 Lewis could do very little because the court will not enforce a clause which is so wide. Forty miles and ten years is far too wide.

Exercise 3

1 Susan could get a court order enforcing what is a reasonable covenant against June.
2 An assignment.
3 Landlord and Tenant Act 1954.
4 Franklin is not at risk because although the Landlord and Tenant Act does allow a landlord to repossess property where (1) the landlord wants the property for herself/himself and (2) the landlord wishes to extensively redevelop it, the landlord must have owned the property for at least five years, and this in Elizabeth's situation is not the case.

Exercise 4

1 Twenty years.
2 An assignment.
3 Three months.

Exercise 5

1 Fifty years.
2 High Court – damages and injunction.
3 Only for home viewing. If it is for public viewing permission of the BBC is required.
4 (a) Linda is not infringing the law because this is for home viewing.
(b) Wellings (Publications) Ltd has infringed copyright. (c) Dr Hartley has not infringed Copyright since he has asked for permission.

Exercise 6

1 False - a shareholder would have as many votes as he has shares.
2 (a) The profit of the company; (b) the decision of the directors.
3 False - an ordinary shareholder with £250 000 in the company would be liable only to lose this amount.
4 A preference share is one which is given preference when the assets of a company are shared out on liquidation.

Exercise 7

1 (a) Preference shareholders have no vote; (b) preference shareholders always take preference for profits and when the company is being liquidated; (c) preference shareholders have a fixed rate of interest.
2 False - a debenture holder is not an owner; he is a creditor.
3 False - this is known as a fixed charge.
4 The preference shareholders will obtain £2000, the debenture holders £500. Therefore, there will be £30 000 left for the ordinary shareholders. Each ordinary shareholder will get 30 000 ÷ 60 000 = 50p, i.e. 50 per cent or 50p in the £.

Exercise 8

1 George would have no case because he has tried to obtain far too wide a restrictive covenant and the court will not enforce it even though Frank starts next door.
2 Mark has a good case because Susan has not had the freehold long enough to refuse to renew his lease. Five years is the minimum period.
3 Dave could sue the rival firm for damages and get an injunction to stop the firm from producing his invention.
4 Janet is breaking the copyright law and she could be sued by the BBC.
5 Dave cannot demand any vote because as a debenture holder he has no voting rights.
6 Joyce has to pay the £10 000 unpaid proportion of the share because although her liability is limited to £50 000 she has only lost £40 000; therefore the liquidators are entitled by law to ask for the balance or in other words the unpaid portion.

CHAPTER 12

Exercise 1

Drawer: J. Fraser; drawee: Barclays; payee: Rock Base (Garage) Ltd.

Exercise 2

1 (a) To keep confidentiality; (b) to honour cheques drawn on the customer's account.

2 Breach of contract and the tort of libel.
3 Wendy would be the creditor, the bank would be the debtor.
4 It usually means that the creditor has insufficient funds in his account to meet the cheque.
5 Dishonoured.
6 (a) The bank charges charged by the bank. (b) The keeping of the account by the bank for the customer.

Exercise 3

1 This is where the bank does not pay out on the cheque.
2 He may instruct the bank provided that he does this before the cheque is cleared.
3 (a) By the drawer; (b) when the bank is notified of the drawer's death; (c) where a petition for a receiving order against the drawer has been presented; (d) where a receiving order has been made against the drawer.
4 If Celia could show that her instructions to the bank had been received before the cheque was 'cleared' then the bank would be liable and would not be entitled to debit Celia's account.

Exercise 4

1 To preserve confidentiality on the customer's account.
2 To honour all cheques.

Exercise 5

1 Michael must meet the loss of £150 because he has a duty to his bank if a cheque is drawn on his authority and this one was.
2 Jim will lost the £95 because he has been negligent in the handling of his own account.
3 Ian could sue the other bank for recovery of the £100 because the cheque was marked 'Account Payee Only' and should not have been honoured by the bank.
4 Roy cannot do anything; the cheque was marked 'Not Negotiable' and therefore he can claim no title to it.

Exercise 6

1 The bank is protected because it cannot be expected to recognise forged endorsements.
2 Barclays is not protected unless it can show that the account holder had been negligent.
3 The National Westminster by not taking up references had been negligent. It thus could not get the protection afforded by the 1975 Act and could be liable to all twenty drawers.

Exercise 7

1 False - if a cheque is more than 6 months old it will not be paid.
2 (a) To maintain confidentiality in respect of a customer's account; (b) to pay cheques for customers on demand.
3 The drawer could sue the bank for breach of contract and libel.
4 True - provided the cheque has been stopped in time, i.e. before payment the bank could be liable.
5 False - the drawer who has been negligent is liable.
6 False - it can only be paid into the payee's account.
7 False - because the cheque is negotiable Bill Brown does receive good title and therefore the payee cannot claim.
8 (a) The paying bank is protected if it pays out on false endorsements. (b) Provided it has not been negligent the collecting bank will be protected if it accepts a stolen or forged cheque.

CHAPTER 13

Exercise 1

1 Alex is the agent acting on behalf of his principal, Manchester United FC.
2 Business Property Services is the agent acting for Janet Baker (Fashions) Ltd, the principal.
3 Derek Butterfield is the principal, the stockbroker is the agent.

Exercise 2

Authorisation; by implication, apparent authority, ratification, necessity.

Exercise 3

1 (a) To act in good faith.
  (b) To work skilfully and show reasonable care.
  (c) To act personally.
  (d) To obey the principal's instructions.
2 (a) Death.
  (b) Insanity.
  (c) Lapse.
  (d) Performance.

Exercise 4

1 Geoff cannot avoid the payment - Sheila acted on his authority and if she made a bad deal that is Geoff's loss. He is bound by her agreement.

2 Kent Sports plc would be obliged to pay because Sports Equipment plc could not possibly know of this instruction. This is a good example of agency by implication.
3 Greenfield (Stockbrokers) Ltd are in a difficult position. This is hardly a necessity and anyway, they could have contacted Sir Roger. It seems that there is no agency between Greenfields and Sir Roger in respect of this deal, and action would be to Greenfields.
4 John, following the death of his principal, is no longer the agent. The agreement to sell the property is not valid and the beneficiaries could avoid it.

CHAPTER 14

Exercise 1

1 (a) Criminal law. It is likely that the appeal would be in the Crown Court. You will remember that appeals from the magistrates go to the Crown Court unless it is on a point of law in which case it goes to the Queen's Bench Divisional Court.
(b) Civil law. This is a case of breach of contract and because of the amount involved the case will be heard in the High Court, Queen's Bench Division.
(c) Civil law. This would be heard in the County Court because only a small sum is involved.
(d) Criminal law. The highest court in the land is, of course, the House of Lords.
2 Four examples of civil courts are: County Court; High Court; Court of Appeal (Civil Division); House of Lords.
3 Precedent; legislation; delegated legislation; European Community law.
4 *Ratio decidendi.*
5 Imran would take his case to the industrial tribunal.
6 A statement of Claim; A Defence; A Defence to the Counter Claim.

Reference: Chapter 1.

Exercise 2

1 (a) No legal intent because this is a domestic arrangement.
(b) There is no acceptance. Michael made the offer having been invited to do so by the shop.
(c) Tony's acceptance is conditional; in fact, it is a counter-offer and therefore there is no acceptance.
(d) No capacity – minors (persons not yet eighteen) cannot make agreements in respect of credit.
(e) There is no *consensus ad idem* (meeting of the minds). Mrs Ward only agreed to sell because she was under threat.

(f) There is no two-way consideration. Brian has only agreed to fulfil an existing obligation.
2 False - an offeror can withdraw an offer at any time before acceptance even though he has made a promise to keep it open.
3 Any three of the following: withdrawal (revocation), rejection, lapse, acceptance.
4 A gift can only be enforced if it is on a document, 'signed, sealed and delivered'.
5 (i) Consideration must be two-way. (ii) It must not be an existing obligation. (iii) It must not be past. (iv). It must be of value but not necessarily adequate. (v) Only the party supplying the consideration can sue.
6 False - a boy of sixteen has only limited contractual capacity.
7 The garage has no case against Stanley because contracts of hire purchase, credit, etc. must be in writing, otherwise they are void.
8 Where duress, undue influence or misrepresentation has existed.

Reference: Chapter 2

Exercise 3

1 Sale of Goods Act 1979.
2 False - if they are written or spoken they are known as express terms.
3 A condition is an essential part of the contract. It goes to the heart of the contract. A warranty is a minor part. A breach of condition is the same as a breach of contract.
4 It is unlikely that any court would treat the contract as breached. Failure to deliver first one minor part would be a breach of warranty.
5 M. & G. (Groceries) Ltd could rely on the first exclusion clause which relates to loss and damage of property but since the Unfair Contract Terms Act 1977 the company cannot rely on the second part which relates to personal injury.
6 Performance, breach, agreement, frustration.
7 False - this remedy is discretionary the court can award it if it wishes.

Reference: Chapter 3

Exercise 4

1 False - a contract of employment may be verbal though in practice offers of employment are confirmed in writing.
2 Thirteen weeks.
3 The Race Relations Act 1976 states that it is illegal for firms to discriminate on grounds of race, colour or ethnic origin in selection for employment so rejecting a man because he was foreign is illegal.
4 (a) To obey lawful and reasonable instructions; (b) to work competently and carefully; (c) to conduct oneself in the interest of the employer; (d) to show 'good faith' to the employer.

5 You could have included any three of the following: (a) to provide a safe system of work; (b) not to discriminate on grounds of sex, race or union membership; (c) to reminburse employees for expenses while they are on the firm's business; (d) to deduct PAYE plus National Insurance contributions. (e) To operate a reasonable system of management.

6 Since the engineering firm has lost money due to Alex's bad work and since they relied on a 'good' reference from Dual Accounting Services in employing Alex then the engineering firm could sue Dual Accounting Services for negligence.

7 Tony is entitled to ten weeks' notice or £1500 in lieu and £2025 redundancy pay (7 weeks x 150 x 1½ + 3 weeks x 150 x 1).

8 James has misconducted himself and can be dismissed *without* notice. His appeal against unfair dismissal is not likely to be successful and he certainly has not been made redundant.

Reference: Chapter 4

Exercise 5

1 (a) Under the Sale of Goods Act 1979, it is an implied term that the seller has good title to the goods. Therefore Disdales would have to give Peggy her £500 back.

(b) The Sale of Goods Act 1979 implies that goods bought from a shop must be of 'merchantable quality'. It does not seem that this was the case here. Good Bargain Radio Supplies Ltd would have to give Richard a refund.

(c) John Martin could get his money back because the Sale of Goods Act implies that goods sold by description must correspond with the description and the Christmas cake did not.

2 (a) Trade Descriptions Act 1968.

(b) True - this is one of the offences under the Trade Descriptions Act and criminal proceedings can result from double pricing.

3 False - the goods are hired and become the property of the hirer on payment of the last payment.

4 (a) Jeff is fortunate because if he can prove he has never received a copy of the agreement then he cannot be forced to pay the final five instalments because the court will never enforce an agreement where the hirer (Jeff in this case) has not received a copy.

(b) Susan is given up to five days to 'cool off'. She can withdraw from the agreement since it was signed at her home as long as it is within five days. Household Supplies Ltd can do nothing.

Reference: Chapter 5

Exercise 6

1 Failure to make profit is non-insurable.

2 Pooling of risks.

3 (a) Star Insurance Co. need not pay out because Michael Jones has not obeyed the principle of 'utmost good faith'.
(b) Safety Insurance need not pay out because Michael Hunter has no 'insurable interest' in his friend's house.
(c) Frank Brown in receiving £10 000 would be getting more than the value of the car. He can only claim £5000. This principle is known as indemnity. *Reference:* Chapter 6

Exercise 7

1 A duty of care; breach of that duty; damages or loss arising from the breach.
2 False - in some instances a duty of care can be owed to a trespasser especially in the case of children.
3 That no duty of care was owed; that the duty was not broken; that no loss damage or injury resulted; that the plaintiff had agreed to take the risk, i.e. consent.
4 Trespass to land, persons and goods.
5 True.
6 Mrs Wardle would have a good case in defamation. She is referred to. The statement is communicated to a third party. The statement is capable of lowering Mrs Wardle's reputation in the eyes of right-thinking people. After all, telephoning New Zealand at the company's expense is not what one would expect from a supervisor. *Reference:* Chapter 7

Exercise 8

1 True - the Health and Safety at Work Act is concerned with criminal offences.
2 This is an Order which forbids the use of equipment or a process which the Health and Safety inspectors feel is dangerous.
3 (a) To take reasonable care for the safety of other employees; (b) to cooperate with employers in safety matters; (c) not to interfere with anything provided for safety.
4 Factories Act 1961.
5 He may apply for industrial benefit which is paid by the state.
6 This is where an employer might be liable for the torts of his employees. *Reference:* Chapter 8

Exercise 9

1 Brian and Fred would probably be successful. Since 26 February 1982 it has not been necessary to register a business name.
2 A sleeping partner is one who invests money but plays no active role in the partnership.
3 Private companies, public companies, nationalised industries.
4 *Ultra vires*.

5 A shareholder stands to lose only the value of his shares - his liability is limited to his shareholding.
6 Maximum twenty; minimum two. *Reference:* Chapter 9

Exercise 10

1 He cannot become an MP, a magistrate or local councillor. A bankrupt will not be able to get credit.
2 False - only individuals and partnerships may be bankrupt; companies are liquidated.
3 He may declare a dividend of 60p in the £ to creditors of the company.
4 That a debt existed; that an act of bankruptcy has been committed; that the petition has been presented. *Reference:* Chapter 10

Exercise 11

1 True - a buyer is not legally bound to buy until contracts are exchanged.
2 Goodwill.
3 The purchaser unfortunately could do nothing because the clause 'twenty years anywhere in the UK' is far too restrictive and the courts will not uphold it.
4 False - the tenant is protected by the Landlord and Tenant Act 1954.
5 Patent.
6 False - copyright laws allow people to copy for home use.
7 True.
8 Preference shareholders would get their money back but ordinary shareholders would get only 50p in the £: 50 000 × £1 = £50 000 to preference shareholders; this leaves £50 000 – (50 000 ÷ 100 000) = 50p per £ for ordinary shareholders. *Reference:* Chapter 11

Exercise 12

1 The person paying out is the drawer, the bank is the drawee and the person whose name appears after 'pay' is the payee.
2 (a) To maintain confidentiality in respect of a customer's account; (b) to honour all cheques drawn.
3 True - when the bank is notified of the receiving order it will stop all cheques in respect of that person.
4 Cross the cheque and mark it 'Account Payee Only'.
5 Negotiability means that the cheque can be transferred from person to person.
6 A cheque may be stopped: (a) under instructions of the drawer; (b) if the bank is notified of the drawer's death; (c) where a receiving order has been made; (d) where a petition for a receiving order has been made.
Reference: Chapter 12

Exercise 13

1 (a) K. Dalglish is the agent, Liverpool FC is the principal.
(b) Ward & Co is the agent, Kent Engineering plc is the principal.
(c) Mr Y is the agent, the pop group is the principal.
2 You could have listed:
express authorisation; implication; statute; necessity; ratification.
3 To pay him for his duties and to reimburse him for expenses.
4 True. Each partner binds the others by his/her actions.
5 False. Most often they are binding on the other party even though they had been entered into by the principal himself.

House of Lords

Woman's entitlement to equal pay

Hayward v Cammel Laird Shipbuilders Ltd

Before Lord Mackay of Clashfern, Lord Chancellor, Lord Bridge of Harwich, Lord Brandon of Oakbrook, Lord Griffiths and Lord Goff of Chieveley.

[Speeches May 5]

A woman was entitled under the equal pay legislation to have the same term as to basic pay as her male comparators irrespective of whether she was as favourably treated as the man when the whole of the benefits of their contracts were taken into account.

The House of Lords so held in allowing an appeal by Miss Julie Hayward, a cook at Cammell Laird Shipbuilders Ltd, from the decision of the Court of Appeal (Lord Justice Purchas, Lord Justice Nicholls and Sir Roualeyn Cuming-Bruce; *The Times* March 5, 1987; [1988] QB 12) to uphold the dismissal by the Employment Appeal Tribunal of her appeal from the order of an industrial tribunal that she was not entitled to a declaration under section I(2) of the Equal Pay Act 1970, as amended by the Sex Discrimination Act 1975 and the Equal Pay (Amendment) Regulations (SI 1983 No 1794) that she should receive a higher rate of pay.

Mr Anthony Lester, QC and Mr David Pannick for the employee; Lord Irvine of Lairg, QC and Mr Charles James for the employers.

THE LORD CHANCELLOR said that the issue was whether in terms of the Equal Pay Act 1970, as amended, the woman who could point to a term of her contract which was less favourable than a term of a similar kind in the man's contract was entitled to have that term made not less favourable irrespective of whether she was as favourably treated as the man when the whole of their contracts were considered.

There was no definition of the word "term" in the legislation. The natural meaning of the word in the present context was a distinct provision of part of the contract which had sufficient content to make it possible to compare it from the point of view of the benefits it conferred with similar provision or part in another contract.

For example the employee had been employed on her accepting terms set out in a letter which included the following:

"We can offer you a position on our staff as a cook at a salary of £5.165 per annum. The base rate on which overtime is based is £4.741 . . . ". The letter had set out the normal hours of work, providing that the overtime payment should be plain time rate plus a third (two-thirds on Saturday and Sunday).

The corresponding provision with regard to basic pay in the men's contracts was less specific and referred to a national agreement from which the rate of wages and overtime payments were to be determined.

The natural application of the word "term" in her contract was that it applied for example, to the basic pay, and that the appropriate comparison was with the hourly rate of basic pay.

But the respondents said that that was not correct and that the use of the expression in section I(2) defining an equality clause as a provision which "relates to terms (whether concerned with pay or not) of a contract" showed that Parliament had in mind that all provisions relating to pay were to be considered as a single term and that accordingly it was only by taking account of all the contractual provisions relating to pay that one could make the comparison which was envisaged.

They went on to say that if that was not correct, many difficulties were likely to arise. For example, where a woman was paid less than a man but had the use of a car, it would be wrong to say that she was entitled to have the term dealing with basic pay put up and the man on applying under the same legislation would be able to say that there was no term in his contract giving him the use of a car and therefore he was entitled to one.

The employers submitted that the only way out of that difficulty was to consider together as one term all matters relating to pay however expressed, in order to produce a result that the woman was put up to equality with the man and no further, and the man put up to equality with the woman and no further, so that there was no general enhancement of their total remuneration.

It had been difficulties involving that and similar examples that had weighed with the Court of Appeal and the Employment Appeal Tribunal in deciding in the employers' favour.

While one could envisage difficult examples, in the ordinary case such as the present no such difficulty arose and it would be wrong to depart from the natural reading of the words Parliament had used because of the difficulty in their application to particular examples, especially when those examples did not arise in actual cases.

The difficulty of reconciling the employers' construction with the words used in the Act was emphasized when one con sidered the provisions of part (ii) in each of the sub-clauses (a), (b) and (c) of section I(2) as was pointed out by Lord Bridge in the course of the hearing.

It was impossible to believe that Parliament had envisaged a contract with no provision for pay at all and therefore if the employers' construction was adopted, part (ii) in each of the sub-subsections could apply only to other benefits.

That seemed a most unlikely construction when one noticed that the introductory words of subsection (2) which applied to parts (i) and (ii) spoke of "terms (whether concerned with pay or not)".

The employee's construction of section I(2) was to be preferred and the case would be remitted to the industrial tribunal for determination in accordance with that opinion.

On that view of the matter it was not strictly necessary to consider the question of Community law. His Lordship concluded, however, that there was nothing in the European legislation which detracted from the force of the employee's argument on the domestic legislation.

Lord Goff delivered a concurring speech and Lord Bridge, Lord Brandon and Lord Griffiths agreed.

Solicitors: Brian Thompson & Partners, Manchester; Davies Arnold & Cooper for Davis Campbell & Co, Liverpool.

FURTHER READING

General

Make sure that you always obtain the most recent edition of these books.

MARSH, S. B. and SOULSBY, J., *Business Law* (McGraw-Hill).
SCHMITTHOFF, C. M. and SARRE, D. A., *Charlesworth's Mercantile Law* (Stevens and Sons).
SMITH, K. and KEENAN, D. J., *Essentials of Mercantile Law* (Pitman).

For those studying for examinations Longmans publish an extremely good exam guide in this subject:

TILEY, J. and BAILEY, S., *Longman Exam Guides Business Law* (Longman).

In addition the following books are suggested for further reading in particular areas. Again make sure you obtain the latest edition in each case

European Community law.

LASOK, D. and BRIDGE, J. W., *Introduction to the Law and Institutions of the European Communities* (Butterworths).

Contract.

DAVIES, F. R., *Law of Contract* (Sweet and Maxwell).
SMITH, J. C. and THOMAS, J. A. C., *A Casebook on Contract* (Butterworths).

Tort.

BAKER, C. D., *Tort* (Sweet and Maxwell).
BRADBURY, P. L., *Cases and Statutes on Tort* (Sweet and Maxwell).

Sale of goods.

ATIYAH, P. S., *The Sale of Goods* (Pitman).

Agency.
FRIDMAN, G. H. L., *The Law of Agency* (Butterworths).

Consumer credit.
DIAMOND, A., *Commercial and Consumer Credit: An Introduction* (Butterworths).

Industrial and employment law.
SELWYN, N., *Law of Employment* (Butterworths).
SELWYN, N., *Law of Health and Safety at Work* (Butterworths).

INDEX